POLICING SOUTH AFRICA

ABOUT THE AUTHOR

Gavin Cawthra is a South African writer and scholar who has pioneered research into the South African security forces. During the 1980s he and other young South Africans resisted military conscription at a time when South Africa's armed forces were intervening more and more brutally beyond the country's borders and within the black townships. As part of this activity, he co-edited the journal *Resister*.

His writings have been translated into several languages. He is the author of:

Brutal Force: The Apartheid War Machine (International Defence and Aid Fund, 1986)

South Africa's Police: From Police State to Democratic Policing? (Catholic Institute for International Relations, 1992)

War and Resistance (co-edited with Gerald Kraak and Gerald O'Sullivan) (Macmillan, forthcoming)

POLICING SOUTH AFRICA

*The South African Police & the
Transition from Apartheid*

GAVIN CAWTHRA

ZED BOOKS LTD
London & New Jersey

DAVID PHILIP
Cape Town

Policing South Africa was first published by
Zed Books Ltd, 7 Cynthia Street, London N1 9JF, UK, and
165 First Avenue, Atlantic Highlands, New Jersey 07716, USA,
in 1993.

First published in Southern Africa
by David Philip Publishers
208 Werdmuller Centre, Claremont 7700, South Africa,
in 1994.

Map on p. xiii from *History of Southern Africa* by
J.D. Omer-Cooper, reproduced by courtesy of James Currey Ltd.

Cover design by Andrew Corbett.
Laserset by Opus 43, Cumbria, UK.
Printed and Bound in the United Kingdom
by Biddles Ltd, Guildford and King's Lynn

A catalogue record for this book
is available from the British Library

US CIP data is available from
the Library of Congress

ISBN 1 85649 065 3 Hb
ISBN 1 85649 066 1 Pb

Southern Africa ISBN 0 86486 261 X

CONTENTS

PREFACE

I wrote this book out of anger and hope. Anger at the decades of police bullying of black South Africans and the arrest, torture and killing of people challenging the apartheid system, events I have monitored and researched for many years. Thousands of South Africans have endured assaults on their humanity by the South African Police (SAP): many of those who have sat at the negotiating tables and are now trying to create the new South Africa have been detained without trial and harassed; others active in the anti-apartheid struggle did not live to see the fruit of their commitment.

With the unbanning of the African National Congress and other organisations, negotiations to end apartheid and preparations for non-racial elections, there has been hope. Hope that the police will reform themselves – or at least allow themselves to be reformed – and eventually find their rightful place in the new South Africa which is being born. Hope that the growing number of police who sympathise with the cause of democracy, or who want to provide a professional service to the community, will be allowed to lead the force into a future free from racism and knee-jerk violence.

Although the SAP with its batons, rifles and armoured personnel carriers has been an icon of white-minority rule in South Africa, and an essential part of the apartheid system, little has been written about the force, especially from the perspective of those opposed to apartheid. It is almost as if it has been regarded as beneath contemplation – until the 1990s, with a few notable exceptions,[1] little attempt was made to get to grips with the problem of policing in South Africa. The SAP itself has contributed to this process by habitually retreating into institutional secrecy and, for decades, dismissing any criticism as a communist-orchestrated 'total onslaught' aimed at weakening the state's defences. On those rare occasions when it saw fit to advertise itself, as on its 75th anniversary in 1988, it produced sanitised versions of its history which paid uncritical homage to the force.[2]

The focus of anti-apartheid research into security issues has been on the South African Defence Force: militarisation was one of the big themes of the 1980s.[3] The SAP was mostly left out of the reckoning. Yet it was the police, and not the army, which precipitated nationwide uprisings in 1976–7 by their brutal actions in Soweto. And police spearheaded the State of Emergency in the 1980s, the bloody counter-revolutionary offensive movement which left thousands dead. 'Troops out of the townships' was the rallying cry of the resistance, but the vast majority of assaults, detentions and killings by the security forces were carried out by the police.

This book is a beginning: it is the first book written from outside the SAP which deals with its history, organisation, strategy and operations, and with the policing imbroglio of the first years of the 1990s. It does not supply all the answers or seek to provide a definitive analysis of the SAP. The inside story still needs to be written: the generals need to explain their thinking and their actions, but they are not yet ready to talk. Nor is this a book about criminology and the role of the SAP in combating crime. It focuses instead on the central problem of policing in South Africa: the role of the police in enforcing white-minority rule, and the challenge to overcome this legacy. The issue of crime goes far beyond the realm of policing – it has its roots in economic and social conditions and will be tackled only by a fundamental reworking of social relations.

I hope this study will inform a wider public debate about the nature and future course of policing in South Africa. It is based partly on my own research, carried out over several years, and partly on the trailblazing work being done in South Africa – researchers are for the first time beginning to crack the shell of secrecy surrounding the SAP and are now gaining access to some of its institutions. In particular, I have used recent information and insights from the Project for the Study of Violence at the University of the Witwatersrand, the Institute of Criminology at the University of Cape Town, the Community Law Centre at the University of the Western Cape and the Project on Peace and Security at the Centre for Intergroup Studies in Cape Town – although I cannot of course claim to represent their views. I have also drawn, even if indirectly, on the wisdom of many South Africans who have struggled against apartheid or become victims of its iniquities, and the experiences and views of police and soldiers with whom I have come into contact over the years.[4]

Many other individuals and organisations helped in my research in England and South Africa, while the Catholic Institute for International Relations in London and the Anti-Apartheid Beweging in Amsterdam gave valuable institutional support. The Ruth First Memorial Trust provided a small and much appreciated grant without which it would have been impossible to write this book. Linda Mugridge, Janine Rauch, John Daniel and Robert Molteno read the manuscript and offered valuable advice. Thank you all. My biggest debt is to those who stood by me and endured the irascibility that protracted writing seems to engender.

Let us hope that this book will contribute to a South Africa where the future will not be determined by police gunshots, and where the police will earn the respect of the community by carrying out a difficult and much-needed service, in a society which recognises the rights and worth of all human beings.

NOTES

1 Notably Sachs 1973 and 1975; Haysom 1987a, 1987b, 1989a, 1989b, 1989c, Brewer 1988, Scharf 1989, Seegers 1989.
2 The history of the SAP commissioned to commemorate the anniversary, Dippenaar 1988, although sometimes absurdly laudatory, nevertheless provides a wealth of information which is otherwise unavailable. Some of this has been used in this book, particularly in Chapter 1.
3 For example Frankel 1984; Cawthra 1986; Grundy 1988; Cock & Nathan 1989
4 Because these contacts have been of such a varied nature, and as they owe more to life experience than research, they are not referenced in the text. They cover the years 1977–92.

Abbreviations

ANC	African National Congress
APLA	Azanian People's Liberation Army
AWB	Afrikaner Weerstandsbeweging
AZAPO	Azanian People's Organisation
BOSS	Bureau for State Security
CCB	Civil Cooperation Bureau
CCI	Crime Combating and Investigation
CID	Criminal Investigation Department
CIS	Crime Intelligence Service
COSAS	Congress of South African Students
COSATU	Congress of South African Trade Unions
CP	Conservative Party
CPSA	Communist Party of South Africa
GDP	Gross Domestic Product
IDASA	Institute for a Democratic Alternative in South Africa
IFP	Inkatha Freedom Party
ISU	Internal Stability Unit
JCC	Joint Coordinating Centre
JMC	Joint Management Committee
KZP	KwaZulu Police
MK	Umkhonto we Sizwe
MPLA	Popular Movement for the Liberation of Angola
Nampol	Namibian Police
NCM	National Coordinating Mechanism
NIS	National Intelligence Service
NP	National Party
NSMS	National Security Management System
OAU	Organisation for African Unity
PAC	Pan-Africanist Congress
PLAN	People's Liberation Army of Namibia
POPCRU	Police and Prison Officers' Civil Rights Union

PWV	Pretoria–Witwatersrand–Vaal
SACC	South African Council of Churches
SACP	South African Communist Party
SADF	South African Defence Force
SAIRR	South African Institute of Race Relations
SAP	South African Police
SASFED	South African Security Federation
SAYCO	South African Youth Congress
SB	Security Branch
SSC	State Security Council
SWAPO	South West African People's Organisation
SWAPOL	South-West Africa Police
TEC	Transitional Executive Council
UDF	United Democratic Front
UN	United Nations
USA	United States of America
UWUSA	United Workers of South Africa
WCC	World Council of Churches
ZANU	Zimbabwe African National Union
ZAPU	Zimbabwe African People's Union

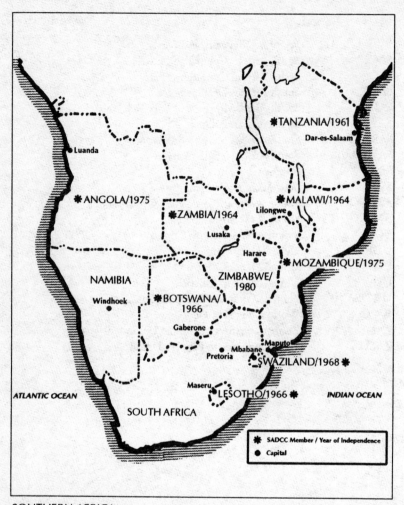

SOUTHERN AFRICA

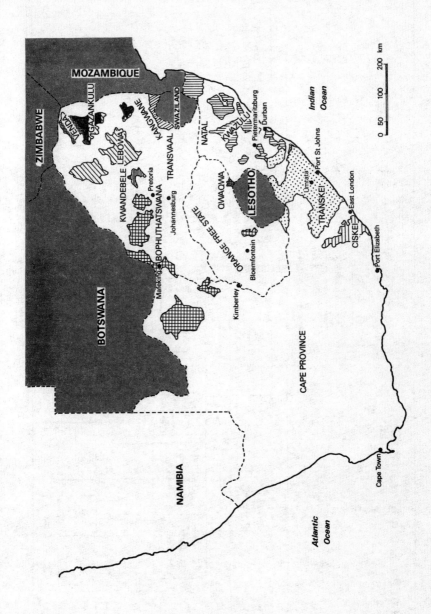

SOUTH AFRICA, SHOWING PROVINCES, BANTUSTANS, CITIES AND
PRINCIPAL TOWNS

Structure of the South African Police, 1993

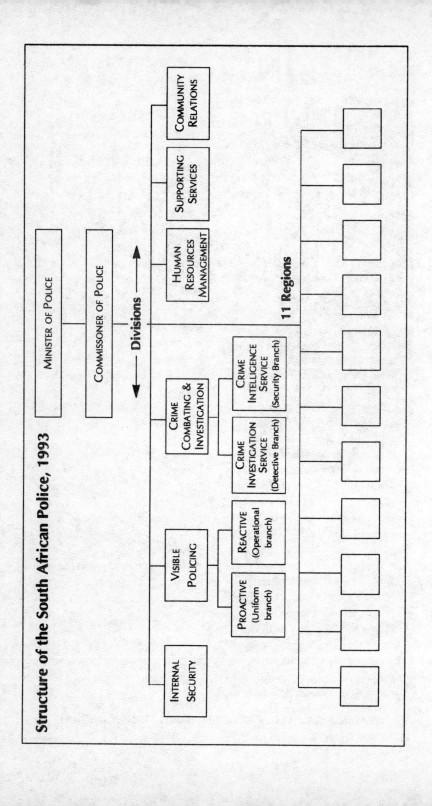

INTRODUCTION

THE PROBLEM OF POLICING IN SOUTH AFRICA

The South African Police (SAP) has been cast as the arch-villain in the struggle against apartheid. Today, as South Africans attempt to build a new non-racial society, the force throws its shadow across the process of political trans-formation. The transition from apartheid to democracy has been threatened more than once by police and military involvement in political killing, but, without effective policing, democracy itself is impossible. The process of change depends on a climate of law and order and free political competition: in the absence of external armed intervention, it will be largely up to the SAP to ensure this.

At critical turning points in the conflict in South Africa the police have taken centre-stage – if their actions have not exactly determined the course of history, they have certainly helped to precipitate new phases in the struggle against apartheid. The shootings at Sharpeville in 1960, when police gunned down unarmed Africans demonstrating against the pass laws, led in quick succession to a State of Emergency, the banning of the African National Congress (ANC) and the Pan-Africanist Congress (PAC), and the launch of armed struggle. The Soweto uprisings, the nationwide protests that left 1,000 people dead in 1976–7, were sparked off by police shooting demonstrating children – most of those killed were hit by police rifle fire.

Police shootings in townships around Johannesburg towards the end of 1984, and a massacre at Langa in the Eastern Cape a few months later, signalled another cycle of bloodletting that plunged South Africa into virtual civil war. For six years the police and army occupied townships and enforced a State of Emergency which gave them sweeping powers. The widening spiral of violence was only broken with the onset of negotiations between the ANC and the government in 1990. But in June 1992 the talks temporarily ground to a halt when the police again covered themselves in infamy by carrying out a massacre of ANC supporters at Boipatong.

These seminal events illustrate a general truth, that the police were always in the front line in the enforcement of apartheid. Over the decades they ensured that black South Africans were kept in their places in segregated and

1

inferior institutions and it was they who helped to implement the massive social engineering that perpetuated white minority rule. They arrested several million South Africans under the pass laws and helped to remove forcibly three and a half million people, victims of the great project to force blacks from the land that was theirs. The Security Branch, the political police, targeted opposition organisations that supported majority rule. The branch monitored a third of a million citizens, detained tens of thousands and tortured many of them, drove opponents into exile or ensured that they were locked up in the country's jails or swung from its gallows. To justify the sustained campaign of repression, the South African state, like some of the right-wing regimes in Latin America and elsewhere, portrayed its enemies as part of a world-wide communist conspiracy. The police came to regard themselves as defenders of the 'free world' and 'Christian civilisation' against the communist threat, but in the process they made a mockery of the precepts of modern civilisation.

The political tasks of the police were overlaid with military imperatives. Between 1966 and 1990 the SAP waged war against the liberation movements fighting for the independence of Zimbabwe and Namibia and for freedom in South Africa. The militarised nature of the force is reflected in its rank structures, its equipment and training, and in its readiness to revert to the power of the gun rather than persevering with the power of persuasion. Periodic political massacres are but one reflection of this – the police are equally trigger-happy in their day-to-day operations.

In the early 1970s, South Africa's police killed an average of 84 people a year – twice the rate of police killings in the USA.[1] The killing rate increased dramatically after the 1976 Soweto uprisings. The annual tally ranged from a low of 163 in 1979 to 763 in 1985; in that year another 2,500 people were wounded in police action. The overwhelming majority of those killed and injured have been black (only three of those killed in 1985, for instance, were white).[2] To these figures must be added, in most years, additions to the mounting toll of deaths of people in police custody.[3]

As decades of counter-insurgency war progressively undermined the civil rights of South Africans, the SAP largely abandoned the concept of the rule of law. The police were drawn increasingly into covert operations. Members of the ANC were hunted down in Southern Africa and further afield, and anti-apartheid activists were assassinated by hit squads. In Namibia, police and army units specialised in 'dirty tricks', using local recruits or mercenaries from neighbouring states to pose as liberation fighters and carry out atrocities. Gruesome tactics, ranging from poisoning to the doctoring of weapons, were used in a no-holds-barred campaign to destroy the liberation movements.

Like all South African government organs, the SAP became more and more secretive. Its first instinct when criticised was to close ranks. For decades the SAP's white recruits have come almost exclusively from the Afrikaner community, and usually from the lesser-skilled and lower-class sectors of that community. Its officer corps is made up mostly of men who worked their way to the top and whose whole life is the SAP. Its distinctive 'cop culture' thus reproduces itself year after year with little external input.

The police have increasingly become a law unto themselves; a process aided by the State of Emergency which exonerated police from civil or criminal prosecution for acts of violence and criminality, provided they were carried out 'in good faith'. Even so, the number of police convicted of serious offences has been alarmingly high. Between 1988 and 1991, 74 were convicted of murder, 148 of culpable homicide and 1,652 of assault.[4]

For all its centrality in maintaining apartheid, the SAP has been curiously neglected by the National Party government. Authorised force levels have seldom been met, and police salaries – at least for whites – are still well below what they could earn in comparable jobs in the private sector. Not surprisingly, many have moved to the burgeoning private security industry, which is increasingly taking over policing tasks in white suburbs and industrial estates.

The lot of a South African policeman or woman is not an enviable one. Not only do they have to work long periods of unpaid overtime at unsocial hours, and take on a wide variety of duties ranging from riot control to petty bureaucratic tasks, but they are regarded as enemies by a large proportion of the population. Every year there are hundreds of attacks on the police by criminals as well as political opponents of the government – in the five years prior to 1991, more than 225 policemen were killed and 60,000 injured in operations, although many of the injuries may have been minor.[5] Their task is becoming more dangerous all the time, despite the end of the ANC's armed struggle – 144 police died 'in the line of duty' in 1991,[6] and 226 in 1992. Not all these incidents were political: the Human Rights Commission recorded the deaths of 116 security force members – police and army – in political conflict in 1992.[7]

Black police – who now make up over 60 per cent of the force – are at the receiving end of both popular opposition to authority and the racism of their white colleagues. The bulk of them are obliged to serve in inferior auxiliary formations, where they have the status of 'police assistants', and those who serve in the regular SAP are generally in subordinate positions – only just over 5 per cent of officers are black.[8]

Whether the SAP, now 120,000 strong, is under strength or not is a matter for debate. In the 1960s, when South Africa was widely regarded as a police state, it had a lower ratio of police to population than many Western countries. Today, there are more police than ever before but crime rates are rising inexorably. South Africa has a homicide rate five times higher than the United States of America, and Cape Town (followed closely by the Witwatersrand) can claim to be the murder capital of the world.[9] With a homicide rate of 50 per 100,000 (compared to 9 per 100,000 in the USA and only about 1 per

100,000 in the Netherlands or England and Wales), South Africa is one of the most violent societies in the world.[10]

The high crime rate has many causes, not least the social and economic degradation caused by apartheid. More recently the collapse of authority in many communities as a result of the bloody contest for political power and police attempts to wipe out popular leadership have contributed to crime. But the police must shoulder much of the blame in a more direct sense. Historically, they have concerned themselves less with preventing crime than with enforcing the restrictions of apartheid and crushing political opposition.

The 1990s have thrown up the greatest challenge to the SAP in its history. The police have had to do a U-turn, allowing their enemy, the 'communist' ANC, to hold mass rallies and protests and watching the structures of apartheid disintegrate. The release of Nelson Mandela and most other political prisoners, the unbanning of the liberation movements and moves towards a constitutional settlement have prepared the ground for an end to white minority rule: soon the police will be answerable to a new government. But little has been done to reorient, retrain and re-equip the SAP. Many public declarations have been made about a new partnership with the community and changing attitudes in the force. Numbers have been boosted, a new riot unit set up, some units renamed or reorganised, and more black police recruited. But the old habits have persisted: with their rifles, shotguns and teargas, and working alongside the army, the police have continually found themselves in violent conflict with crowds of protesters. The resultant killings threatened the negotiations process on more than one occasion.

The police have done far more damage to the prospects for peace than simply shooting at demonstrators. Sections of the security forces, including elements of the SAP, have incited communal and political violence with the aim of destabilising the ANC and other opponents of the government and weakening their negotiating positions. In Natal, the police have colluded with, or turned a blind eye to, attacks by Inkatha adherents on ANC supporters, and they have helped to export this incipient civil war to the Transvaal. Victims of the violence, eyewitnesses, international monitoring organisations and civil rights groups have all damned the SAP for its role in the bloodshed. Since the unbanning of the ANC in early 1990, more than 8,000 people have died in political conflict – more than in other period of apartheid rule.

The tactics used in the destabilisation campaign have been inherited from the counter-insurgency wars in neighbouring states. They include random attacks on train commuters and political assassinations – more people (mostly ANC members and supporters) were assassinated in 30 months after the ANC was unbanned than in the previous five years.[11] Police death squads, set up in the 1980s to 'eliminate' ANC activists, have almost certainly had a hand in many of these operations, although the covert nature of their operations makes detailed information hard to come by. These acts have been compounded by police failures to investigate, charge and prosecute offenders, and to disarm violent Inkatha supporters: Amnesty International has declared it 'wilful negligence'.[12]

The police role in attempts to destabilise the ANC and the broader anti-apartheid movement has contributed to the chronic instability and violence which could tilt South Africa into a nightmare of anarchy and disintegration: the spectre of Lebanon, Yugoslavia or, closer to home, Mozambique. Such an outcome would destroy, of course, the very cause for which white minority governments in South Africa (including De Klerk's) have always stood: continued white prosperity and security. The government and its security forces would reap the whirlwind, for the destabilising actions of the security forces are not merely an aberration or the work of a 'third force' acting independently. Although the covert sections of the security forces undoubtedly operate with some autonomy, and decisions to carry out specific assassinations and other actions are often authorised at a local level, the overall pattern of operations is so transparent that it would be an insult to their intelligence to suggest that senior cabinet ministers and President de Klerk himself were not aware of it.

Throughout the 1970s and 1980s, the white-minority government and its security forces pursued a strategy in neighbouring states which combined military attacks and covert operations, including terrorism, with peace negotiations. In the ANC's assessment, the De Klerk government continued this twin-track strategy, which the organisation described as 'talking peace and waging war' – seeking to destabilise the ANC and its allies to weaken their position at the negotiating table.[13]

Effective policing, and an end to destabilising actions, are essential to a peaceful transition to a non-racial South Africa; and, because a culture of violence has taken hold, the problem of policing will remain one of the major challenges to any new government. Despite this, questions of policing have long been ignored by the anti-apartheid movement. The force was regarded as an irredeemable enemy, to be defeated and disbanded. Only in the last few years has the ANC and the broader opposition started to come to terms with the fact that when white minority rule goes, the new government will inherit the SAP largely intact. Since it will lack the trained personnel and resources to replace the force, it will have to learn how to control it, redirect it and transform it into a force answerable to and enjoying the confidence of the community.[14] It is that set of questions – difficult as they are – that this book ultimately addresses.

NOTES

1   Foster & Luyt 1986.
2   IDAF 1991, p 69; author's calculations.
3   *Annual Survey of Race Relations* 1980-90/91.
4   *BBC Summary of World Broadcasts* 21.2.92.
5   Jeffery 1991, p 80.
6   *Eastern Province Herald* 1.1.92.
7   Commonwealth Observer Mission 1993, p 13.
8   *Financial Mail* 19.4.91.
9   *Financial Mail* 15.2.91.
10 Commonwealth Observer Mission 1993, p 13.
11 *HRC Press Statement and Briefing on Political Assassination in the Nineties*, 21.5.92.
12 Address by Mary Rayner, 'International Hearing on Violence in South Africa and Implementation of the National Peace Accord', London, 14–15 July 1992.
13 *ANC Press Release* 11.10.90.
14 See, for example, Maduna 1991.

1

THE EVOLUTION OF
POLICING STRATEGY

Many of the problems of policing in South Africa today are rooted in the country's fractious and violent past. The character of the SAP has been moulded through decades of war, rebellion and civil conflict; it has always had a quasi-military role and been used as a political instrument of the government of the day. Colonial frontier-style policing, with its emphasis on armed force, characterised police strategy in the nineteenth and early twentieth centuries. With the growth of an African urban working class, police tasks became more bureaucratic and overtly political – the enforcement of the pass laws became a major aspect of their work.

The armed struggles launched by African nationalists in the 1960s further militarised and politicised the SAP, a process accelerated by its role in suppressing mass rebellions like the 1976 Soweto uprisings. By the 1980s the state had adopted a Total Strategy in which all aspects of policy were subjugated to the security imperative, and government was dominated by military and police 'securocrats'. This strategy failed to suppress anti-apartheid resistance, and in 1986, with security chiefs believing the country was on the brink of insurrection, the army and police began a counter-revolutionary campaign. The counter-revolution lasted until the end of the decade, by which stage the country was in a state of virtual civil war and facing economic catastrophe. The government was forced to change tack and seek a way out of the cycle of violence into which its strategy of repression inevitably led. This chapter looks at the evolution of policing strategy in the context of the wider strategic concerns of successive National Party governments.

But first a note of caution: strategy, pared down, is the means by which ends are achieved. These ends are set not by the police, and usually not by the military, but by the executive or other branches of the state. Although the police help to determine strategic objectives, they do not themselves set the agenda. Strategy usually also entails the use or threat of force: in this the military is the main instrument and the police play a secondary role. In a general sense, then, police strategy must be understood as a derivation of national strategy, and sometimes as an adjunct to or an aspect of military strategy. It focuses on particular issues or areas rather than on the big picture.

In the South African context the police have often lacked a coherent vision of means and ends. At critical junctures the force spoke with many voices, often pursuing a series of changing micro-strategies. What follows is therefore schematic, highlighting some of the more significant voices: the positions articulated by key figures should not necessarily be taken as an indication that the force as a whole shared these views; but they do show some of the shifts and debates within the SAP.

Foundations of Police Strategy

THE EARLY DAYS

The SAP was born out of the Act of Union of 1910, which brought together Boer (Afrikaner) and British settlers, the former adversaries of the Anglo-Boer War, and laid the basis for continued white domination over the conquered African population. It united several disparate forces, and its first commissioner, Colonel T.G. Truter, complained that 'a more complex system can hardly be imagined ... there is no uniform policy regarding the organisation and control of the police.' [1]

Whether British or Boer, most of the forces which preceded the SAP were essentially military units. In the two British colonies, the Cape Mounted Police and the Natal Mounted Rifles were responsible for continuing the conquest and subjugation of the black population, and the rudimentary police units in the Boer republics were extensions of military commandos. In the capitals of the Cape and Natal, efforts had been made to introduce policing along the lines of the London Metropolitan force – which pioneered the 'bobby on the beat' system. But the municipal model was applied almost exclusively to whites: a two-tiered pattern of policing emerged, with Africans being subjected to authoritarian, militarised policing and whites to a less repressive system. [2]

The new SAP retained many of the features of a colonial military force, and a separate frontier unit, the South African Mounted Riflemen, was maintained to patrol the most densely populated black rural areas until 1920. The police were essentially an 'internal army of occupation' [3] and worked closely with the new Union Defence Force – whose duties were also primarily internal. As their name implies, the Mounted Riflemen were equipped with firearms, as were other white police during emergencies or on specific operations. Police operating in municipal areas were not usually armed, but this began to change in the 1920s and 1930s and by the 1950s all white police carried handguns as a matter of routine – black police were armed only in the 1970s. [4] As well as quelling rural resistance, police increasingly became involved in administrative and control functions. These included enforcing various pass laws for Africans which had been introduced gradually in many parts of the country.

At the outset the force was one-fifth black – Africans had been incorporated into separate police units under white command before the formation of the SAP.[5] However, blacks in the SAP could then rise only to the rank of sergeant. Many of the white members, including most of the officer corps, had previously been members of the British armed forces, but recruitment of Afrikaners into lower ranks rapidly outstripped that of English-speakers. Most recruits were drawn from impoverished Afrikaner rural communities – pay and conditions were bad and the force was often undermanned. Police complained of long hours, low morale, the poor esteem in which they were held by the white public and the open resentment of blacks – grievances which have persisted throughout the SAP's history.

These problems were exacerbated by the political role the police were forced to play. The white Union of South Africa was beset by internal conflicts between Boer and Briton, capitalist and worker. The SAP became an instrument of the government, which was dominated by British capitalist interests. The first major police actions, in 1913 and 1914, were to put down strikes by white workers. During the First World War SAP members were not only conscripted for the South African invasion of German South West-Africa – part of South Africa's contribution to the British Empire's war effort – but had to suppress an anti-British Afrikaner rebellion. Curiously, the police themselves helped kindle the rebellion by accidentally shooting dead General Koos de la Rey, an Afrikaner hero in the Anglo-Boer War, at a roadblock set up to catch a gangster.[6] It would not be the last time that police trigger-happiness provoked a political crisis.

In 1922 a strike by white workers on the Witwatersrand rapidly turned into an armed insurrection. Again, the police, supported by the army, were called in to put it down, resulting in the deaths of up to 250 people.[7] Mobile police units also engaged in rural campaigns to crush black resistance, continuing the frontier colonial tradition of punitive raids. At Bulhoek in the Eastern Cape, 200 members of a defiant religious group were massacred by police, and a joint police-military force crushed a rebellion by the Bondelswarts people in South West Africa.

POLICING URBAN AREAS

Policing in the burgeoning black urban areas followed the frontier tradition rather than the metropolitan model. Police mounted 'raids' on what was essentially seen as 'enemy territory' to demonstrate their power, enforce regulations and suppress pockets of defiance.

A host of colonial-style laws regulated the lives of black South Africans and were aimed at forcing them into the wage economy and providing revenue for the state. Police spent much of their time checking passes and tax receipts and enforcing restrictions like the liquor laws which prohibited Africans from drinking certain types of alcohol. Punishment was often dispensed summarily by police officers, and in the magistrates' courts cases under the pass laws and other restrictions were rushed through with little attention to the requirements of justice. Often police themselves were the prosecutors – another feature of policing in South Africa which has persisted long after other countries have abandoned it. The pass laws were also used to secure virtual slave labour for white farms. Black prisoners, many arrested under the pass or tax laws, were made available as cheap or unpaid labour to white farmers. Later the farmers chipped in to help build jails, drawing prison labour in proportion to their contribution. By the 1950s, 200,000 prisoners were working for farmers every year.[8]

Policing in black urban areas took an increasingly political turn as resistance hardened. In 1929 around Durban, in one of the first large-scale urban cordon-and-search operations, a force of police was assembled to break a boycott of municipal beer-halls (the state gained considerable income from controlling alcohol sales to Africans). Townships were surrounded and sealed off while police went from door to door interrogating residents and rounding up those whose papers were not in order. Teargas was used for the first time.[9] In what was to become a familiar refrain, the Commissioner of Police, Colonel I.P. de Villiers, declared that the trouble was all the result of 'propaganda by communist agents'.

The SAP increasingly called for greater powers of surveillance and repression on the grounds that the Communist Party of South Africa, which was expanding from its base in the white working class to embrace the struggle for black rights, was a threat to the state. The party was also accused of manipulating the growing black trade union movement. The SAP's Detective Branch turned its attention to black opposition groups in the towns. A special branch was set up at police headquarters in Pretoria to counter those whom the Commissioner of Police labelled 'communist and other agitators, unscrupulous persons who issued propaganda to ignorant and peaceable natives'.[11] This was the precursor of the Security Branch which was to play a critical role in suppressing black resistance in the second half of the century.

The involvement of the police in war, rebellion and civil strife undercut efforts to develop and stabilise the force. Organisational problems were the main theme of commissioners' reports during the 1920s and 1930s. Although English-speaking whites still dominated the government, after 1927 over 90 per cent of the annual white intake into the police were Afrikaners, and this has remained the case ever since. Policemen chafed against the militaristic discipline they had to endure and their poor pay and conditions, and Afrikaner nationalist sentiment took root amongst lower-ranking white policemen. Public complaints against the police mounted and tension rose as officers struggled to enforce the pass laws, liquor laws and taxation on the growing black urban population: three-quarters of all prosecutions against Africans were for violations of discriminatory legislation.[12]

In 1936 the government appointed a commission of inquiry, the Lansdown Commission, to get to the bottom of the problems. The commission concerned itself mainly with internal grievances in the force, but it identified what has been the fundamental problem of policing in South Africa:

> We are of the opinion, after a careful survey of the evidence, that the relations between natives and police are marked by a suppressed hostility which excludes whole-hearted co-operation .... This is due partly to the odium incurred by the police in enforcing unpopular legislation, but is contributed to by the manner in which such enforcement is carried out and the general attitude of some individual policemen to the native population.[13]

Black police were also criticised by the commission for their alleged 'tendency ... to consider arrest in itself as a punitive measure justifying the application to the arrested person of some measure of unnecessary force, if not assault.'[14] In what was to prove an enduring principle of policing in South Africa, responsibility for the policing of black communities was devolved increasingly to black officers. The black police themselves were treated worse in every respect than their white counterparts and were instructed to 'leave the European population alone'.[15]

The outbreak of the Second World War traumatised the SAP, as most Afrikaners, who now made up the majority of the force, opposed the government's declaration of war against Germany. The history of the SAP, commissioned to mark its 75th anniversary, states that 'the majority of policemen were members of the Ossewa Brandwag', an organisation which openly supported the Nazis. Only a small minority volunteered to serve abroad in the war against fascism.[16] However, support for the Brandwag dropped off quickly when its wartime attempts at sabotage failed and it was disowned by the National Party, which was increasingly becoming the voice of the Afrikaner people. The security section of the SAP, the 'special branch', played a prominent role in cracking down on pro-German activists. Ironically, amongst the thousands it helped to detain in this period was Hendrik van den Bergh, who in the 1960s was to head the reconstituted Security Branch.[17]

In the war years, which saw rapid industrialisation, partly through arms and ammunition manufacture, an increasingly militant black urban working class initiated many strikes and protests, and in 1946 the police put down a strike by over 60,000 black mineworkers, killing six and injuring 600. The Communist Party benefited from this new militancy – and from the Soviet contribution to the defeat of Hitler – and extended its influence in the black trade union movement. The ANC, which until then had relied largely on the politics of petitioning, had been revitalised by Nelson Mandela and other youthful leaders who were set on mobilising mass actions for black rights. This was the cue for the SAP to set up the Security Branch to counter threats to 'internal security'. The first members of the branch, including its commander, were trained in Britain and learnt their techniques from the British police and intelligence services.[18] Most of its members were drawn from the SAP's Detective Branch, who were accustomed to operating covertly, and it set about establishing a network of informers in the townships. But the branch remained small – no more than 100 strong – during the 1940s and 1950s.[19]

Policing Apartheid

The police were a vital part of the structure of laws, courts, bureaucracy and armed forces that maintained white domination. The force that the National Party inherited when it took over the reins of government after winning the 1948 white election was already quasi-military and racially segregated. Policemen saw nothing unusual in being deployed in the political role of countering threats to the government of the day. Their approach to the black population was essentially authoritarian and confrontational and their main task was to enforce repressive and restrictive legislation.[20] By 1947, annual prosecutions under racially linked statutes had risen to nearly half a million, and made up over 40 per cent of all prosecutions.[21] The stage was set for the close alliance between government and police in the long campaign to enforce apartheid and suppress political opposition.

'AFRIKANERISATION'

Alongside the new laws it introduced to entrench segregation, notably the pass laws and the Group Areas Act, the National Party brought in legislation which strengthened the powers of the police and largely removed them from public scrutiny. The new government viewed the police as its 'first line of defence' and substantially increased the strength of the force: between 1952 and 1958 authorised manpower rose by 50 per cent.[22] Apartheid increased the need for black police, especially because each racial group would as far as possible be responsible for its 'own' policing. For the first time, some police stations in black areas were placed under the control of black non-commissioned officers – but under close white supervision.[23]

The loyalty of white police to the National Party was encouraged through an Afrikaner cultural organisation set up within the SAP, known as Akpol, which is still active today. Although ostensibly concerned with promoting the use of Afrikaans, and 'Afrikaans art and culture', Akpol spread the message of Christian Nationalism, the ideology of the National Party. Its motto is 'The trek continues'. As the SAP's history puts it:

The Force was regarded as an important component of the [Afrikaner] nation which supplied its manpower and it was believed that policemen felt called upon to contribute, as individuals and as a unit, to the maintenance and expansion of the nation's common spiritual concerns.[24]

Religion itself came to play an increasingly important ideological role in justifying police actions. The underlying assumption was that because the Afrikaners were the chosen people, guided by God, the police were God's instruments to achieve His will.

The nation that the police served consisted only of whites, of course: blacks were outsiders and they were increasingly criminalised. Afrikaner nationalist criminologists argued that Africans were unsophisticated and traditionalist, and that their value systems were undermined by exposure to the ways of the whites. Integration led to crime. From there it was a short step to the notion that integration itself was a crime. Thousands of black South Africans were arrested and treated as offenders for using amenities reserved for whites, or for living in the wrong areas – even private mixed gatherings were broken up on the grounds of the liquor laws. While Africans were the main targets, coloured and Indian South Africans were forced to live in ghettoes under the Group Areas Act and were subjected to rigid segregation. One of the justifications for stamping out the Communist Party, banned in 1950, was that it led to integration; but even the liberal opposition began to be seen as a threat on the grounds that 'racial mixing' was the thin end of the wedge of communism or anarchy.[25]

RESISTANCE AND CRACKDOWN

Harsh, insensitive policing and the intensification of segregation helped to harden African attitudes. Black South Africans became increasingly determined to rid themselves of the destructive and demeaning strictures of apartheid. The 1950s were a decade of defiance: the ANC embarked on a programme of strikes, civil disobedience and non-cooperation. Nelson Mandela led the ANC and its allies into a mass passive resistance campaign in 1952, which included breaking 'unjust laws'. The police responded by rounding up thousands of protesters. Over 8,000 were jailed. In parts of the country there were violent clashes between police and demonstrators and new repressive laws were introduced, including the Public Safety Act, which allowed for a State of Emergency to be imposed. The Suppression of Communism Act was used to harass and remove from public life hundreds of people, including many non-communists. The ANC fought back, often outwitting the Security Branch in a game of cat and mouse.[26]

After extensive Security Branch raids in 1956 to gather evidence, the police arrested Mandela and 155 other resistance leaders. Tried with treason, all were eventually acquitted four years later, but the trial had achieved the objective of tying up the leadership and preventing them from directing resistance campaigns. Despite all the police activity, the momentum of mass resistance appeared to be unstoppable. Poverty and the constant irritation of police raids and bureaucratic controls motivated black South Africans to organise strikes, boycotts and protests throughout the 1950s.[27]

On 21 March 1960 a line of police, vastly outnumbered and apparently ill-prepared, opened fire on an angry crowd. The shooting at the gates of Sharpeville police station, in which 69 people were killed, sparked off other protests which the police again suppressed with rifle fire. The government declared a State of Emergency. Police and army units sealed off townships in Cape Town and Durban and rounded up 11,000 people.[28] Resistance spread to rural areas as well, and in Pondoland in the Eastern Cape mobile police and army units had to put down a peasant rising that verged on guerilla war.

The police viewed the uprisings as a challenge to legitimate authority by 'agitators' and 'intimidators' who instigated 'riots'.[29] This had already become the standard lexicon with which successive police commanders described any resistance to white rule. The police argued that the bulk of black South Africans were law-abiding and accepted the legitimacy of the state and its institutions – there were a small number of troublemakers who caused unrest and had to be eliminated. The police needed strong powers to deal with the agitators and the 'communist' organisations which gave them sustenance.

This logic led in April 1960 to the banning of the ANC and the Pan-Africanist Congress. Their leaders were hunted down, but Mandela, Walter Sisulu and others evaded the police dragnet and went underground, while Oliver Tambo had been sent out of the country to set up an external organisation. In December 1961 the ANC launched its armed struggle, declaring: 'The time comes in the life of any nation when there remain only two choices – submit or fight.'[30] In the next two years, the ANC carried out over 200 operations – virtually all were sabotage jobs involving no loss of life. A PAC offshoot, Poqo, was less discriminating – it encouraged an insurrection which flared briefly in parts of the country before the police clamped down. The SAP took this as an indication that guerilla war was imminent. 'Anti-riot training', which included instruction in aspects of counter-insurgency warfare, was introduced. Some police were taught to use Browning heavy machine-guns and closer operational links were forged with the SADF.[31]

But the Security Branch, through its intelligence work, was able to crack the underground structures set up by the ANC and PAC. Surveillance, interrogation (and often torture) of suspects, followed by trials and imprisonment, formed the bedrock of the SAP's political strategy in the early 1960s. Only in rural areas was counter-insurgency more important than intelligence work – here mobile units, modern mechanised variants of the old Mounted Rifles, were used.[32]

THE POLICE STATE

The police were granted increasingly draconian powers, thanks mainly to the single-mindedness of Balthazar Johannes Vorster, who was Minister of Justice between 1961 and 1966 before he became Prime Minister. The SAP's official history records that the police were 'jubilant' at Vorster's appointment, for here 'was the strong political head it had been looking for.'[33] Vorster, who had been interned along with van den Bergh during the war for his membership of the Ossewa Brandwag, believed that firm action was needed, especially by the Security Branch, to counter what he saw as a gathering revolution. Working closely with his police commanders, he steered through parliament a string of laws which increased the state's powers to banish, restrict and detain its opponents and ban meetings and organisations. New laws defined offences such as 'subversion' and 'terrorism' very broadly to facilitate prosecutions. Police were given powers to detain people without trial initially for 12 days, then for 90 days, then 180, and finally, with the passage of the Terrorism Act in 1967, for as long as they wanted. Torture of detainees became routine and it contributed to the 68 deaths in political detention by 1990.[34]

The new laws also made it easier for the courts to convict government opponents, and mass political trials followed police arrests. One study shows that between March 1963 and August 1964, 1,315 people were charged with political offences, of whom 44 were sentenced to death and 12 to life imprisonment.[35] Amongst those jailed were the underground leaders of the ANC and PAC, including Nelson Mandela. They were all victims of the Security Branch's intelligence system, which relied on informers, interrogation of suspects and detective work. Robben Island and others jails began to fill with political prisoners. The security police grew increasingly powerful.[36] By 1985 over 5,000 members of the SAP had been trained in 'internal security', although not all of these were in the Security Branch.[37]

By the mid-1960s armed resistance had been shattered, but the police were still obsessed with ferreting out potential enemies of the state. Individuals who dared to oppose the regime were forced out of the country, placed under house arrest, banned from working, writing or meeting other people, or banished to remote corners of the land. The security police stamped on the merest flickers of opposition. South Africa exhibited all the features associated with an authoritarian police state – paranoid fear of opposition, political intolerance, invasion of privacy, the midnight knock on the door.

It was not only political repression that made South Africa in the 1960s a police state. Partly as a result of the criminalisation of Africans through apartheid laws, the prison population doubled in ten years, to a daily average of 66,500 in 1963.[38] By 1967, a million Africans were being prosecuted annually for offences under discriminatory legislation such as the pass and poll tax laws and liquor restrictions.[39] Hangings were being carried out at such a rate that a South African professor of law, Barend van Niekerk, calculated that nearly half of all executions in the world were taking place in South Africa.[40]

In the 1960s the police found new quarry. With the black resistance movement quiescent, they honed the skills needed to preserve the purity of the apartheid state. Rising rates of serious crime were not allowed to deflect them from implementing elaborate schemes to trap white men suspected of sleeping with black women. They also found the time to conduct propaganda campaigns against 'foreign influences' like pop music.

The trend towards authoritarianism and the centralisation of power was accelerated when Vorster took over the premiership in September 1966. Holding on to his justice portfolio, he promoted the chief of the Security Branch, Lieutenant-General Hendrik van den Bergh, to head a new agency, the Bureau for State Security. The organisation's acronym, BOSS, encapsulated its attitude not only to the population at large but also to the other security agencies of the state: it was a uniquely privileged and powerful organisation. However, although BOSS recruited initially mainly from the security police, its operatives did not have powers of arrest and the Security Branch retained its operational role. Van den Bergh worked closely with Prime Minister Vorster. The SAP and BOSS were the dominant forces in the intelligence community – although the SADF tried to compete with BOSS it did not have the ear of Vorster and was sidelined when it came to strategic decision-making.[41]

In the SAP during the 1960s there was a new emphasis on professionalisation, training, diversification and the introduction of new technology. The force was plagued by personnel shortages, however. These were boom years for white South Africa, and the police could not compete with the private sector for labour. Like the railways and some other state sectors, the police mopped up the dregs of the white, especially Afrikaner, workforce. This may have ensured full white employment, but the SAP could not meet its authorised personnel requirements. Although wages and conditions improved, they remained low relative to the private sector – the government feared that wage rises in the police force would set off a spiral of claims in other state sectors.[42]

The number of black policemen steadily increased, but many of them were destined for the fledgling police forces of the new African homelands, or bantustans, which the apartheid masterplan created to strip black South Africans of their citizenship.

Counter-insurgency and Riot Control

THE CULTURE OF COUNTER-INSURGENCY

Many members of South Africa's liberation movements went into exile in the

1960s and began to prepare for guerilla war. They were hampered by their lack of access to South Africa, surrounded as it was by white-ruled Rhodesia and the Portuguese colonies of Angola and Mozambique. But in the mid-1960s African nationalists launched armed struggles in the Portuguese colonies and in Rhodesia, where Ian Smith had unilaterally declared independence from Britain and proclaimed another thousand years of white-minority rule. In South West Africa, by now known internationally as Namibia, the South West African People's Organisation, SWAPO, took up arms in 1966 in order to end the South African occupation which had continued since the First World War.

These countries were South Africa's buffers against the new independent states to the north, and Pretoria was naturally keen to prevent them falling into the hands of the liberation movements. It was police and not military units which were despatched to Rhodesia and northern Namibia. To the SAP, which occupied such an important position in upholding the security of the nation, this was a natural progression. The police saw guerilla warfare as a new phase in the battle against ideological crime. As one of the SAP's historians has it: 'Police action against terrorists was simply equated with combating crime, and the Police Force readily identified with this concept.'[43] As far as the South African state was concerned, it was not at war, countering armed struggle by oppressed peoples; it was dealing with small groups of nefarious and criminal terrorists.

The SAP was engaged in counter-insurgency warfare continuously for a quarter of a century. In 1966 police units were despatched to Namibia, and the next year to Rhodesia. The SADF took over Namibian operations in 1973, when it became clear the police could no longer cope alone, but police counter-insurgency operations were resumed four years later and continued until the war ended in 1989. Most members of the SAP were frequently called upon for periods of three months or more to fight a harsh war in the bush against African nationalists. This experience affected their attitude towards the black population at home: they were seen not so much a community to be served as an enemy to be countered. Many of the strategies and tactics learnt in the bush were transferred to South Africa's townships – a culture of counter-insurgency was instilled.

The guerilla wars also led to the arming of black police, and the SAP learnt the value of black counter-insurgency forces: they were cheaper, their lives were politically expendable, and they understood better the local terrain and its people. The SAP discovered that by using semi-autonomous black forces, whether police or vigilantes, it could distance itself from politically sensitive or extra-legal tasks. Many of the policing strategies used in the 1980s and 1990s were pioneered in the Rhodesian or Namibian wars: the use of rudimentarily trained black auxiliary forces and special constables; the establishment of ethnic units under the control of 'homeland' authorities and chiefs collaborating with the authorities; the development of units drawn mainly from captured ex-guerillas and trained for irregular operations.[44]

The counter-insurgency campaign fuelled the SAP's obsession with the notion of a communist onslaught against South Africa. The guerilla liberation armies were supported in different degrees by either the Soviet Union or China – as well as by many African countries. South Africa's rulers, who had watched African countries to the north slough off colonial rule and in some cases attempt to develop socialist alternatives, believed that the forces of communism, whose handmaidens were 'anarchy' and 'terrorism', had their eyes on South Africa. Zimbabwe, Namibia, and later Angola and other countries in Southern Africa were referred to simply as 'the border', even though the fighting was sometimes a thousand kilometres from South African territory.

Two dramatic events in the mid-1970s shook South Africa's security apparatus and switched the spotlight from the police to the SADF. In 1974 the dictatorship which had ruled Portugal for decades collapsed in a military coup led by disaffected officers. One of the first decisions of the new regime was to rid itself of the colonies, even if this meant handing over to the liberation movements in Angola and Mozambique. The SADF was determined to prevent the Marxist MPLA movement from coming to power in Angola, and towards the end of 1975 it invaded Angola from its bases in neighbouring Namibia, intent on installing the rival Unita movement in power. But its armoured columns were beaten at the gates of the capital, Luanda, by Cuban forces brought in by the MPLA. The new government in Luanda allowed SWAPO guerillas to operate from its territory, and the war in northern Namibia escalated rapidly. The Cubans stayed in Angola: proof incarnate to Pretoria's strategists of the communist threat. In Mozambique, the Marxist Frelimo movement swept to power, soon opening its border with Rhodesia to Zimbabwean nationalist guerillas. Within a few years the white-minority regime of Ian Smith was losing the war.

Soweto

The regional crisis was less the concern of the SAP than the SADF, which began to gear up for a regional war. The police had more than enough to worry about inside South Africa. A wave of strikes swept the country in 1973, and police became preoccupied with monitoring and harassing an emerging wave of black consciousness organisations. In mid-1976 Soweto erupted: police attacks on a relatively peaceful demonstration provoked further demonstrations, more killings and a cycle of violence that twisted through most of South Africa in the next six months. The police responded ferociously: an estimated 1,000 people were killed and between 10,000 and 20,000 arrested or detained. Many of those affected were children, who had sparked the uprisings by protesting against apartheid education.[45]

While the scale of the killings led to a public and international outcry, the police adopted the same approach as they had in the 1960 crisis: the riots were the result of agitators and firm action was needed to nip them in the bud. There appeared to be little effort at restraint. 'Instructions have been given to maintain law and order at all costs,' declared Vorster two days after the uprisings began. Much of the shooting during the Soweto uprisings was carried out by riot squads, established in the previous 18 months in several centres around the country. The units drew on the skills of a new élite urban 'anti-terrorist' corps, the Special Task Force.[46] The riot squads and the Special Task Force were set up with Israeli and other external assistance and advice. In 1975 General Moir Armit, former head of Israeli intelligence, visited South Africa and disclosed that Israel was providing guidance on urban warfare techniques. SAP officers also toured European countries to study riot control methods, visited Argentina and claimed that they had visited the US, although this was denied by the State Department. In 1977 a trip to Scotland Yard by an SAP brigadier intent on drawing on the British experience of counter-insurgency in Northern Ireland was stopped by anti-apartheid activists; nevertheless, the SAP gained extensive information on British methods. They also drew on the experiences of the Rhodesian police.[47]

Riot squad members were selected on the basis of their bush-war experience and had to complete intensive counter-insurgency training. Like the rest of the police, these units were issued with rifles instead of less lethal anti-riot equipment, and they were unprotected by visors or shields. They took to the streets in their camouflage outfits and, armed with automatic rifles, operated on a 'shoot first, ask questions later' basis. In Soweto alone, police fired 16,433 rounds of ammunition, mostly from automatic rifles, in the first two-and-a-half months of the uprising.[48] The crossover from bush to township was perhaps symbolised most graphically in the person of Colonel Theunis 'Rooi Rus' Swanepoel, who had commanded the first operation against SWAPO at Omgulumbashe in northern Namibia, become an infamous Special Branch interrogator and was drafted into Soweto on the first day of the uprisings in command of a riot squad. Interviewed in the 1980s, Swanepoel made it clear that he had no regrets, or rather, he regretted only not using more force. Employing simple military logic, he asserted that, 'You can only stop violence by using a greater amount of violence.'[49] Another ugly feature of the police response was the use of indirect methods of policing, especially through 'vigilantes' – mostly hostel-dwellers who were encouraged by the police to attack other Soweto residents (see Chapter 2).

The use of firepower was backed up by mass arrests, the detention, interrogation and often torture of suspected leaders, and later the banning of organisations thought to be involved. Steve Biko, the most prominent of the black consciousness leaders, died in police custody in September 1977, and the next month all the black consciousness organisations were banned.

Police actions inflamed the disorder and contributed to it spreading. The repression also resulted in an upsurge of ANC sabotage actions, and the head of the security police reckoned that in the two years after the uprising began the ANC and PAC recruited at least 3,000 young exiles into their military structures.[50] The brutality of security operations had led to international condemnation, resulting in a flight of investment capital and the imposition of a mandatory arms embargo by the UN.[51] The arms embargo, adopted by the Security Council in November 1977, included 'paramilitary police equipment' in the list of 'arms and related materiel' which states were prohibited from supplying to South Africa. (This, and pressures from anti-apartheid activists, would make it increasingly difficult for the SAP to secure the level of international cooperation it had come to rely upon.)

The urban unrest was confirmation for a growing group of reformers within the business community, the National Party and sections of the security establishment that apartheid as it stood was too costly and would prove unpoliceable and indefensible. For years the system had been creaking – the sheer volume of pass law offences, for example, was absorbing ever-increasing bureaucratic and police resources. Government under Vorster had grown unwieldy and uncoordinated, and the military establishment was keen to streamline decision making and marshal the resources of the state to deal with the external and internal threats. The rate of economic growth had declined in the 1970s and many business analysts believed the economy was being held back by structural strains resulting from apartheid – there was an urgent need to reform aspects of the labour system. The military, anxious to build up the state's armaments production capabilities, increase the funds available for war and stabilise the political situation, shared some of the concerns of business leaders.[53]

The reformist alliance of business, security and political chiefs believed that without sweeping changes to the system there could be no security. But reforms had to be managed carefully within clear limits, and they had to take place behind a security shield. The reformist initiative was not inimical to firm security action – on the contrary, it depended upon it. The reformers, especially in the security establishment, took to heart the admonitions of an American political scientist, Samuel Huntington:

> Reform and repression may proceed hand-in-hand .... Effective repression may enhance the appeal of reform to radicals by increasing the costs and risks of revolution and to stand-patters by reassuring them of the government's ability to maintain order.[54]

The changes that the reformers wanted to make stopped short of addressing the question of political power,[55] but the reformers regarded coercion without cooption as unworkable. While the old police strategy of destroying opposition organisations through infiltration, interrogation, disruption and the use of the courts still had its place, this was not enough to deal with what was increasingly seen as a revolutionary situation.

Total Strategy

A strategy that could accommodate the requirements of reform and repression was being propagated in the think-tanks of the SADF, and to a lesser extent amongst the general staff of the SAP. Its starting point was, inevitably, the 'communist onslaught' which was increasingly seen as multi-dimensional or 'total'. Onto this were grafted the strategies adopted in other counter-insurgency wars, especially those of the French in Algeria.

As early as 1968 the basic tenets of what was to become known as Total Strategy were expounded by the SADF's General Alan Fraser. Arguing that revolutionary war was 20 per cent military action and 80 per cent political action, he claimed:

> Victory can be obtained by a government only by retaining and, if temporarily lost, by recapturing the support of the masses – and by the complete destruction of the insurgent organisation and the eradication of its influence upon the people .... The objective for both sides in a revolutionary war is ... the population itself.[56]

The principles of Total Strategy were derived largely from the writings of the French counter-insurgency strategist André Beaufre, who argued that struggles could be waged 'indirectly' in different fields: economic, social, political and psychological. To defeat an enemy in a counter-insurgency war, it was necessary to coordinate action over all this terrain, with the aim of restoring control and redressing grievances which could be exploited by revolutionaries. Thus the '20 per cent military, 80 per cent political' formula, which became almost a motto of South Africa's security chiefs: the security forces, given the right powers and resources would hold the line, but in the long run only good government and the redressing of some of the gross injustices of apartheid would guarantee stability.[57]

While apparently sophisticated, Total Strategy was an extreme outcome of the simplistic and by now unquestioned assumption of a 'total communist onslaught'. All aspects of life could be viewed through the prism of security, all opposition could be seen as part of an omnipresent threat. International pressure for sanctions, organisations committed to peaceful change in South Africa, all were seen in the context of the onslaught against a country which stood virtually alone against communist expansionism. As a government commission of inquiry put it in 1980:

> South Africa, and indeed the whole of Southern Africa, faces the external threat of

a violent transformation to a Marxist state. This has already happened in Angola and Mozambique. However, there is also interference from the so-called 'action for peaceful change' from Western circles, which, in itself, also contains the potential danger of a revolutionary transformation of the South and Southern African community.[58]

Similar views were expressed by the then head of the Security Branch, General P. J. Coetzee (soon to become Commissioner of the SAP). A self-proclaimed expert on communism and one of the SAP's few intellectuals – his PhD thesis focused on the small Trotskyist tradition in South Africa – General Coetzee asserted that 'black–white confrontation' was a result of the Soviet onslaught, using the tool of the ANC, as part of its global strategy against the West.[59]

The 'onslaught' theorists were responsible for a major misreading of Soviet intentions towards Southern Africa. Although the Soviet Union made no secret of its wish to see the end of white minority rule and supplied extensive military aid to Angola, Mozambique, the ANC and SWAPO, the region had a relatively low priority in its foreign policy. South Africa's assertion of its crucial strategic position was wishful thinking – it was peripheral to the Cold War conflict.[60]

SAP and SADF strategists erred fundamentally in concluding that Soviet military support for the ANC and SWAPO made them puppets of Moscow – in the ANC's case via the South African Communist Party. Although the party came to dominate the ANC, at least in its external and military structures,[61] the movement's agenda remained broadly nationalist and democratic, and most of its supporters could not be considered to be Marxists. These intelligence mistakes flowed in part from the habit of evoking the communist bogey for propaganda purposes, both to unite white South Africans and to try to secure Western support. They also came from the government's determination to deny the legitimacy of the anti-apartheid struggle. To accept that the ANC and other anti-apartheid groups had legitimate grievances and objectives would be to undermine the cause that the police, army and other institutions of the state were defending.

Defence Minister P. W. Botha became the leading exponent of Total Strategy. He launched his manifesto in March 1977 in a government White Paper on defence which argued that the demands of security required action in the political, military, economic, psychological, scientific, technological, religious, cultural and other fields, including transport, financial and community services.[62] Vorster, and his ally Van den Bergh, were toppled by revelations of government involvement in illegal slush-funds – the 'Muldergate' scandal, named after one of the ministers involved, Connie Mulder – and Botha swept to power.[63]

With Botha in control, the military establishment, and not the police, now had the direct line to the government. And the SADF was much more ambitious and willing to tackle the broader issues of state policy: by and large the police (although not BOSS) had restricted themselves to the issues of countering 'subversion' and combating crime. But the police were by no means left out in the cold. They had accepted many of the precepts of what was to become known as Total Strategy. While they were not keen on the idea of winning hearts and minds, they readily accepted the notion of a total communist onslaught. By the mid-1980s the police were enthusiastic propagators of the total onslaught theory – a factor reflected in the terminology used in the annual reports of the Commissioner of Police.[64] With BOSS downgraded – it was eventually renamed the National Intelligence Service (NIS) – the Directorate of Military Intelligence came to dominate the intelligence field. The Security Branch continued to play an important role, however, and on an operational level inside South Africa, the SAP remained in charge of riot control and other operations.[65]

In 1972 Vorster had set up the State Security Council to coordinate security strategy, but it had fallen prey to political infighting and inter-departmental rivalries. Botha revived the council and increased its powers, sidelining the cabinet. Henceforth, all major strategic and security decisions were to be taken in the State Security Council. Underneath the council a network of secret committees was established to implement its decisions and coordinate government security action on a local level.[66] Although the system, known as the National Security Management System (NSMS), underpinned government strategy, it was not fully activated – in part it was envisaged as a substitute for the civilian administration in the event of a crisis.

The Botha government concentrated its security effort on building up the SADF: its budget was increased by around 40 per cent annually between 1974 and 1977, while the police got between 6 and 28 per cent more.[67] A massive mobilisation of the white population into local commandos was coupled with a campaign of aggressive militarisation, and the army gradually took over the patrolling of border areas from the police. War threatened the entire region during the first half of the 1980s as the SADF adopted a policy of 'forward defence' and mounted campaigns of destabilisation against neighbouring countries. It backed rebel forces seeking to harry or overthrow the new governments of Angola and Mozambique. The SADF viewed the Marxist government in Angola with particular alarm, largely because of the threat it posed to South African control of Namibia, and in the early 1980s it invaded and occupied parts of southern Angola. It also threatened Zimbabwe, which had become independent in 1980 after the Smith regime had been forced to agree to internationally supervised elections.[68] The SADF hoped both to eliminate the prospect of the ANC establishing rear bases for its guerilla war in Southern Africa and to bludgeon neighbouring states into a *Pax Pretoriana* in which South Africa's hegemony would be restored.[69]

While the SADF marauded around Southern Africa, the pressures on the police at home were mounting. Despite the banning of the black consciousness organisations in September 1977, the political aftershocks of Soweto continued, and the ANC stepped up its campaign of sabotage. The burden of enforcing racial legislation had been reduced by the ending of liquor restrictions and the poll tax, but arrests under the pass laws were still running at around 200,000 a year in the early 1980s (they were eventually phased out in 1985).[70] The police were also losing the battle against crime. Robberies went up by 47 per cent and burglaries by 66 per cent between 1970 and 1980.[71] Despite salary increases, manpower problems were endemic. A pioneering study of policing in coloured areas of Cape Town in 1982, for example, found that in one area, Grassy Park, with a population of about 100,000 people, a single police van and a few police were all that were available on each shift. [72]

Police and Army: The 'Security Family'

THE RABIE STRATEGY

The government was increasingly prepared to use the army to suppress resistance to its rule, but it still held to the old principle of criminalising opposition by using the police and courts. This strategy was set out in the early 1980s by a commission headed by Justice Rabie which reviewed security legislation. The commission argued that:

> activities which threaten the internal security of the Republic should, as far as circumstances permit, be combated as crimes. Such a line of action is, so long as it can be maintained, preferable to a situation where subversive activities are combated by military measures.[73]

Measures such as prolonged detention without trial were needed to counter the total onslaught, argued the commission. Executive action was needed as well as judicial action:

> since it is the duty of the executive authority to watch over the security of the State, the final decision as to what must be regarded as a threat to the security of the State and what steps should be taken to ensure the security of the State, should also rest with the executive authority.[74]

As a result of the commission's recommendations, a new Internal Security Act was introduced in 1982, which amalgamated and rationalised previous security legislation. The act remained the main instrument in political trials and was widely used for detentions until 1991 when some of its provisions were amended (see Chapter 2). The act defined offences such as 'terrorism', 'communism' and 'subversion' in very broad terms, for which sentences up to the death sentence could be imposed. As a South African law professor has pointed out, many of the security offences were defined so vaguely as to undermine the meaning of innocence and guilt.[75]

The Internal Security Act continued to allow the minister of law and order, on the basis of secret Security Branch reports, to 'ban' individuals – to restrict them to certain places or prohibit them from specified activities, including meeting other people. It empowered the minister to ban organisations, publications and meetings or impose restrictions on them (magistrates could also prohibit meetings). Most significantly for police work, four sections of the Act established different ways in which people could be detained without trial. The Rabie Commission argued that this was the most important, and often the only means the police had of obtaining information on 'subversive activities'.[76] The Act authorised police to detain people for several purposes:

- Under Section 28 people could be detained, on the authorisation of the minister of law and order, to prevent them committing an offence.

- Section 29 allowed the police to detain people indefinitely for interrogation (subject only to a board of review after six months). People held in detention in this way would be denied access to lawyers and relatives.

- Under Section 31, the attorney-general could authorise people to be held for the duration of a trial to be used as state witnesses.

- Section 50 allowed police, of the rank of lieutenant-colonel or above, to detain people for up to 14 days, while Section 50 (a), which had to be declared to be in force by the State President in specific circumstances, allowed the police to detain people for up to six months.[77]

The Act was buttressed by three other laws introduced in 1982, the Intimidation Act, the Protection of Information Act and the Demonstrations in or near Court Buildings Act, while the Public Safety Act, allowing for the declaration of States of Emergency, remained on the statute books.[78]

With this arsenal of laws at his disposal, the new police commissioner, General P. J. Coetzee, could declare:

> From my point of view as Commissioner of Police, the revolutionary ANC terrorist is necessarily an outlaw or criminal, because South African law which I am duty and honour bound to uphold, very specifically categories [sic] terrorist conspiracies and actions as criminal offences.[79]

But the strategy mapped out by the Rabie Commission, to treat revolutionary actions as crimes 'so long as (the strategy) can be maintained' soon proved inadequate. In the early 1980s, in all the areas in which apartheid had inflicted its wounds – housing, education, on the factory shopfloor, in the bantustans – people organised in opposition. Mass organisations based in local communities or organising youth, students and women, and which had gained strength by mobilising around specific grievances, allied themselves with an increasingly powerful trade union movement and identified themselves with the ANC's policies. The ANC also managed to step up its campaigns of sabotage and 'armed propaganda' despite all the efforts of the SAP. To police and military strategists, this was confirmation of the 'total onslaught'.

In 1983 hundreds of opposition organisations – church organisations, mass-membership youth and community associations, single-issue campaigns, even sports associations – came together in the United Democratic Front (UDF). It immediately set about mobilising against the jewel in the crown of the Total Strategists' reforms: a new 'constitutional dispensation' in which Indian and coloured South Africans – but not Africans – would have the vote (albeit to chambers of parliament effectively subservient to the white one).

In the townships, opposition hardened against black local authorities which were imposed as part of the reformist initiative. These protests coalesced with ongoing struggles around education and housing issues. The police riot squads and the Security Branch were strengthened, and the police budget was substantially increased (in 1982/3 by 55 per cent); but the Botha government showed an increasing willingness to deploy troops when it felt the police could not cope alone. The concept of a 'partnership' of the police and army in the coordinated effort to stamp out revolution was gaining sway, particularly as the ANC's armed struggle was becoming a significant factor in stretching the regime's defences. The military began to take on some policing functions. In 1977 the defence force argued that 'the responsibility for combating internal and especially urban unrest rests primarily with the SAP', but by 1982 it was talking of 'joint action' and of uniting 'the Security Forces into a well-knit community'.[80]

Demarcation of responsibility in the early 1980s was established in a policy declaration signed by the chief of the defence force and the Commissioner of Police. According to Major-General Albertus 'Bert' Wandrag, then the SAP's head of counter-insurgency and riot control, this specified that:

> the SA Police is primarily responsible for riot control and the combating of insurgency .... The SA Defence Force is employed in a supporting role, until armed conflict commences, after which the responsibility is to be taken over by the SA Defence Force with the SA Police in a supporting role.[81]

The police retained their distinctive intelligence tasks, and the Security Branch continued to be responsible for interrogating detainees and infiltrating organisations. Police Commissioner Coetzee, basing his views on his years in the Security Branch, reportedly preferred stealth to confrontation, favouring covert manipulation of ideological and other differences within opposition organisations in order to divide them. Believing that the UDF was too powerful to crush and that banning it would merely force it underground, he was reportedly behind the government's relatively tolerant attitude to the organisation in its first years.[82] Nevertheless, he made preparations for more intense confrontations and when it came to the test proved a ruthless operator. He argued the police corner against the SADF: even in times of 'violence, unrest and insurrection', the police had a specific role for which 'specialised and quasi-military units are to be deployed'. Even when the SADF had to be called in when 'mass uprisings' took place, it would need to draw on intelligence provided by the police's network of informers, and the police would retain a role in carrying out small-scale actions and specialised tasks. There was, said Coetzee, an urgent need to expand the SAP, especially the 'intelligence and para-military branches', and for coordinated joint action with the SADF and psychological and propaganda campaigns.[83]

The envisaged role of the police in counter-insurgency warfare and unrest was almost certainly influenced by growing contact between the SAP and the police forces of Argentina and Chile, both then under right-wing dictatorships specialising in the 'disappearance' of political opponents. The then commissioner of the SAP, General Mike Geldenhuys, accompanied by Brigadier Wandrag, were guests of the Argentinean and Chilean police in 1981, and especially admired Chile's militarised Special Task Force. Another visit to Chile, to study training methods and to 'strengthen existing ties' was made in 1983.[84] The Taiwanese police and security services, responsible for the tight grip kept on the Chinese republic by its anti-communist leaders, provided further inspiration. An official visit to South Africa in 1983 by General Ho En-Ting, commissioner of the Taiwanese police, was reciprocated a year later when General Coetzee and Major-General Lothar Neethling (who was later to be accused of involvement in political assassinations)[85] visited the island. General Coetzee, who received Taiwan's highest medal for foreigners, acclaimed the close links between the two forces:

> The main similarity between our two countries naturally remains the pledge to combat the Communist offensive against free nations everywhere .... It is therefore not surprising in such a situation that the two organisations that are directly involved in this threat, namely the Police Forces of the two countries, combine forces and share their experiences and resources.[86]

THE TOWNSHIPS ERUPT

In September 1984, simmering protests in the townships of the Vaal Triangle near Johannesburg led to an explosion of mass anger – police, councillors and other perceived collaborators were attacked. For the security chiefs, the ghost of Soweto had risen. They were determined not to let the situation get out control. The Minister of Law and Order, Louis le Grange, pledged to root out 'revolutionary ... criminal and intimidatory forces'.

The State Security Council authorised the marshalling of a force of 5,000 soldiers and 2,000 police. The joint force besieged Sebokeng, the township at the centre of the unrest, and entered it at midnight on 22 October for house-to-house searches. Four hundred people were arrested – but not one was charged with any political offence. The operation was seen by some observers as 'a glorified pass raid', but the UDF regarded it as 'a declaration of war'.[87] In a joint statement the ministers responsible for policing and for defence declared: 'Just as the police force support the Defence Force on the border, so the Defence Force is supporting the police in internal unrest situations.'[88] Although the police and troops made a cursory effort to win support, handing out pamphlets signed 'The friendly forces', the operation alienated the community, contributing to the success of a protest strike two weeks later.[89]

The Vaal Triangle did turn into another Soweto. Unrest spread across the country in the next months, and police and soldiers moved into townships, inflaming the situation by their strong-arm tactics. Assessing the spread of violence between August and November 1984, South Africa's Catholic bishops declared that the police were responsible for 'indiscriminate use of firearms; assaults and beatings; damage to property; provocation, callous or insensitive conduct; indiscriminate or reckless use of teargas ....' They gave examples of police shooting children, firing teargas into schools, firing into houses and on pedestrians from armoured vehicles, breaking up funerals, and looting shops. The police, they said, were 'now regarded by many people in the black townships as disturbers of the peace and perpetrators of violent crime.'[90] The SAP dismissed the claims in its customary manner as unfounded propaganda, implying that it was part of the 'total onslaught'.

The young UDF supporters, known as comrades, who spearheaded the uprising were fearless and desperate – the police battled to gain control, and in some areas the comrades ruled the streets. Police action was met with mass demonstrations, school boycotts, mass political strikes or stay-aways from work, rent strikes which undermined the finances of local authorities and consumer boycotts of white shops (which proved very effective in some areas in persuading white business to use its political clout to restrain the security forces). These tactics of mass action were combined with guerilla attacks and assaults by comrades on the 'collaborators'. The UDF talked of insurrection and 'people's power'; the ANC believed it was making a strategic breakthrough in its guerilla campaign which would lead to a 'people's war'.[91] The police and army generals pronounced that South Africa was on the brink of revolution.

The uprising had come at a critical time for the reforms introduced under the rubric of Total Strategy, and with its concessions seemingly thrown back in its face, the government came to rely for advice on police, military and intelligence 'securocrats'. Some of them argued that reform itself was leading to insecurity; most of them believed that the priority was to regain control.[92] The situation was complicated by the virtual collapse of the Security Branch's network of spies and informants in the townships. Many of them had been killed or intimidated – the 'necklace' of burning tires became a symbol of the fate of collaborators.

Counter-revolution

The securocrats got their way on 21 July 1985 when the government declared a State of Emergency over large parts of the country. It was lifted in March 1986, partly because the detention of nearly 8,000 people and strong police action had largely suppressed overt resistance, and also because the government was exploring prospects for negotiation with an Eminent Persons Group despatched by the Commonwealth. But unrest soon increased, and when it became clear that the Commonwealth initiative would depend on the introduction of full political rights for all South Africans, the securocrats scuppered it by authorising – apparently without cabinet approval – provocative military attacks on neighbouring Commonwealth countries.[83] The emergency was re-imposed nationally in June 1986. It remained in force until the onset of government-ANC negotiations in 1991.

The national emergency was not a knee-jerk reaction by security officials – it was a calculated act of long-term political planning aimed at restoring the initiative to the state. Police and military personnel were given sweeping powers under the emergency to use force, detain people, and enforce curfews, bans and other restrictions. Police and soldiers of any rank were empowered to detain people for 14 days to interrogate them, and were indemnified from prosecution, except where it could be shown they did not act 'in good faith'.[94] No distinction was made between soldiers and police in the regulations: the generic term 'security forces' covered them both (as well as members of the prisons service). If soldiers were back to 'internal security' tasks, as they had been in 1960 and before, the police were at war again.

Differences of opinion over strategy between and within the police, SADF and NIS did not end with the State of Emergency.[95] Many army officers would have preferred not to have used troops in combating internal unrest, although most saw no other option given the weakness of the police. General Jannie Geldenhuys articulated their objections:

> This is not the task for which we were primarily trained. We prefer to be a deterrent. When we have to fight, we want to use tanks and cannon rather than water cannon and plastic shields in internal disturbances.[96]

As they had in 1976, some army generals also regarded the police as incompetent, unnecessarily heavy-handed, prone to the excessive use of force and lacking in understanding of the long-term, hearts-and-minds imperatives of counter-insurgency. They feared – quite rightly – that what remained of the SADF's reputation as a national defence force standing above political conflicts would be undermined as soldiers were tarred with the same brush as the police.[97]

According to one analysis, the emergency was opposed by the SAP Commissioner, General Coetzee, who favoured the more traditional methods of infiltration, detention and imprisonment (although given the assault on his spy network, this would have been more difficult than in previous times). But the crackdown was backed by police generals such as Major-General Johan van der Merwe, then head of the Security Branch (he was promoted to Commissioner in 1989), and Major-General Bert Wandrag, head of counter-insurgency in the SAP.[98]

Shortly before the declaration of the emergency Wandrag expressed the view that harsh action was needed. Reflecting the typical world view of military and police commanders, based on the supposition that 'the communists consider the RSA to be target number one in their quest for world superiority, because of this country's strategic situation and its abundance of natural resources' he argued that:

> [The communists] prefer to foment domestic grievances – real as well as imagined – and to instigate the country's inhabitants to full-scale insurrection and revolution. The only way in which to render the enemy powerless is to nip revolution in the bud by ensuring that there is no fertile soil in which the seeds of revolution can germinate.
>
>   The role of the SA Police in this regard should be clearly understood. It is their task to police a community which is not of their making. They do, however, have a clear understanding of their task to maintain law and order ....[99]

This task, he made clear, involved 'firm action', in which the concept of 'minimum force' had little relevance.[100]

Within the overall framework of Total Strategy, which remained the guiding principle of the state, the reformist imperatives gave way under the national State of Emergency to a more tactical counter-insurgency focus. Beaufre, the grand strategist, was out of favour: instead, the SAP and SADF started quoting verbatim from a US army officer, John J. McCuen, who emphasised the more practical aspects of counter-insurgency. The new buzzwords were 'counter-revolutionary warfare'.

McCuen's approach was in essence quite simple – take what was presumed to be the strategy of the insurgents and reverse it:

> a governing power can defeat any revolutionary movement if it adapts the revolutionary strategy and principles and applies them in reverse to defeat the revolutionaries with their own weapons on their own battlefield.[101]

That the strategy was based largely on countering a Maoist-type campaign, which the ANC showed little inclination to follow, did not seem to disconcert the security forces, just as the lack of evidence of a Soviet fixation on Southern Africa had not weaned them from the 'total onslaught' thesis. At the time the ANC was in fact debating the virtues of urban-based insurrection as a revolutionary strategy, rather than the phased rural-oriented approach of Mao. (In securocrat circles there was some interest in the urban guerilla warfare theories of the Brazilian revolutionary Carlos Marighella – but, again, the ANC did not follow this brand of revolutionary theory.) [102]

Following McCuen, the securocrats argued that there were four phases in revolutionary warfare: 'organisation, terrorism, guerilla warfare, and mobile warfare'.[103] The authorities had to identify which phase they were in and then take the appropriate measures to reverse it back to the first phase, when they could engage in 'counter-organisation'. Psychological and social actions, the establishment of auxiliary police and military units and propaganda work would restore control over the population.

The new approach adopted by the securocrats still had a socio-economic and political dimension, but it was much attenuated. Instead of trying to solve national political issues, they argued that reform had to be undertaken from the bottom up, starting in specific areas once 'law and order' had been restored. It was characterised as 'reform by stealth'. While winning the support of the people was the final objective, this could only be achieved when the security forces regained control: 'You simply can't address the real grievances of people if there is no law and order,' said Adriaan Vlok, the Minister of Law and Order.[104]

The securocrats were not much interested in tinkering with the constitution or changing the existing political dispensation; instead they would unblock 'socio-economic bottlenecks' by improving local conditions and upgrading facilities. Improvements in housing, electricity supply and refuse removal were seen as the way to win hearts and minds.

The police, the military and the bureaucracy had to devise joint strategies and tactics to defeat the enemy in the day-to-day operational context as well as over the long term. The Directorate of Military Intelligence underlined this by quoting approvingly from General Templer, commander of the British forces in Malaya during the insurgency there:

> Any idea that the business of normal government and the business of the emergency are two separate entities must be killed for good and all. The two activities are completely and utterly interrelated.[105]

NATIONAL SECURITY MANAGEMENT SYSTEM

For this coordinated effort, the National Security Management System

(NSMS) introduced earlier by P.W. Botha was tailor-made, and it swung into action in 1986. Under the overall purview of the Office of the State President (aided by advisory committees) and the State Security Council (backed by a secretariat and work committee), a National Joint Management Centre was established, chaired by the Deputy Minister of Law and Order, Roelf Meyer (later Leon Wessels). The national centre oversaw the State of Emergency and coordinated the activities of 11 regional Joint Management Committees (JMCs), beneath which were 60 Sub-JMCs broadly following police divisional and sub-divisional breakdowns, 350 Mini-JMCs which corresponded to municipal boundaries, and a host of Local Management Centres covering the area of jurisdiction of a police station.[106] At each level, the JMCs were broken into committees dealing with security issues, political, economic and social matters, communications, and intelligence. Each also had a Joint Operational Centre responsible for coordinating police, army and other security force actions.

Military and police personnel were prominent at all levels in the NSMS, with the police taking control of lower levels and playing the dominant role in operational command. The military was deployed more widely than before and remained the main influence over the government, but the very fact that the primary threat was now seen as domestic and not external meant that the police began to reassert their role in strategic intelligence and hence in influencing state strategy. The emergency also required the substantial strengthening of the SAP, which began to draw away some of the state funds which previously would have flowed to the defence force.

The functioning of the committee-based NSMS was described thus:

> Each intelligence committee gathers and interprets the intelligence on which coordinated state activities are based. Staffed by representatives of military intelligence, the security police and the NIS, it seeks to promote unity of effort between these traditionally competing intelligence agencies. The security committee ... acts on the intelligence provided by the intelligence committee. Staffed by a combination of riot police officers, military officers, security branch officers and officers of the municipal police, kitskonstabels, and commando and civil defence units, it coordinates the implementation of security strategies....
>
> The welfare committee, on the other hand, takes responsibility for coordinating the functions of the civilian administration....
>
> The overall national security management strategy is sold to the public via the fourth of the JMC's committees, the communication committee....[107]

IMPLEMENTING THE COUNTER-REVOLUTION

With the NSMS activated, and vastly strengthened though the recruitment in particular of more security personnel, the police and army began to implement their counter-revolutionary strategy, with the aim of destroying the ANC and its allies and restoring the initiative to the state. The strategy entailed establishing a firm police and army presence in the townships and suppressing protest or resistance; 'taking out' leadership through mass detentions, trials, harassment and assassinations; re-establishing intelligence networks; the 'counter-organisation' of communities through setting up groups with links to the security forces and the use of vigilantes; and the alleviation of socio-economic grievances through the upgrading of selected trouble spots.

Police and troops poured into townships around South Africa, setting up joint bases and in places commandeering football stadiums and other facilities. They patrolled the streets in armoured vehicles – either the police fighting vehicle, the Casspir, which had been devised for use in the war zones of Namibia, or the army Buffel. Curfews and other restrictions were imposed, meetings were banned and where resistance had been intense townships were sealed off by troop cordons and razor-wire barricades, while police went from door to door searching for dissidents. Police action was often indiscriminate: the Institute of Race Relations reported that 720 people were killed by the security forces 'in the suppression of unrest' between September 1984 and October 1986.[108]

People were picked off the streets and interrogated about 'agitators'; leaders of community organisations, trade unions, religious and other groups were rounded up and thrown into jail or put in cells at police stations. A particular target was the alternative system of administration which emerged in some townships in the wake of the collapse of local government authority – street committees, 'people's courts' and the like. Nearly 30,000 people were detained in 1986, 10,000 of whom were under 18. Some were interrogated, most were simply locked away in an attempt to remove leadership from communities.[109] As Captain Craig Williamson, once the Security Branch's most renowned spy, put it:

> the State has to act fast and efficiently to preserve law and order by identifying and removing the revolutionary political leaders and the structures that support them from the positions they hold in the community.[110]

The police were fully stretched by all this activity. To strengthen them, and also as part of efforts to 'counter-organise' communities, the SAP established two new auxiliary black forces, the special constables and the municipal police. Vigilante groups were also set up and existing groups associated with local administrative structures were armed – even criminal gangs were used by the police to 'counter-organise'. In some areas, black police – who had borne the brunt of township anger – donned civilian clothing and rampaged through communities.

To 'cut the ground from under [the] feet' of the opposition, as General Wandrag put it, 34 townships were targeted for 'upgrading', and another 200 for lower-level attention. The 34 areas were selected for strategic reasons and known as 'oilspots' after one of McCuen's dictums about the expansion of 'strategic bases' once the population there has been 'counter-organised'. A few billion rands were earmarked for the provision of civic amenities, housing, transport and other facilities.[111]

By the end of 1986 the ferocity of repression had taken its toll; opposition organisations were in disarray, communities were demoralised and most of the structures of 'people's power' had been wiped out. The SADF increasingly shifted to its welfare brief, seeking to upgrade townships. But the opposition was already regrouping, and activists who had evaded the police net were reorganising. Besides, the state had been reluctant to confront the trade union movement head-on, for fear of its effects on the economy, and most of the church organisations had survived. The underground and military structures of the ANC stepped up operations. The ANC sought to expand its armed struggle under the slogan 'people's war' – guerillas would train others and arm whole communities to step up the attack.

At the end of 1987, there was the first indication that the state was testing the prospects of national negotiations, when it released ANC leader Govan Mbeki from prison.[112] The securocrats, however, were shaken by the massive popular reception he received. Lieutenant-General van der Merwe, then still head of the Security Branch, warned that the 'revolutionary climate' was on the increase and 'radical organisations are busy re-organising'.[113] A new clampdown was not long in coming. In February 1988 all the major resistance organisations were effectively banned, and severe restrictions were placed on the main trade union movement, the Congress of South African Trade Unions (COSATU).

The bans were not effectively enforced, and by then the police had adopted a less direct strategy to suppress and disorganise resistance – the emergency regulations were not used to the same extent and far fewer people were detained. Instead, extra-legal methods of repression such as assassination, arson and the bombing of offices became more common. The courts were also kept busy, processing the thousands of people charged with offences arising from the conflict, ranging from arson and public violence through to treason and murder. But by now opposition organisations had learnt to deal with extreme repression and were preparing for campaigns of mass protest.[114] COSATU defied the restrictions on it and, with the churches, helped to unify anti-apartheid organisations into a front opposing the government.

The state pushed ahead with its counter-revolutionary strategy, and with declining levels of townships unrest, attempted to regain the political initiative. The Minister of Law and Order stated in the middle of 1988 that the state now had a 'three-pronged counter-revolutionary plan': action against the 'revolutionaries', the 'upgrading' campaign and the introduction of a new constitutional scheme.[115]

The regime was making heavy weather with all three fronts, however: resistance was continuing to grow, and the upgrading campaign had had only limited effects. An attempt in April 1988 to introduce a new constitutional scheme allowing for limited African participation at central government level backfired – even Africans collaborating in bantustan structures rejected it as inadequate – and when elections were held in October in an attempt to restore local government, there was a massive boycott. Moreover, there was an upsurge of resistance in the bantustans and the ANC was still managing to extend its armed actions: General van der Merwe described the armed struggle as one of the most pressing problems facing the security forces.[116] The police, however, appeared to be sticking to their strategy: in a parliamentary White Paper on the SAP produced in 1988, the Minister of Law and Order declared that the SAP was 'an enthusiastic participant and implementor' in the state's 'total counter-revolutionary strategy'.[117]

The internal crisis was overlaid by a growing regional crisis, as it was in the mid-1970s. The SADF came unstuck in Angola. After over-extending itself, it failed in a counter-offensive against the MPLA and its Cuban allies and suffered heavy casualties when it tried to capture the town of Cuito Cuanavale. Angolan government forces recaptured all the territory occupied by South Africa since the early 1980s and with Cuban reinforcements swept down to the Namibian border early in 1988.[118] Pretoria was also under intense international pressure as the US and many other countries had imposed stringent financial and other sanctions in protest at the State of Emergency, and the South African economy had suffered. The new accommodation of the US with the Soviet Union added to the pressure – South Africa could no longer rely on tacit or actual US support for its operations against the MPLA and its Cuban allies. The government was forced to agree to pull out of Angola and allow Namibia to become independent after UN-supervised elections, although in return it did get a Cuban agreement to withdraw from Angola.

The settlement in Namibia and Angola increased the pressure for a negotiated solution in South Africa itself. Despite the advances it had made in its guerilla campaign and the mass support it had gathered during the State of Emergency, the ANC was not in a position where it could conceivably seize power. As the Commissioner of the SAP, General Hennie de Witt, put it in 1988:

It has become clear to the African National Congress, the United Democratic Front and their sympathisers that they will not be able to force South Africa and its peoples to their knees by means of violence.[119]

But the price paid for putting down the rebellion had been high and the ANC and its allies had certainly not been destroyed. Growing sections of the Afrikaner and National Party intelligentsia were openly criticising the continuing State of Emergency, and businessmen were making overtures to the ANC. The centralisation of authority through the NSMS, which gave president Botha extensive personal power, also alienated sections of the political establishment, especially as Botha became increasingly autocratic and irascible. Even at the height of their power, the securocrats were resisted by some government departments, notably foreign affairs.[120] Nor were the securocrats able to justify their dominance by beating the anti-communist drum so loudly: with the Cubans going from Angola, the Berlin Wall coming down and the Soviet Union in terminal crisis, the notion of a 'total communist onslaught' appeared increasingly absurd.

Faith in the counter-revolutionary strategy of the securocrats was being eroded. Old resentments against the way the military establishment in particular had ridden roughshod over the state bureaucracy and the government re-emerged. The ethos of an apolitical bureaucracy, subject to the direction of an elected government – no matter how much it might fly in the face of the facts – remained strong in the corridors of Pretoria, and the military establishment was seen to have undermined this tradition. In 1989, apparently for the first time, the cabinet overruled the State Security Council, authorising the release of detainees on hunger strike, and in October that year eight leaders of the ANC and PAC serving long terms of imprisonment were released from jail.[121]

The counter-revolutionary strategy had brought the country to the very brink of civil war, isolated it internationally and led to worldwide sanctions. Tens of thousands of young South Africans were alienated from authority and many had not attended school for years. There were dire predictions that unless a more consensual mode of government could be found, the country would slide into chaos. The spectre of 'anarchy' which the SAP always used to justify its strong-arm tactics was more real than ever before as a result of the inroads the police had made into community leadership.

The emergency also contributed to a rise in crime. Rates of reported crime rose relentlessly in the second half of the 1980s, by up to 7 per cent annually, and the SAP's ability to solve crimes steadily diminished.[122] The occupation of townships was a contributory factor to the increase in crime, as criminal gangs, sometimes with tacit police support, took advantage of the breakdown of community and authority structures, and police directed most of their efforts towards countering political opposition rather than combating crime.

Strategy Under De Klerk

By 1989, with the influence of the securocrats on the wane, it was clear that

Botha could not survive much longer as president. As it had been twelve years earlier, the National Party was thrown into ferment and different factions vied for power. At the end of the power struggle, F. W. de Klerk narrowly gained the presidency. He had no background in the SAP or the SADF – he was believed to speak for the section of the Afrikaner oligarchy concerned about the usurpation of executive decision-making power by the securocrats.[123] As De Klerk took power, the resistance movement re-emerged from underground. Sensing that the police would not be able to act in the old way, hundreds of thousands of South Africans took to the streets in defiance of emergency restrictions. De Klerk buckled and instructed the police to allow the marches to go ahead. Organisations declared themselves 'unbanned' and the ANC began to operate more or less openly.

Although De Klerk was careful not to alienate the military and police establishment, he was at times scathing in his assessment of the securocrats' strategy: 'You cannot simply have a counter-insurgency approach, because it may be that the enemy is the majority of the population.' The upgrading campaigns, he added, could only calm the situation: 'the only way to prevent a revolution is a negotiated political settlement that can win majority credibility among all population groups.'[124] Even the Minister of Law and Order, Adriaan Vlok, embraced this assessment – security action was only 'holding action' and political action had to be taken as the *status quo* could no longer be maintained. It was political action, he said, that would 'kill communism in the hearts of our people'.[125]

'The season of violence is over,' declared De Klerk, releasing Nelson Mandela and unbanning the ANC and all other restricted organisations in February 1990. In some ways, the strategy advanced by De Klerk and his supporters represented a return to the grander vision of the Total Strategy of the early 1980s, with its emphasis on political, social and economic reform. But, for the first time in South Africa's history, there was at least a tacit recognition that reform would have to entail some form of democracy for all – even if this was hedged with qualifications and meant 'power sharing' instead of majority rule. This was an important psychological and political break. Previously, policing strategists had taken it for granted that it was white minority rule which the police were defending: now it was the process of change itself which had to be protected and controlled as many of the old shibboleths of apartheid were cast away – more complex and subtle ways would have to be found to ensure the continued ascendancy of the whites.

Although the De Klerk government was a hostage to the securocrats, who still formed the most powerful faction in government, civilians increasingly asserted themselves. Under the new regime, security was still seen as a prerequisite for reform, but the balance had changed. Social, economic and political initiatives would no longer be determined largely by the imperatives of security: now – at least to some degree – security action would be dictated by the broader political agenda.

The break with the past strategy had been signalled in November 1989 when De Klerk declared that the NSMS would be 'dismantled' – a step which military and police commanders were reported to have welcomed as a move towards normalisation (there was always a section of the SADF which did not welcome its involvement in police work).[126] Many features of the old system remained, however.

De Klerk was careful to prepare the police for his initiatives. They would still have an intelligence-gathering and infiltration role, but the objectives of this were recast: the aim now was to monitor opposition organisations, contain them, and aid the government in its negotiations with them. But, as became apparent in 1991–2, sections of the security police and the army would continue to wage a secret campaign to destabilise and disorganise the ANC and its allies through violence: the so-called 'third force'.

Under De Klerk, the police regained many of their key functions in maintaining internal order as the army's grip over the security apparatus slipped and its budget was slashed. The NIS, closest in the security establishment to De Klerk, was also a beneficiary of the withering of the power of the military establishment – it regained its old position as the main agency responsible for intelligence processing and assessment, although its influence was constrained by its lack of operational punch.[127]

A document compiled by the new head of the Security Branch, Lieutenant-General 'Basie' Smit, reflecting discussions held at a January 1990 conference of the Branch's commanding officers, gave some indication of the new police strategy. The Branch regarded the reform initiative with some trepidation, but noted that its operations were to be extended as the 'Minister of Law and Order has ordered us to improve our information gathering capacity'. Projects 'aimed at undermining black political groups' would be relegated to the background, but the Branch would have to 'ensure that radical members do not take over' the ANC and 'protect Nelson Mandela and moderate members'. It would also start directing its attentions at the far right as well as 'all formerly illegitimate organisations and persons involved with them'. This would include 'continuous analysis of the ANC, PAC, black consciousness and nationalistic strategies, and development of counter-strategies.'[128]

De Klerk publicly called for the police to be removed from the 'political arena': they would no longer be responsible for suppressing demonstrations and political protests and their role in enforcing apartheid would end. He told the 500 highest-ranking police officers, assembled at the Police College in January 1990:

Up to now the police have been required to perform two types of functions. The one is to handle typical crime situations – murder, rape, theft, etc – the task of a police force all over the world. But you also had other tasks to fulfil, and that was a control function connected to a specific political party and the execution of laws ....

You will no longer be required to prevent people from gathering to canvass support for their views. This is the political arena and we want to take the police out of it. We don't want to use you any more as instruments to reach certain political goals. We as politicians must take full responsibility for politics.... This is the direction we are taking and I want you to make peace with this new line.[129]

De Klerk moved swiftly to upgrade the SAP, freeing funds by cutting the defence budget, and the force announced that it intended to increase its manpower by 10,000 within 12 months. R800 million was withdrawn from government's emergency funds for the SAP and salary rises of up to 80 per cent were announced.[130]

The police tried hard to break the mould in which they were cast. Glossy advertisements were placed in newspapers claiming that the force was at the service of the community. Efforts were made to improve professional standards and to emphasise the importance of community relations.[131] A police White Paper presented to parliament in April 1990 claimed that policing 'is a service performed out of and for the community'.[132] The force was also reorganised and decentralised through the establishment of 11 police regions, which it was claimed would lead to greater community accountability.

But within a few months it was evident that the declared change in strategy had not filtered through to police on the ground, and that it was by no means as complete a break with the past as De Klerk had intimated. Many of the military-style tactics persisted. 'Crime sweeps' continued – militarised joint police-army operations involving road blocks and house-to-house searches along the lines of the operations which were a feature of the emergency. Whether they were motivated by a desire to stamp out crime or as a political show of force, their effects in alienating local people were much the same.[133] According to SADF officers, military units were only deployed in 'unrest areas' at the request of the police, and 'whenever possible ... an SADF patrol operates with a policeman, although the members of each force receive orders from their own commanders.'[134] But in January 1992 the defence minister remarked that 'at least 10,000' troops were 'deployed on a daily basis to ensure security and stability' inside South Africa – many, if not most of these, would be involved in actions in support of the SAP, and these numbers probably exceeded those deployed at most stages during the State of Emergency.[135]

Although major political rallies went ahead without police interference, smaller gatherings were broken up ruthlessly, fuelling the continuing cycle of violent confrontation – according to a human rights monitoring group, at least 323 people were killed and 3,390 wounded by police between February 1990, when the ANC was unbanned, and the end of that year.[136] Although the State of Emergency was lifted in June, except in the province of Natal, the government imposed mini-emergencies on many of townships by declaring them 'unrest areas', giving police the same powers as they held under the national emergency.

Events in the Witwatersrand in the middle of 1990 led many to question whether the SAP – and De Klerk – had indeed changed strategy, or whether the counter-revolution was being continued under the cover of negotiations. Violence which had been flaring in Natal between ANC adherents and supporters of the KwaZulu bantustan-based Inkatha movement suddenly and unexpectedly spread to the Witwatersrand. In Natal, where at least 4,000 people had been killed since 1987, the police were widely accused of standing idly by or siding with Inkatha, and the same accusations were made in the Witwatersrand: certainly there was extensive evidence of police partiality towards Inkatha.

Suspicions were aroused that secret units in the Security Branch and the counter-insurgency wings of the SADF were continuing the old policies of assassination, deployment of vigilantes and use of criminal gangs and other extra-legal actions aimed at weakening the ANC. As the violence continued through 1991 and into 1992, these suspicions, at first dismissed by many observers, were borne out by successive revelations, which are examined in Chapters 3 and 4.

It became clear that the change in strategy was not quite the U-turn De Klerk liked to present it as. Many elements of the counter-revolutionary approach developed in the second half of the 1980s were retained, and sections of the security forces, especially in the Security Branch, the KwaZulu police, the Directorate of Military Intelligence and the SADF's Special Forces, continued their extra-legal activities. Increasingly, they operated in tandem with extreme right-wing paramilitary organisations which mushroomed in the 1990s.

Whether or not the De Klerk government authorised or approved of these operations, it clearly benefited from the effect they had in wrongfooting the ANC and its allies. The ANC accused the government of following a strategy similar to one it had used in Namibia in the closing stages of the war: negotiating to end the conflict, but continuing military and political action on the ground to weaken and disorganise its opponents.

This strategy was not necessarily orchestrated in its finer points. To some extent it arose naturally from political and functional divisions in the state bureaucracy and the security forces. The counter-insurgency units of the security forces have always operated with relative autonomy. The special forces oriented towards covert action continued their operations and a powerful clique within the security forces demonstrated, through their capacity to generate political violence, that they were in a position to decide the pace of reform and its limits.

De Klerk thus remained under the spell of the counter-insurgency experts. He had to weigh the possible effects on his support base of tackling the hard-liners head on – many whites regarded the police and army as guarantors of their survival. And alienating the security forces *en masse*, through purges of the officer corps for example, would have left him 'naked in the conference chamber', or at least without the capacity to fall back on force if negotiations failed. As long the violence thrown up by covert security force actions did not threaten to destroy totally his credibility or demolish his negotiating initiative, it suited De Klerk to allow the security forces to use violence to undermine the ANC. Hawkish cabinet ministers and securocrats (including the SAP Commissioner, General van der Merwe) formed a faction which agitated within the De Klerk administration for firmer security force action, including the use of 'dirty tricks'. While SADF officers contented themselves with lobbying hawkish cabinet ministers, many of those in the SAP, especially in the security section, were reported to have aligned themselves with the right-wing Conservative Party.[137]

It would have been unrealistic to expect the SAP to break overnight with a political pattern that, since the early days, had three motifs: paramilitary action, political repression, which involved extensive intelligence work, and bureaucratic enforcement of discriminatory measures. Such a turnaround would have required, in the first place, a purge of the officer corps, but De Klerk continued to rely on men who had spent their lives running counter-insurgency campaigns. It would also have required a swift reorientation of the force's manpower, training and deployment policies, and its opening up to broader control and influence. De Klerk was unwilling or unable to move decisively on these issues. But political crises, precipitated in large part by police and army actions and by revelations about covert activities, undermined the credibility of his government and led it to take some steps, grudgingly and with mixed results, to clean up the security forces.

Notes

1   Cited in Dippenaar 1988, p 7.
2   Sachs 1973, pp 54–5, 239; Koch 1978; Brogden 1989.
3   Brogden 1989, p 13.
4. Grundy 1983, p. 145; Dippenaar 1988, pp 76–7.
5   Sachs 1973, p 55.
6   Dippenaar 1988, pp 25–6.

7   Simons & Simons 1983, pp 286–96.
8   Fernandez (n.d.), pp 2–3; Cook 1982.
9   Parsons 1982, p 248.
10 Dippenaar 1988, pp 97–8.
11 Cited in Sachs 1975, p 235.
12 Sachs 1973, p 170.
13 Cited in Dippenaar 1988, pp 127–8.
14 Cited in Dippenaar 1988, p 126.
15 Van der Spuy 1989, p 272.
16 Dippenaar 1988, pp 144–5.
17 Sachs 1973, p 242.
18 Dippenaar 1988, p 211.
19 Sachs 1975, p 237.
20 Van der Spuy 1990, p 93.
21 Sachs 1973, p 170.
22 Cawthra 1986, p 12.
23 Dippenaar 1988, pp 238–9, 255.
24 Dippenaar 1988, p 246.
25 See, for example, Bunting 1986.
26 Benson 1985, pp 157–78.
27 Benson 1985, pp 140–209.
28 *Survey of Race Relations* 1961, p 52.
29 *Annual Report of the Commissioner of the SAP* 1960.
30 IDAF 1991, p 122.
31 Dippenaar 1988, pp 288, 291.
32 Sachs 1975, p 231.
33 Dippenaar 1988, p 298.
34 Amnesty International 1978; Lawyers' Committee 1983; IDAF 1991, p 68.
35 Bunting 1986, p 239.
36 Sachs 1975, p 237.
37 Seegers 1989, p ii.
38 Benson 1985, pp 270–1.
39 Sachs 1975, p 242.
40 *Human Rights Commission Fact Paper*, no E, undated.
41 Seegers 1989, p ii.
42 Frankel 1980, p 488.
43 Dippenaar 1988, p 372.
44 Cawthra 1986, pp 199–210; Herbstein & Evenson 1989, pp 61–95.
45 Brooks & Brickhill 1980, pp 256–60.
46 Brooks & Brickhill 1980, pp 239–7.
47 *Guardian* 8.7.75; *Rand Daily Mail* 2.12.75; Brooks & Brickhill 1980, pp 247–8; Jeffery 1991, p 45.
48 Brooks & Brickhill 1980, pp 249, 361.
49 *Star* 26.3.86.
50 Brooks & Brickhill 1980, pp 304–5.
51 Barber & Barratt 1990, pp 225–53.
52 Landgren 1989, p 251.
53 Price 1991, pp 34–71.
54 *International Security*, Spring 1992, vol 6, no 4, p 9, cited in Price 1991, p 91.
55 Seegers 1988, p 420.
56 Cited in Bunting 1986, pp 424–5.
57 Beaufre 1965; Louw 1978.
58 *Report of the Commission of Inquiry into Reporting on Security Matters Regarding the South*

African Defence Force and South African Police.
59 *Sunday Times* 5.6.85; Dippenaar 1988, pp 652–63.
60 Campbell 1987; Grundy 1991.
61 Ellis & Sechaba 1992.
62 SADF 1977, p 5.
63 Ellis & Sechaba 1992, p 92.
64 Van der Spuy 1988, p 13.
65 Williams 1990, p 13.
66 Grundy 1988, pp 49-55.
67 *Annual Estimates.*
68 Hanlon 1986; Cawthra 1986.
69 Price 1991, p 94.
70 IDAF 1991, p 47.
71 Pinnock 1982, p 305.
72 Pinnock 1982, p 300.
73 *Report of the Commission of Inquiry into Security Legislation* 1982.
74 Cited in *Resister* 36, February/March 1985, p 21.
75 Matthews 1986, pp 271–2.
76 IDAF 1991, p 68.
77 Internal Security Act 1982.
78 *Survey of Race Relations* 1982, pp 226–9.
79 Coetzee 1983, p 4.
80 Cawthra 1986, p 223.
81 Wandrag 1985, p 9.
82 *Southscan* 5.6.87.
83 Coetzee 1983, pp 17–9.
84 *Servamus* May 1982, July 1983.
85 Pauw 1991, pp 240–9.
86 *Servamus* October 1984, pp 24–5.
87 Cawthra 1986, pp 244-5.
88 *BBC Summary of World Broadcasts* 11.10.84.
89 Cawthra 1986, pp 245–6.
90 SACBC 1984.
91 Ellis & Sechaba 1992, pp 143–5.
92 Wandrag 1985, p 8.
93 Barber & Barratt 1990, pp 328–31; Ellis & Sechaba 1992, p 176.
94 *Government Gazette* 21.7.85.
95 *Africa Confidential* 16.6.88.
96 Cited in Coker 1987, p 13.
97 Coker 1987, p 14.
98 Swilling & Phillips 1989a, p 143.
99 Wandrag 1985, pp 15–6.
100 Wandrag 1985, p 10.
101 McCuen 1966, pp 28-9.
102 See for example *Servamus* April 1986, pp 16–7.
103 McCuen 1966, pp 28–9.
104 *Leadership SA*, vol 6, no i, 1987.
105 Cited in Swilling & Phillips 1989a, p 143.
106 Seegers 1988; Selfe 1989.
107 Swilling & Phillips 1989b, pp 85–6.
108 *IDAF Briefing Paper*, No 22, March 1987.
109 *IDAF Briefing Paper*, No 22, March 1987.
110 *Leadership SA*, vol 5, no 1, 1986.

111   Swilling & Phillips 1989b, p 81; Hansson 1990, p 51.
112   *Guardian* 27.11.89.
113   *BBC Summary of World Broadcasts* 1.12.87.
114   IDAF 1989; IDAF 1990.
115   *Cape Times* 10.6.88; *Guardian* 10.6.88.
116   *Guardian* 10.2.89.
117   SAP 1988, preface.
118   *Focus* no 78, September/October 1988, p 12.
119   *Annual Report of the Commssioner of the SAP* 1988.
120   Williams 1990, p 16.
121   *Financial Mail*, 13.10.89.
122   *Annual Reports of the Commissioner of the SAP*.
123   Williams 1990, pp 17–8; Hansson 1990; Grundy 1991, p 119.
124   Cited in Hansson 1990, pp 55–6.
125   *Natal Mercury* 3.11.89.
126   *Cape Times* 29.11.89.
127   Nathan & Phillips 1991, p 7.
128   *Guardian* 17.1.92.
129   *Focus on SA*, February 1990.
130   *BBC Summary of World Broadcasts* 9.6.90.
131   *SouthScan* 1.2.91.
132   SAP 1988.
133   *Daily Dispatch* 4.4.90; *Sowetan* 30.4.90.
134   *Paratus* April 1991, p 45.
135   *Argus* 27.1.92.
136   HRC 1991.
137   *SouthScan* 24.5.91; Williams 1992, pp 10–3; *New Nation* 24.7.92.

2

FORCES

The police do not act alone in maintaining law and order: they work alongside the civil administration, the military, the prisons service and the courts. In South Africa these structures have always overlapped to a greater degree than in most other Western-oriented countries. Police can be called upon to carry out a variety of administrative tasks, ranging from health inspection to assisting in tax collection. Soldiers back up the police in law and order operations and some conscripts have been obliged to do their military service in the SAP. Prison officers have been regarded as members of the security forces and given the same powers as police and soldiers during States of Emergency. In the courts, police act as prosecutors, messengers and clerks.

The Legal Framework

The police operate within the framework of the law, even if the law has given them extraordinary powers and paved the way for extra-legal operations. One of their main jobs, as in all societies, is to enforce the laws of the land, and they work in tandem with the courts and civil administration. Coercive violence is mediated by the courts, although increasingly the powers of the police have become more important than the written laws of the land in suppressing resistance.[1]

THE COURTS

Although extra-legal methods have been favoured by sections of the police and army in recent years, and many of those detained by the police have never seen the inside of a courtroom, the courts form part of the repressive apparatus that has enforced apartheid and suppressed political resistance. Political prisoners and the tens of millions imprisoned under apartheid measures like the pass laws have all been victims of the legal process. With the dismantling of apartheid controls, the justice system has been thrown into disarray, and is still attempting to come to terms with the needs of a new South Africa in which crime is rising dramatically.

The Supreme Court, with its provincial and local divisions, has heard the more serious political cases, especially treason and 'terrorism', and is empowered to impose the death penalty. A moratorium on death sentences was introduced in March 1992 but parliament voted to lift it in June the next year. Appeals are heard by the Appellate Division, the highest court in the land, which sits in Bloemfontein in the Orange Free State. Supreme Court judges are appointed by the State President from the ranks of advocates (advocates are senior lawyers, the equivalent of British barristers; attorneys the equivalent of solicitors). Until very recently, all judges have been white, and many were appointed on the basis of their political allegiance to apartheid – the mould was broken only in 1991 with the appointment of Justice Ismail Mahomed, a black advocate who had made a name defending anti-apartheid activists.[2] Nine out of ten criminal cases involve Africans who make up 75 per cent of the population, and, of course, have had no say in drawing up the laws.[3] Nelson Mandela's objection to a judge in 1962 remained as valid in the early 1990s as it was then:

> a judiciary controlled entirely by whites and enforcing laws encacted by a white parliament in which we have no representation, laws which in most cases are passed in the face of unamimous opposition from Africans, cannot be regarded as an impartial tribunal in a political trial where an African stands as an accused.[4]

The South African judiciary has often vaunted its independence and judges are generally trained to a high standard and regarded as relatively incorruptible. Some judges have won small victories for democracy in challenging the legal bulldozer of the state, but their record is largely one of loyalty to the *status quo*. With few exceptions, judges have enforced apartheid legislation without criticism, even with enthusiasm, and made little effort to defend the rights of the individual as they were eroded by the state's security machine.[5]

Albie Sachs, an ANC constitutional expert who wrote a history of the South African legal system, concluded:

> The main criticism which could perhaps be advanced in relation to the conduct of most judges is not so much that they help to enforce race discrimination because they are corrupt, cowed or consciously biased, but that they do so willingly; not that they lack courtesy or decorum, but that they use polite and elegant language to lend dignity to laws which imposed segregation and harshly penalise radical opponents of a system of government almost universally condemned. Instead of investing their office with the prestige associated with the pursuit of justice, they allow the prestige associated with their office to be used for the pursuit of injustice.[6]

Given these factors, it is not surprising that even government commissions have found that black South Africans lack confidence in the judiciary and regard it as illegitimate.

The crisis of legitimacy is even worse in the lower courts, presided over by magistrates, who are usually selected from the band of public prosecutors working for the department of justice. Magistrates can sentence people only to a maximum of one year's imprisonment, but they are empowered to order whippings of male offenders under 30 years old. More than 40,000 people, mostly black juveniles, were flogged each year during the 1980s – this must have reinforced the belief of many youngsters that the state relies on violence to rule.[7] In 90 per cent of cases in magistrate's courts, the accused are undefended: the police, who often prosecute, thus have a clear advantage.

Until 1986, commissioner's courts, presided over by white civil servants, heard cases which involved only Africans – these could be civil or criminal actions, but they mostly enforced the pass laws. In rural areas, so-called chief's courts' still dispense informal justice in civil or criminal cases involving only Africans, based on the chief's intepretation of traditional law or custom. Informal courts also exist in urban areas. These have been closely linked with policing functions, structures of the homeland administrations and town councils (see the discussion of vigilantes in this chapter). They arose, and were promoted by the authorities, to fill the law and order vacuum resulting from inadequate formal policing.[8] With the ascendancy of the ANC in the early 1980s, most of them collapsed and in some areas they were replaced by 'people's courts' aligned with ANC-oriented local committees.

The police moved against the people's courts during the national State of Emergency, detaining their members and sometimes putting them on trial for treason, assault or abduction. The courts were gradually revived under the auspices of civic associations, dealing with criminal and community matters and carrying out street patrols.[9] Since the unbanning of the ANC, in some areas the police have sought to co-opt rather than destroy the courts, although the relationship between the community structures and the authorities is uneasy and often confrontational. Four such courts operated in Guguletu in Cape Town in 1991, with the tacit support of the police.[10] In a pilot case in Alexandra township outside Johannesburg, moves have been made to incorporate aspects of the people's courts – although not the structures themselves – as a recogised extension of the justice system, through the appointment of community-based mediators or adjudicators.[11]

In general, little has been done to restore popular faith in the legal system. The pattern of justice that persists is one where the accused is invariably black, has no legal representation, often has to rely on an interpreter as intermediary and usually cannot afford bail. It is a system that is effective in securing convictions, but in the words of a Natal Supreme Court judge: 'To think that at the end of the trial of an unrepresented accused there may be justice is an exercise in self-delusion.'[12]

POLICE POWERS

The most excessive discriminatory legislation has now been wiped off the statute book and the teeth drawn from security legislation. Some of these laws, like those requiring Africans to carry passes, went as part of the Total Strategy reforms in the 1980s; others, including the most repressive aspects of the Internal Security Act, and the Population Registration Act which underpinned apartheid, were revoked only in the 1990s. But the police still enjoy substantial legal powers in their day-to-day operations and retain a formidable arsenal of laws which can be used against opponents of the state.

The Police Act of 1958 – which has been amended regularly, usually to increase police leeway – sets out the powers and functions of the police, but it must be read in conjunction with other laws, such as the Criminal Procedure Act and Internal Security Act. The Police Act describes the functions of the police as 'the preservation of internal security; the maintenance of law and order; the prevention of crime; the investigation of any offence or alleged offence.'[13] No weight is given to the different functions: the 1990 White Paper on the police argues that 'these four functions form an entity ... priority cannot be given to any one of them'.[14] The political tasks of the police, through the 'preservation of internal security' are thus an explicit and formally equal aspect of its role.

The Police Act confers powers on the police not usually found in a country which claims to be a democracy. It allows policemen and women to stop and search vehicles without a warrant on any public road.[13] It prohibits publication without authorisation of SAP preparations or actions concerned with the 'prevention of terroristic activities'.[14] Until the act was amended in February 1992, it outlawed the publication of anything 'untrue' about the police – the onus on proving the accuracy of any news reports or comments lay on the defendant.[15]

The Indemnity Act of 1977 gives police and other state officials indemnity from civil or criminal proceedings for actions arising from policing 'internal disorder' or aimed at maintaining or restoring 'good order or public safety or essential services'.[18] Where proceedings can be brought, the Police Act specifies that this has to be done within six months of the incident. Until 1984, when the Supreme Court ruled the time-limit could not apply to periods of detention, this act made it difficult for long-term detainees to bring charges of assault against the police.[19]

The Criminal Procedure Act, as amended, gives the police extensive powers. Confessions made to police by accused are, in terms of the act, admissable in court without the state having to prove beyond reasonable doubt that they were made voluntarily.[20] The act also authorises police to use such force 'as may in the circumstances be reasonably necessary' to overcome resistance or stop someone escaping arrest.[21] The police have taken this provision as a licence to kill, as the figures for people killed or wounded by the police every year demonstrate.[22]

Although the State of Emergency was lifted in June 1990, the legislation allowing for emergencies to be imposed has remained on the statute books and at times the De Klerk administration has threatened to use it again.[23] The government has also extensively used the Public Safety Act to declare what amount to localised States of Emergency. During 1990 and 1991, over 50 townships, including Soweto and Alexandra, were declared to be 'unrest areas' in terms of this legislation, and many remained under the restrictions during 1992. Regulations, usually identical to those of the 1986–90 national State of Emergency, are imposed in unrest areas, night curfews are declared and militarised police and troops sent in to enforce the restrictions. The regulations empower soldiers and police to detain people without trial, use whatever force they deem necessary, and enforce restrictions such as the curfews and bans on meetings.

In May 1991 the most draconian clauses of the Internal Security Act (see previous chapter) were scrapped or amended. While the Minister of Justice retained his powers to ban organisations, these were subject to Supreme Court review. The clauses providing for publications to be banned and for the restriction of individuals were removed. Police were limited under Section 29 to detaining people without trial for 10 days and not indefinitely as in the past. However, the period of detention could be extended by a Supreme Court judge, and detainees were still prevented from seeing lawyers or relatives. Human rights organisations pointed out that the first 10 days are the danger period in which most reports of torture and most deaths and assaults have been recorded. Tough new provisions were also introduced for 'intimidation', with fines of R10,000 or up to 10 years' imprisonment.[24]

Even these reforms were threatened a year later when the government tabled legislation before parliament to re-introduce indefinite detention without trial for people suspected of knowledge of illegal arms. At the same time the government proposed to further strengthen the Intimidation Act, introducing a presumption of guilt, raising maximum sentences to 25 years and allowing for conviction without the evidence of eyewitnesses. It also sought to formalise the authorisation of police phone-tapping, bugging and interception of mail.[25] In February 1993 the government again used growing crime and the spread of illegal weapons to threaten harsh measures: the death penalty would be made operative again, minimum sentences of five years would be imposed for possession of AK-47 automatic weapons and bail would be refused in certain cases, announced De Klerk, in the context of a wide-ranging anti-crime initiative.[26]

Organisation of the SAP

CONTROL AND COMMAND

Parliament has exercised little control over the police. There has been no parliamentary committee which monitors policing or defence issues (except when introducing new legislation), and little information about the force has been made available to MPs. The Minister of Law and Order has often responded only in general terms to questions in parliament, or refused to answer them at all.[27] As recently as 1988 he refused to tell parliament how many people served in the SAP on the grounds that it was 'not in the interest of the safety of the Republic to reveal the exact establishment of the South African Police'[28] (although the figures were published in the annual report of the Commissioner of the SAP).

The ministers responsible for the police have themselves not been kept fully informed of developments relating to the force,[29] although they have traditionally had a hardline image and cast themselves as champions of the police rather than the public. Their names are associated with some of the worst excesses of apartheid: B. J. Vorster, who piloted through the fierce security legislation of the 1960s; Jimmy Kruger, who authorised the 1976 massacres in Soweto and other townships and said of the death of Steve Biko in police detention, 'it leaves me cold'; Louis le Grange, who gained notoriety for his tough stance during the States of Emergency in the 1980s. His successor, Adriaan Vlok, also adopted an uncompromising posture, advocating mass detentions, but was somewhat miscast: he was widely regarded as ineffectual, even by his generals. He was removed from his post by President de Klerk late in 1991 after a scandal had erupted over police funding for Inkatha (see Chapter 4) and was put in charge of the nation's prisons. His replacement, Hernus Kriel, reportedly a hardliner and a member of a securocrat cabal trying to resist the De Klerk reforms,[30] enjoyed the confidence of the generals. No doubt the unprecedented injection of state funds received by the police under his leadership helped.[31]

The remnants of the National Security Management System (see Chapter 1) continued to wield powerful influence in the early 1990s. Renamed the National Coordinating Mechanism (NCM), and substantially modified and downgraded under De Klerk, it continued to coordinate government security and socio-political initiatives, and thus had a considerable influence over the police. The system also gave the police leverage over government policy, though much reduced since the days when the securocrats reigned.

The introduction of a Transitional Executive Council, as result of negotiations between the ANC and government, was due to change the structure of control during the course of 1993 (see Chapter 5). Before these changes, De Klerk's cabinet controlled the NCM through four cabinet committees. The

Cabinet Committee for Security Matters replaced the old State Security Council and was responsible for policing and other security issues. It was served by a secretariat which in turn drew on the resources of the National Intelligence Service, under the control of the Minister of Justice. These bodies were mainly responsible for establishing the thrust of state security strategy – but they did so in coordination with the subsidiary bodies of other cabinet committees through a network of Task Forces, each of which had specific responsibilities. Decisions thus mediated by the Task Forces were passed down for implementation to nine regional Joint Coordinating Centres (JCCs) and a network of local JCCs for implementation.

While the De Klerk government stressed that the NCM was oriented towards welfare rather than security issues, and was in the main controlled by civilians, evidence from at least some local areas indicated that the same police and military personnel and local bureaucrats who ran the NMS were involved.[32] The police thus remained involved at all levels in determining and implementing state strategy in fields that went far beyond the bounds of law and order. According to the ex-head of the Strategic Communications Committee of the State Security Council, Lieutenant-Colonel John Horak, many decisions – such as a decision to assassinate a political opponent – were taken at a local level by senior police officers.[33]

To what extent the remaining structures of the NCM continue to be a shadowy factor behind police actions is hard to determine. Within the SAP itself, structures and line-of-command functions are clearer. The Commissioner of Police has traditionally been drawn from the ranks of men who have worked their way to the top. A spell in the Security Branch seems to work wonders for those with their eyes on top jobs in the SAP, and counter-insurgency experience is virtually essential. The Commissioner is usually rotated every two years, which effectively prevents him from imposing his own personal stamp on the force, although it does result in a constant jostling for influence by potential successors.

General Johan van der Merwe, who was appointed Commissioner by De Klerk in 1989, exemplifies the background of many of the top policemen. Joining the force at the age of 16 in the early 1950s, in 1964 he transferred to the Security Branch, where he spent most of the rest of his career. He won his counter-insurgency credentials in northern Namibia between 1979 and 1983, when he commanded the security police there: this was a time when the war against SWAPO was at its peak. It was also when the notorious Koevoet unit, which was later moved to South Africa, was deployed under Security Branch control. Koevoet pioneered methods of irregular warfare and gained a reputation for untrammelled brutality and ruthless torture. After returning to South Africa, Van der Merwe was promoted to head the Security Branch in the critical year 1986, when the counter-revolution swung into action. The

Branch was responsible for the detention and interrogation of thousands of anti-apartheid activists in the following years.[34]

Under the Commissioner is a deputy, and a Board of Control, drawing in all the lieutenant-generals who head the various functional divisions in the force. The board determines policy and strategy.[35] The Commissioner controls a bloated general staff – until 19 of them were retired in September 1992 there were 55 serving officers with the rank of major-general or lieutenant-general (only the Commissioner is a full general).[36] Most of them share similar backgrounds: white male Afrikaners who have worked their way up through the ranks, usually with a spell in counter-insurgency work. Few of them are specialists, and political loyalties have been an important, perhaps overriding, factor in promotion. As a result, the top echelons of the SAP are widely regarded as inadequate to the job and resistant to change. A British expert who was granted access to the SAP in 1992 found that leadership, management and strategic planning in the SAP was 'woefully inadequate'.[37]

THE SAP RESTRUCTURED

As a result of recommendations made by a commission set up in 1988 under the retiring commissioner, General Hennie de Witt, the SAP was restructured in 1990–1. Some of the reorganisation was influenced by the new spirit of democracy in South Africa. The SAP has realised that to survive under a democratically elected government it has to put its house in order. But the restructuring is also aimed at ending centralised control, the long-term effect of which could be to break the SAP into regional forces – a step which would fit in with National Party plans to limit through federalism the powers of a black majority government (see Chapter 5). Furthermore, the De Witt recommendations arose more from the exigencies of the State of Emergency than an attempt to come to terms with a democratic future. The police proved a cumbersome and blunt instrument during the emergency, and its personnel and resources were stretched to the limit.

According to the Minister of Law and Order, senior policemen saw a need to 'streamline' the force, to release trained police from bureaucratic tasks, and to devolve management decisions so that the top structures could concentrate on strategic decision-making. While the De Witt report has not been published, the police journal *Servamus* has given a flavour of its conclusions:

> The ever increasing demands made by the public on the Police Force made it necessary to increase manpower, vehicles, equipment, etc. Management and control, which eminated [sic] from one central point, subsequently became complicated and difficult to handle. Lines of communication between Head Office and the operational level were cumbersome and, in some cases, ineffective.[38]

As a result of De Witt's proposals, the SAP is now organised administratively into 11 regional commands, corresponding to the government's development regions and the divisions of the NCM. Each region is under the command of a regional commissioner, with the rank of major-general. Beneath that are some 82 police districts, each with a Security Branch centre (the Branch itself has been restructured, as explained below) and more than 800 police stations.[39] The regional commissioners enjoy considerable autonomy: already different parts of the country are characterised by different styles of policing, and the new structures may accelerate this process. Nevertheless, the SAP, unlike the police forces in Britain or the USA, remains a national force under a single command.

The SAP now consists of five divisions: Crime Combating and Investigation (CCI), Visible Policing, Internal Stability, Human Resources Management and Support Services. A further division, Community Relations, is in the process of being formed. The functions of the branches overlap and they do not usually operate independently.

The *Support Services* division covers finance, logistics, public relations, technical services and several specialised units responsible mainly for administrative tasks – its personnel are mostly desk-bound.[40] The public relations unit has been expanded in the last few years, reflecting a somewhat more open attitude in the SAP. For decades the force became progressively more secretive, regarding the media virtually as an enemy. The De Witt commission recommended that the police become more proactive in their relations with the media, and the public relations division has adopted a much higher profile in the 1990s.[41] The division of *Human Resources Management* is responsible for training and personnel functions. In December 1992 the new *Community Relations* division, headed by a lieutenant-general, was established in an effort to improve communications with the public, especially the black community. Community relations officers were to be appointed in each police district.

By far the majority of police are in the division which was provisionally called *Visible Policing* (the name seems to have stuck), formed in May 1991 from the merger of the Uniformed and Operational branches, including reserve formations. The basic uniformed/operational distinctions persist in the new structure: uniformed sections are responsible for proactive and crime prevention work, operational sections for reactive tasks, including counter-insurgency operations and riot control. The uniformed sections of the force form the front line of conventional policing and are in constant contact with the general public. According to the SAP:

> the Uniformed Branch mans all the police stations, mobile police stations, reporting offices, patrol vehicles, border posts, radio stations, airports, harbours, courts, government mortuaries, and many other police offices and institutions. The execution of this task not only forms the long arm of the law, but it also serves as the eyes and ears of all the other branches of the South African Police.[42]

The operational sections of this division are explicitly responsible for political policing: riot control, counter-insurgency, the protection of government installations and personnel. It includes two contentious black auxiliary forces which have often held the front line in the townships: the police assistants (special constables or *kitskonstabels*) and the municipal police. It also involves some specialised units, notably the Internal Stability Units, widely known as Riot Squads, the Special Task Force and the Special Guard Unit. (These are examined in this chapter, in the section on counter-insurgency and riot units.) The SAP does not mince its words about the tasks of the operational sections:

> The primary aim of this Branch is to protect the community against any violent onslaught. The Branch is, amongst others, responsible for counteracting the infiltration of terrorists, dealing with internal riots, uprisings and strikes and for undertaking the training of members of the South African Police in this regard. The aim of planning, activating and coordinating the activities of the South African Police within the National Coordinating Mechanism is also included.[43]

While the merger of the uniformed and operational sections was presented by the SAP as part of its depoliticisation, it could equally be interpreted as having the opposite effect: integrating the average policeman or woman more closely with the militarised, more politicised units of the force. One indication of the balance of power within the new integrated division was the appointment as its head of the ex-operational branch chief, Lieutenant-General Louwrens Malan, a veteran of both Security Branch and counter-insurgency operations. Malan also served as Director of Intelligence in the Office of the Prime Minister between 1979 and 1981, a period when the office was taking on increasingly authoritarian powers in order to implement the militaristic Total Strategy doctrine.[44]

Visible Policing includes a small *Air Wing* which uses 18 helicopters and three light aircraft to assist in crowd control and crime operations.[45] A *Transport Policing* unit is responsible for patrolling the premises of the parastatal Transnet corporation, which runs the country's railways, airports and harbours. The unit is a pale shadow of the Railways and Harbour Police, a separate force some 7,000 strong which was incorporated into the SAP in 1986 to save money.[46]

The uniformed force is backed by two part-time reserves, somewhat oddly known as the *Police Reserve* and the *Reserve Police* force. The Police Reserve consists of ex-police who have retired from the force, as well as ex-conscripts who were put into the SAP for their national service. Many are inactive, having fulfilled their statutory obligations, but active reserve members are called up to serve periods of between 30 and 90 days annually. They help relieve pressure on the regular force, especially at times of emergency, by manning roadblocks, patrolling and working in police stations.

The *Reserve Police* force, commonly called the reservists, is a part-time volunteer force of mainly white civilians. Since 1988 members have been committed to putting in a minimum of 16 hours each a month, although it unlikely that anything near this figure is achieved. There are three categories for which people can volunteer. Group A work alongside the police in their normal day-to-day duties and can be called up for full-time duty during emergencies. Some have been sent for counter-insurgency training and deployed on the country's northern borders and nearly 500 were involved in 'riot' duties in 1990; the reservists have their own riot units.[47] Group B carry out tasks only in their own residential areas, while a group of divers is used to help the police recover bodies and other items from dams and rivers. There is also a volunteer force of amateur radio operators who help with police communications, known as SAP Wachthuis.[48]

Most of the over 12,000 reservists are white males, although several hundred white women and a some blacks have volunteered. White schoolboys have been encouraged since 1981 to join a force of Junior Reservists which helps the police during school holidays – it was opened to black youths in 1984. The boys, who have to be over 16, sometimes wear uniforms, but do not carry weapons, although they are trained to use them.[49] The number of reservist volunteers has declined since the late 1970s, when over 20,000 were involved:[50] the decline was most marked during the State of Emergency, so it can probably be attributed to the more onerous and dangerous conditions facing volunteers. To relieve pressure on the regular force, the SAP has tried to make more use of reservists since 1990, but this has not been successful as many of them support extreme right-wing factions and have become disillusioned with De Klerk's reforms.[51]

The fourth wing of the restructured SAP, *Crime Combating and Investigation* (usually referred to as CCI) is a result of the merger on 1 April 1991 of the Criminal Investigation Division (the CID, otherwise known as the Detective Branch) and the Security Branch. The SAP declared that the Security Branch, the most notorious of all police structures, had been abolished. The truth was far from that: the Branch has retained its separate identity and continues to operate, albeit under the new name of Crime Intelligence Service (CIS – sometimes given as Crime Information Service). The old Detective Branch also retains an identity under the name Crime Investigation Service. The head of the Security Branch, Lieutenant-General Basie Smit, was appointed to oversee the amalgamated division, even though detectives outnumber security personnel at least two to one in the 12,000 strong division.[52] It is likely that Smit's appointment indicates that the influence of the Branch is now felt more keenly by members of the old Detective Branch, even though the overall security orientation has changed. Detectives have traditionally supplied many security recruits, as their work is quite similar and they are accustomed to undercover operations – Lieutenant-General Smit himself made his name as a detective.

CCI includes a number of other specialised units, including the 'fraud squads', the South African Narcotics Bureau and Diamond and Gold units.[53] *Stock-theft Units* operate in rural areas, using horses, scrambler motorcycles and four-wheel-drive vehicles. There has been some suggestion that they have been drawn into counter-insurgency operations. *Murder and Robbery Units*, first set up in the late 1950s to counter black gangsterism, specialise in investigating serious crimes, especially murders or where criminal gangs are involved. They are particularly hard-bitten, and one in particular, the Brixton Murder and Robbery Unit in Johannesburg, has been implicated in summary executions and has provided personnel for the SADF's hit-squad, the Civil Cooperation Bureau.[54]

CRIME INVESTIGATION SERVICE (SECURITY BRANCH)

Of all the specialised units of the SAP, the Security Branch, as it is best known, has done the most damage to the anti-apartheid movement. Its victims have ranged from Nelson Mandela to Steve Biko to Archbishop Desmond Tutu, from the South African Communist Party to the South African Council of Churches. 'Our target is that collection of individuals and organisations, operating from within and without, who practise or attempt subversion or revolution,' declared the then Security Branch chief General Coetzee in 1982.[55] In practice, because of the SAP's overarching security analysis, virtually all anti-apartheid organisations became targets.

While the SAP has done everything in its power to prevent details of the Branch from being made public, it has summarised its functions:

- Gathering information in order to expose activities which endanger or may endanger the security of the State or the public, or the maintenance of the public order.
- The detention and questioning of persons who are suspected of being guilty of terrorism or subversion or of possessing information concerning such deeds.
- Taking steps to ensure that persons who threaten the security of the State or the public or the maintenance of public order appear before court.
- Maintaining an efficient and extensive information network by means of research, liaison with other information services and the application of modern technological resources.[56]

The Branch gained a reputation for bungling and Keystone Cops-type antics during the 1950s, but by the 1960s it had become a ruthless and powerful machine. The climate of fear and suspicion it engendered probably did as much harm as its actual operations; the scale of its work was immense. In January 1990 General Smit disclosed that it had 'given attention to' 314,000 individuals and 9,500 organisations since its inception.[57] The Human

Rights Commission has calculated that the Branch has been 'responsible for the detention without trial of 80,000 political opponents, involving the torture of countless numbers and the death of at least 73.'[58]

Opposition activists have become accustomed to dodging the attentions of the Branch, checking for bugs in rooms, watching for unmarked cars prowling outside meeting halls, and trying to uncover agents sent to infiltrate them. In its quest for information, the Branch would raid organisations to confiscate documents, search for information and intimidate employees – and some of this confiscated material would feature in government propaganda campaigns. The security police have also specialised in the interrogation and torture of political detainees. Since the early 1960s, teams of specialist interrogators have operated at Security Branch headquarters at Compol building in Pretoria, and at Johannesburg police headquarters, John Vorster Square. Interrogation has also taken place at regional branch headquarters, and individual security policemen have coordinated interrogations at police stations around the country. Most deaths in detention have occurred during these sessions – explanations given by the police have ranged from 'slipped on soap in the shower' to 'fell out of the window'. This record of torture is examined in the next chapter.

A favoured route of security agents was to progress through established student and youth organisations, moving on to other opposition groups and then into exile to infiltrate the ANC and its armed wing.[59] The most effective agents succeeded in infiltrating the guerilla training and transit structures of the ANC, although many were eventually uncovered.[60] The role of these agents went far beyond intelligence – many were instructed to disrupt the ANC by poisoning or assassinating its members and destroying and sabotaging equipment (see Chapter 3). Most of their activities were not reported – although the actions of a few agents were milked for publicity by the SAP, as part of the campaign to demoralise the anti-apartheid movement. None received more acclaim than Captain Craig Williamson, who posed as a student activist, became a deputy-director of a funding agency in Europe and used his position to infiltrate the ANC's propaganda network before he fled back to South Africa on the brink of being uncovered. Williamson's achievements were ludicrously embellished – 'infiltrating Lagos' by attending a conference in Nigeria, and becoming 'our man in the Kremlin' by virtue of a short transit stop in Moscow.[61]

Little is known of the Security Branch's structure since it was renamed CCI, and only patchy details have emerged of its organisation before that. Before it was restructured – and this is almost certainly still the case – the Branch functioned as an empire within the empire, with its own chain of command, sub-culture and network of loyalties. From Compol, it controlled offices in all the police regions as well as personnel based at larger police stations, running a network of more than 4,000 policemen and women, assisted by thousands of agents and informants responsible for infiltrating anti-apartheid organisations or picking up information in the townships. The Railways Police also had its own security section before it was abolished.

The Branch was apparently organised into various 'desks': desk A monitored political activity related to South Africa in foreign countries; B handled technical aspects (presumably including bugging and telephone tapping); C countered the ANC and PAC; and G had an intelligence function. Each of these structures was further sub-divided – for example, G5 was a unit responsible for infiltrating agents into the ANC in countries neighbouring South Africa and C2 for interrogating guerilla suspects. The most notorious of the divisions was C1, a counter-insurgency unit.[62]

The *Askaris*, as the black personnel of C1 were called, are widely feared as a hit squad. The unit first came to public attention early in 1989 during a terrorism trial in Cape Town. A state witness, Bongani Jonas, told the court that the police had tried to recruit him as an Askari, to 'go around the townships acting on information the security police have, to seek out and kill [guerillas]'.[63] Some months later an ex-security policeman, Butana Almond Nofomela, who was due to be hanged for an unrelated murder, disclosed that he had been an Askari and had helped to carry out eight assassinations and many kidnappings of anti-apartheid activists. He said he was a member of the C1 unit of the Security Branch. The SAP denied it all.[64] But his story was corroborated by Captain Dirk Coetzee, also an ex-member of C1.

The SAP did its best to cover up the nature and existence of C1, and public attention was directed at the SADF's hit squad, the Civil Co-operation Bureau, which was uncovered at about the same time. Nevertheless, there is enough information to draw up a fairly clear picture of the organisation. Based at Vlakplaas, a farm outside Pretoria, C1 relied mostly on ex-members of the ANC and PAC. Coetzee related how some captured guerillas were pressed to work for the security police under threat of summary execution – at least one who refused was shot and his body burnt.[65] These Askaris, as they were called, were used to track down guerillas inside and outside the country. Although they were full members of the SAP, they received no police training. While the SAP claims that they had mainly an intelligence role, there is extensive evidence of them luring their erstwhile comrades into traps where they could be killed.[66] Small groups of Askaris were also attached to the Security Police in the provinces (hit squad operations are examined in the next chapter). Even after the formation of the Crime Intelligence Service, the Askaris continued to operate from Vlakplaas, and it was only in early 1993 that the government began to show a willingness to clean out the unit and remove its top commanders from influential positions in the police force.[67]

Alone amongst the state's intelligence agencies, the Security Branch/Crime

Intelligence Service has powers of detention and arrest. Until the formation of BOSS in the 1960s, it was also responsible for intelligence assessment, but this function, at least on the level of national strategy, is now largely the preserve of BOSS's successor, the National Intelligence Service (NIS). Under P. W. Botha's premiership, Military Intelligence rose to prominence and usurped many of the functions of BOSS/NIS – the two agencies had jockeyed for position in the Vorster years and often differed in their intelligence assessments.[68] For example, BOSS reportedly opposed South Africa's invasion of Angola in 1975 after the collapse of the Portuguese dictatorship, but the SADF went ahead anyway on the basis of its own intelligence assessment (with disastrous results).[69] NIS has regained its dominant position under De Klerk, drawing on information from the security police and Military Intelligence to make strategic assessments; it is believed to back De Klerk and is his strongest foothold in the security establishment.[70] But the intelligence structures as a whole have been at loggerheads since the unbanning of the ANC, as different factions of the security forces have competed for political influence, pursued different strategies and used various means to ensure their preservation in the radically changing circumstances of the 1990s. At times they leaked covert information about each other to the press as part of the backstabbing which accompanied the shake-up of the intelligence world in the De Klerk period.[71] Military Intelligence has been at the forefront of those structures seeking to destabilise the ANC – if not the negotiations themselves – and many of its operatives have taken part in political violence. The security police remain an important front-line intelligence agency – they have the agents in the field, control most of the monitoring programmes and carry out the interrogations.

The Branch also has a little publicised role in counter-insurgency. In the Namibian war, security police played a key intelligence role, working alongside ordinary police and military units, and specialising in interrogation. Security police have similarly been involved in rural counter-insurgency operations in South Africa, and in hunting down and trapping ANC guerillas operating in South Africa or based in other Southern African states.[72]

COUNTER-INSURGENCY AND RIOT UNITS (INTERNAL STABILITY)

The SAP is one of the more militarised police forces in the world. The trend towards counter-insurgency and riot control has not been arrested during the 1990s, although it has taken slightly different forms. Today, strengthened riot squads falling under the Internal Stability division form a powerful core of units equipped for urban conflict or rural guerilla war, but they can be boosted at short notice by other police personnel trained and equipped for counter-insurgency warfare and riot control.

As part of the face-lift the police have received in the early 1990s, the riot squads, reaction units or counter-insurgency units, first set up in the 1970s, are now known as *Internal Stability Units* and form the nucleus of a new division. With a strength of over 5,000 in early 1992, they were scheduled to grow to 17,500 under an ambitious expansion drive initiated in 1990 when the Minister of Law and Order instructed the SAP to develop a separate force. This was presented as part of an effort to remove the regular SAP from the 'political terrain', but it was condemned by the ANC as a unilateral initiative with potentially profound consequences. The move also resulted from the SAP's assessment that shortcomings in crowd control, which resulted in unacceptably high civilian casualties, were not the result of 'defective training', but were due to 'a lack of proper supervision and control, and to a deficiency in the number of trained personnel available'. The numbers available for urban deployment have been further boosted by the removal of police from border patrols in the 1990s.[73]

In Pretoria, a centralised internal stability unit, *Unit 19*, has been built up since the late 1980s when R11 million was allocated for the construction of a new counter-insurgency base in the city.[74] In 1990 its strength was about 800, but it was intended that it would grow to 2,700. The unit can be airlifted anywhere in the country to back up riot units based at all regional headquarters. The extent of its operations can be gauged by a report of its movements in 1989 in the police journal *Servamus*:

> 1989 was a busy year for Unit 19, they have been deployed from Cape Town to Ellisras [in the Northern Transvaal], Walvisbaai [in Namibia] to Durban. Wherever there was a border post which had to be manned, unrest to control or even a foot patrol to walk, one can be sure that Unit 19 was there at one stage or another.[75]

The riot and counter-insurgency units have their own training bases, the most important of which is at Maleoskop.[76]

Although small – perhaps 200 men – the *Special Task Force* is the élite of the riot and counter-insurgency units. It is trained for unconventional operations, especially the freeing of hostages. Some indication of its tasks is given by the training courses it undertakes, which in 1990 included diving and small boat handling, sharpshooting, VIP protection, 'urban terror' and rock climbing.[77] Set up in 1976, and modelled on Israeli and West German units, it played an important role in training riot squads and has since established small sub-units in some regions. It can be airborne in minutes for deployment anywhere in the country.[78]

The *Special Guard Unit* is not as highly trained as the Task Force, although it is responsible for protecting the state president and other senior officials. About 2,000 strong, the unit is basically a force of bodyguards and is deployed around the homes and offices of top officials.[79]

Further counter-insurgency punch is provided by the remnants of *Koevoet*, the Namibian security police unit which was pulled back to South Africa at the time of Namibian independence in 1989–90. Officered by white South African security policemen, Koevoet (Afrikaans for 'crowbar') consisted of Namibian mercenaries, some of whom were ex-SWAPO guerillas captured by the South African forces and persuaded to change sides. Given free rein in the 'operational areas' Koevoet devised ruthless fighting methods which, although they proved effective in killing guerillas, alienated local people. Relying on the mobility and firepower provided by its Casspir armoured vehicles and hunting down guerillas through the use of trained trackers and the violent interrogation of local people, Koevoet killed more Namibians than any other police or military unit.[80]

While some Koevoet members stayed in Namibia at independence, most of its fighters were brought back to South Africa and given South African citizenship. The SAP said they were used only for tracking and were attached to the Stock Theft Unit, operating from ten temporary bases around South Africa. But the *Weekly Mail* newspaper found a Koevoet base near Brits in the Northern Transvaal in 1991, and was told by the men there that they were employed by the security police and had been despatched to various parts of South Africa.[81] There were also reports that Koevoet members had been attached to the security police Askari unit and used to stoke up township violence.[82] After allegations that they were involved in a massacre at Boipatong in 1992 (see Chapter 4), Koevoet was disbanded and its members dispersed amongst the regular SAP.[83]

Black Auxiliary Forces

Today black police play a more important part in the SAP than ever before, but despite the growth in their numbers, they remain in inferior roles. The position of regular black SAP members within the force is examined later in this chapter: this section is concerned with the increasing number of black police who serve in separate auxiliary forces. Conditions in these forces are generally worse than in the SAP, and they are almost exclusively black – belying claims that police force is non-racial and that all police have equal opportunities.

Within the SAP, blacks who are not regular members serve either as police assistants or as municipal police. *Police assistants*, who used to be called special constables, are known colloquially as *kitskonstabels* – 'instant constables' in Afrikaans – because they used to be trained in only six weeks (this has now been doubled to three months). Established in some haste in the second half of 1986, when the state embarked on its counter-revolutionary strategy, the police assistants were seen as a way of extending police personnel strength quickly and cheaply, and re-establishing a police presence in the townships.

They would also contribute to the process of destroying opposition community leadership and replacing it with structures more acceptable to the government.

A training centre was set up in scrubland alongside the Koeberg nuclear power station in the Western Cape and volunteers were recruited from rural areas and townships, especially from the ranks of vigilantes and government employees. Little attention was paid to qualifications, other than loyalty to the state. Some were not told what job they were going to do. Many were illiterate. Training was rudimentary and done orally: one constable said his weapons training consisted of firing 16 shots at a board. The recruits were issued with blue overalls, shotguns, batons, whips and handcuffs and let loose in the townships. The predictable result was mayhem.[84]

In response to vigorous and widespread criticism and a flurry of court interdicts, the SAP moved to tighten up control and supervision. The special constables themselves complained that they were treated like 'dogs' or 'slaves' by the regular police.[85] Applicants now have to have at least one year of secondary schooling and training has been improved, but the force is still badly trained and has a reputation for lawlessness. It has been expanded rapidly during the 1990s and now constitutes more than a tenth of SAP strength.[86]

The *municipal police*, another sub-standard force making up more than 10 per cent of SAP strength, was also established during the policing crisis of the mid-1980s. It replaced the so-called 'blackjack' police forces run by administration boards and community guards controlled by black local authorities, but municipal police have greater powers than their predecessors and are armed. The first units were trained by the SAP and deployed in Soweto and other townships, nominally under the control of black town councils. They were used mainly to guard town councillors and government property, and soon gained a reputation for indiscipline and brutality – locals called them 'greenflies' after their green uniforms.[87]

Municipal police also proved a thorn in the flesh of the SAP. In at least four townships they went on strike, demanding better pay and conditions and complaining about racism by SAP members. In Katlehong, 115 municipal police were arrested by the SAP after staging a protest demonstration, and in Sebokeng the riot squad had to be brought in to put down a mutiny – several police were injured in the ensuing gunfight.[88] In 1989 the SAP took over control of the municipal police, removing them from the jurisdiction of black local authorities. By that stage they consisted of 256 different forces, mostly in the Transvaal, with a total strength of 9,000.[89]

Both the auxiliary forces have a front-line operational role and are controlled through the operational branch of the Visible Policing division. Although they have inflicted considerable damage on communities, they have also been targets for reprisal and have a far higher casualty rate than the regular

SAP. They are the police force's cannon fodder – poorly paid, poorly trained and expendable.

BANTUSTAN FORCES

An estimated 20,000 black police are accommodated in ten bantustan or homeland forces.[90] Here segregation is taken one step further: people classified into the different 'population groups' – Zulu, Venda and so on – fall under the authority of the relevant bantustan administration and the result is virtually homogeneous ethnic forces.

The bantustans were designed as apartheid's final solution – eventually there would be no more black South Africans, only citizens of 'independent states' who would come to white South Africa to sell their labour. It was a fantasy of social engineering that like so many grand experiments with human societies became a nightmare. Reintegration of the bantustans under a majority government is now inevitable, but the power structures set up to protect the ruling élites there, including the police forces, have left a legacy of corruption, institutional rivalry and political bitterness that will take years to heal.[91]

In the four 'independent states' – Transkei, Bophuthatswana, Venda and Ciskei, collectively known as the TBVC states – supposedly separate police forces were founded alongside military units as one of the trappings of statehood. White SAP members gradually relinquished formal control to black members of the SAP of the appropriate ethnic group, who were promoted up the ranks to befit their new status. The new generals and brigadiers put in charge of the bantustan forces were carefully selected, mostly from the Security Branch, but their promotion was often so rapid that their qualifications do not match their jobs and there is now widespread dissatisfaction in many of the forces with the poor quality of the top leadership. This discontent in the ranks is fuelled by the nepotism, corruption and selective patronage which characterises all the bureaucratic agencies in the bantustans.[92]

In practice, to different degrees, the various forces have remained extensions of the SAP, and are almost clones in terms of structure and orientation. Equipment, expertise, training and in many cases operational command still come directly from the SAP. In 1990, for instance, 800 members of bantustan forces were given basic training at SAP institutions, and a further 1,000 received riot and counter-insurgency training.[93] The forces also rely on the SAP's criminal records service for tracing offenders and stolen vehicles, and on its forensic laboratories. Policing matters in the bantustans are overseen by an SAP-dominated coordinating committee, although since 1990 the Transkei and Bophuthatswana have withdrawn from the committee.[94]

South African security legislation has been replaced in the TBVC states by similar, sometimes harsher laws: the 1977 Public Security Act in the Transkei, the Internal Security Act of 1979 in Bophuthatswana, Ciskei's 1982 National

Security Act and Venda's Maintenance of Law and Order Act introduced in 1985. Local police acts and standing orders – virtually identical to those of the SAP – were also introduced.

In the other bantustans, those which have not reached the stage of 'independence', control of local police units has been transferred to a lesser degree to the bantustan authorities: nominally separate forces exist in Lebowa, QwaQwa, Gazankulu, KaNgwane, Kwandebele and KwaZulu. These forces are extensions of the SAP, but in KwaZulu, at the insistence of the homeland leader Mangosuthu Buthelezi, the force enjoys some operational freedom. Four of the six commissioners in these territories in 1992 were seconded white SAP officers.[95]

In *Transkei*, the first bantustan to become independent, the police have developed the greatest autonomy, although the local force has until recently subscribed to the SAP ethos. By 1975 the SAP had handed administrative control over all police stations, equipment and personnel in the territory to the Transkei Police.[96] The SAP continued to train and supply the force. In the early 1980s some SAP personnel were replaced with white Rhodesians (who also took command of the army) as the Transkei regime, led by the corrupt and autocratic George Matanzima, prokoved a spat with Pretoria and grandiloquently declared that it was going its own way.[97] In practice, however, the Transkei remained utterly dependent on Pretoria which subsidised most of the homeland's budget, including its police and military expenditure.

At the end of 1987 an army brigadier, Bantu Holomisa, led a popularly supported coup against the Matanzima regime. The military council which has since ruled the bantustan has moved closer to the ANC. The army is the most important institution in the bantustan, and the police have only a secondary role in internal security, but they have stopped detaining and harassing the ANC and its allies and instead have turned their attentions to the rump of Matanzima supporters and others opposed to the new leadership. Holomisa has called on the Trankei police to adopt new methods of work based on communication and contact with the public, which he hopes will restore public confidence in the force.[98]

Ciskei has been the site of Byzantine political intrigues since its 'independence' in 1981. Brigadier Charles Sebe, brother of Life President Lennox Sebe, played a prominent part in many of the political machinations. As Commander-General in the early 1980s of the Department of State Security, which controlled the police, army and intelligence service, he claimed that God had given him the task of 'eradicating communism from South Africa'. The Ciskei police, formed in 1977, have played second fiddle to military intelligence structures since independence, and have remained basically an extension of the SAP with a counter-insurgency emphasis: to broaden their fighting experience they helped the SAP in Namibia in the 1980s. An important role in political repression has been played by two specialist units, the Ciskei

Security Branch and the Elite Unit, a kind of praetorian guard which was commanded by Lennox Sebe's son.[99]

In March 1990 the Ciskei government was taken over in a coup by Brigadier 'Oupa' Gqozo. Although he posed as champion of the people and courted the ANC, he allowed himself to be manipulated by a South African military intelligence front known as International Researchers – later renamed the Ciskei Intelligence Service. Military intelligence set about transforming the Gqozo regime into an anti-ANC force.[100] Black police and army officers were replaced by hardline whites, and Brigadier (later General) Jan Viktor, a former commander of the Askaris at Vlakplaas, was brought in to head the police force.[101] Gqozo was fed with disinformation about ANC plots against him, and his increasingly erratic regime was drawn into a trial of strength with the ANC, leading to the September 1992 Bisho massacre, when at least 28 ANC supporters were killed and 200 wounded by Ciskei soldiers during a mass protest at the territory's border. After the massacre, Gqozo's links with Pretoria weakened – Brigadier Viktor resigned, accusing him of politicising the police – but he remained in the power of hardline white security advisers, now acting in a freelance capacity.[102]

In *Bophuthatswana*, economically the most healthy of the bantustans, police and military units set up by Pretoria have played a prominent role in enforcing the autocratic rule of Lucas Mangope, although the SAP and SADF have kept their local surrogates on a tight rein, perhaps because of Bophuthatswana's strategic position on the border with Botswana and its proximity to South Africa's industrial heartland. But in February 1988 sections of the Bophuthatswana Defence Force, with evident popular support, rebelled and took Mangope prisoner. The SAP's Special Task Force and units of the SADF quickly moved in to crush the coup and restore the Mangope regime, and the mutineers were subsequently charged and imprisoned. The Bophuthatswana security forces were brought even more closely under Pretoria's control: in any case, they never had more than token autonomy, and the police have been commanded by seconded white SAP officers. In the 1990s a clique of ex-Rhodesians installed themselves as 'advisers' to Mangope and gained control over the administrative and security appraratus. Rowan Cronje, once a minister in Ian Smith's government, took over the defence ministry and helped steer the Mangope regime ever further to the right. The police have continued active suppression of the ANC and its allies under the bantustan's draconian security legislation. Like the SAP, the Bophuthatswana police are militarised and have played a front-line counter-insurgency role.[103]

The small *Venda* police force was set up as part of that bantustan's joint Venda National Force which carried out the functions of police, army, intelligence and prisons services. During the 1980s, as opposition to the homeland authorities mounted, the police became infamous for rounding up and torturing opponents of the government, including church leaders.[104] But in March 1990 the old regime fell after mass protests and the army commander, General Gabriel Ramushana, took over. He has steered a middle course between Pretoria and the ANC.

Of the other bantustan forces, by far the most potent and problematic is the *KwaZulu* police force (KZP), which has grown to over 4,000 men and women since its formation in 1980. Essentially an offshoot of the SAP, and commanded by a seconded SAP officer, the KZP has been used as a political instrument by the KwaZulu-based Inkatha movement and its leader, Mangosuthu 'Gatsha' Buthelezi, who holds the post of Minister of Police. Buthelezi has constantly agitated for greater powers to be transferred to him and his police force. Like the SAP, the KZP controls paramilitary riot or reaction units, which are based at police headquarters at Ulundi and at each of the police districts. The KZP says these have been 'extensively used to quell the sporadic incidents of violence ... by certain radical elements.'[105] The SAP continues to train and equip the KZP, but its senior officers have also attended training courses, which included counter-insurgency techniques, in West Germany, the US and unspecified countries in the Middle East.[106]

The KZP commissioner in the early 1990s, Major-General Jacques Buchner, served in the Security Branch for 25 years and played a prominent role in the establishment of the SAP's Askari unit. In 1982 he led a raid into Lesotho in which 42 people, South African refugees as well as Lesotho nationals, were killed.[107] He was posted to Pietermartizburg security police headquarters in 1987, when violence erupted there between ANC and Inkatha supporters which led to more than 4,000 deaths. He took over control of the KZP in 1989: it has almost doubled in size under his command, and he has gone on record as calling for a force 10,000 strong.[108] As we will see in the next chapter, both the KZP and the Pietermaritzburg security police have been involved in assassinations of ANC supporters. The KZP has also shown itself to be partial in its operations, supporting Inkatha against the ANC, and in many cases it has contributed to the violence.[109]

VIGILANTE GROUPS

In some of the bantustans, and in many townships, the police overlap with, or work alongside, private bodyguard forces or vigilante formations controlled by local strongmen. The nature of these forces and the extent of their links with the SAP varies enormously, and some of them have existed only for short periods. The devastating effects of vigilante activities on local communities, their role in the counter-revolution of the second half the 1980s and their contribution to the political violence of the 1990s is examined later in this book. Some mention should be made here of the more established groups, however, since they form part of the structures of policing in South Africa.

The townships were relatively unpoliticised before the uprisings of 1976, and many groups emerged to carry out law-and-order functions not attended to by the police. Their attitude to the police and the apartheid state varied: some were products of it or benefited from its limited resources, others carved out a degree of autonomy – but none aligned themselves with the anti-apartheid opposition. The *makgotla*, semi-official tribal courts and vigilante groups which operated mainly in townships around Johannesburg, were perhaps the best established. They utilised the grey area of 'traditional law' to administer punishment to perceived malefactors, mostly by whipping, and were given some informal control over the allocation of housing, as part of their role in administering the influx control (pass law) system. Relations with the police were uneasy, as each felt the other was treading on its turf, and in the early 1980s the police tried to persuade the *makgotla* members – who numbered about 500 in Soweto, where they were best established – to join the police reservists.[110] Attempts were made by government structures to extend the *makgotla* to other areas, notably the Eastern Cape,[111] but the uprising in the second half of the 1980s effectively ended the reign of the *makgotla*.

In Cape Town townships, street committees, not to be confused with those which emerged under UDF control in the mid-1980s, patrolled neighbourhoods and tried to settle local disputes. They were given tacit support by the police, and in return they too helped enforce influx control.[112] After 1976, along with other township vigilante groups, they were caught between the pressures of the radicals who saw them as collaborators, and the state, which was casting about for allies in its attempt to extend apartheid control through new local government structures. Many vigilantes were co-opted into the new black local authorities. With the expansion of the bantustan system, groups attached to bantustan political parties, such as Inkatha, also became more active. In the Ciskei, an unofficial police reserve known as the Green Berets (although they soon abandoned the berets) was set up in the mid-1970s by the the authorities. Mostly older men recruited from rural areas, the Green Berets helped to suppress a boycott of buses by commuters in 1983 and tried to stamp out militant trade unionism. Roaming the streets in gangs, they assaulted and abducted many opponents of the authorities, often handing them over to the police who at the height of this campaign used the local soccer stadium as a centre for detaining and assaulting people brought in from the streets.[113]

In the Gazankulu bantustan, a vigilante force linked to the 'cultural movement' Ximoko ka Rixaka, led by the homeland leader, was active in the 1980s. Some of its members were reported to have received counter-insurgency training. In Kwandebele, a notorious vigilante organisation, Mbokodo, assaulted and attacked people opposing moves to make the bantustan independent.[114]

The most powerful of all the bantustan vigilante groups is undoubtedly Inkatha, originally a KwaZulu 'cultural movement' and now a political party officially known as the Inkatha Freedom Party (IFP). While Inkatha has displayed many of the features of the other bantustan vigilante groups – violent opposition to anti-apartheid activists, assistance to the police in crushing political resistance, public diplays of allegiance to the bantustan leader – its large membership (figures are disputed but it is probably over a million strong) and its high political profile make it far more than a vigilante unit. Its role is examined later in this book.

While the police and other authorities made growing use of vigilantes in the 1970s, the explosion of vigilantism came as a backlash during the township uprising of 1984–6. New forms of street committees and informal courts, linked to the UDF and the ANC, swept aside the old vigilante structures, and the authority of local councillors and bantustan officials was undermined as radical comrades took control. Many councillors and police were forced to flee the townships for their lives. As the crisis intensified, comrades in many areas resorted to increasingly heavy-handed methods of enforcing boycotts and other mass actions. The security forces exploited grievances amongst the conservative elements whose positions of authority and privilege had been destroyed by the radical assault. Various groups sprang up – although not exactly spontaneously – to lead a brutal backlash: the Phakatis in Thabong in the Orange Free State, Amabutho in Umlazi in Natal, Ama-Afrika, funded by the SADF in the Eastern Cape and the Witdoeke in Crossroads squatter camp in Cape Town.[115]

With axes, assegais (stabbing spears), sticks, guns and other weapons, and backed to varying degrees by the police, the vigilantes exacted a terrible toll on the comrades and the wider community. Many of these vigilante groups no longer exist. Some, like the Witdoeke, have survived although they are no longer as active as they used to be. Others faded away once they had served their purpose or the balance of street power shifted irreversibly against them. Some groups were incorporated into the ranks of the *kitskonstabels* and municipal police.

In the 1990s, the face of vigilantism has changed. Inkatha has widened its vigilante-type actions into virtual civil war. With the power of councillors and bantustan authorities on the wane, vigilante groups associated with them have faded away. But criminal gangs have been allowed by the police to operate in some townships providing they do the dirty work of harrying anti-apartheid activists.

Private Forces and White Auxiliaries

PRIVATE SECURITY INDUSTRY

The failure of the police to combat crime, and the SAP's willingness – for reasons of economy as well as strategy – to 'sub-contract' policing tasks, has spawned a massive private security industry in South Africa. While private security firms have become a feature of life in many countries, in South Africa security guards outnumber the police by up to five to one: estimates of the numbers employed in the industry range from 300,000 to 600,000, though the higher figure probably includes non-uniformed personnel.[116] Many large corporations, private or parastatal, as well as local councils and regional authorities, have their own in-house security departments, and hundreds of companies specialise in security services for individuals, businesses or properties.

The distinction between private and public has steadily been eroded in modern life. White South Africans are now more likely to shop in privately owned (and privately patrolled) malls than in high streets, and many South Africans live in flats or housing clusters controlled by security guards.[117] Privately owned security firms have thus taken over many of the functions previously the preserve of the police: increasingly, their role is not merely preventive, but reactive. In middle-class suburbs, especially in the Johannesburg area, most houses are protected by private firms who will despatch armed patrol vehicles to deal with intruders; some of them boast 'rapid deployment forces' and use paramilitary equipment.

The relationship between the SAP and the private firms is symbiotic: without the security firms the police would be overwhelmed. Many of the leading figures in the industry are ex-SAP or SADF members, usually with counter-insurgency experience, and some are veterans of the Rhodesian war. The SAP provides some assistance with training, equipment, advice and information.[118] In many ways, the private firms are extensions of the SAP, expanding its influence, methods and ethos in the business community and providing career opportunities for its trained personnel.

The government has actively encouraged the privatisation process. The National Key Points Act of 1980 was instrumental in this: it compelled owners of major plants and installations to implement stringent security precautions on pain of large financial penalties or imprisonment. The result was what one press report called a 'multi-million rand bonanza' for the security industry, and, because firms were now required to protect large industrial installations from guerilla and other actions, the industry became significantly militarised.[119] Many of the personnel at key points carry shotguns and other lethal weapons. Large corporations, including the mining companies, have their own in-house security operations. The mine forces are extensively militarised – some are equipped with teargas, armoured vehicles (including police Casspirs), helicopters and anti-riot equipment[120]

With the industry experiencing rapid expansion in the 1980s, regulation of standards became a problem as fly-by-night operators and opportunist ex-members of the security forces moved in to make a quick buck.[121] The Security

Association of South Africa (SASA) and the South African Security Federation (SASFED) have tried to establish professional standards through self-regulation and training programmes, and in 1987 the government introduced the Security Officers Act to establish some control over the industry.[122] Working conditions for black security guards are still bad: low pay, long hours and inadequate facilities (in a recent case security guards were found to be living in bushes near the premises they were guarding)[123] and unions have opposed some of the government controls, arguing that they cut into meagre wages.[124]

These measures have not stopped abuses. In one of the most notorious cases, Sybrand 'Louis' van Schoor, a white security guard in East London, and an ex-policeman, shot dead 41 alleged burglars over a period of a few years. After each incident, magistrates found that he had acted within the law, and not once was he so much as cautioned by the police or courts. He became the local hero of many whites, but the publicity he drew to himself proved to be his undoing and he was eventually hauled before the courts and sentenced to 20 years in jail.[125]

CITY COUNCILS AND WHITE NEIGHBOURHOODS

Some white town and city councils have taken steps to establish their own 'private' police forces and even intelligence agencies, in part out of desperation at the failure of the SAP to combat crime, and in some cases to monitor political opponents. In the fear-filled climate of the early 1980s in-house security departments were militarised. The city of Durban opted for an 'aggressive' security posture, installing electrified fencing and 'explosive devices' (presumably a euphemism for booby traps or landmines) around key council installations.[126] In Cape Town, the council's Security Services Division established a Rapid Deployment Force, equipped with lethal weapons and 'specially adapted unmarked vehicles', appropriately commanded by an ex-Rhodesian police inspector.[127] Johannesburg set up a Department of Public Safety in 1983, with a task list which included 'the provision of guard services; the provision of reaction services; co-operation with national security force ... monitoring and forecasting of security threats; liaison with national security intelligence'.[128]

The Johannesburg security department developed close links with Military Intelligence, and took it upon itself to spy on anti-apartheid activists, students, trade unionists and even pop singers and the then editor of Johannesburg's main evening newspaper, *The Star*. With ratepayers' money, paid out of a R50 million security budget, the department recruited staff mainly from the police and other intelligence agencies and operated under the control of municipal officials rather than elected councillors. A former training officer at the depart-ment, Hannes Gouws, told local newspapers the department had also set up a special unit which had intimidated anti-apartheid activists and petrol-bombed their houses. Amongst those closely monitored was David Webster, a university lecturer and anti-apartheid activist who was assassinated in May 1989.[129]

The city councils also control *traffic police* forces, as do the provincial authorities. Most of these are armed and have powers to search vehicles without a warrant and to arrest drivers. In Durban, as a result of the historical legacy of a nineteenth-century municipal force, the local police are better trained and have greater powers than other council forces, and increasingly carry out crime-combating duties. The Durban City Council decided to double the size of the force for 'crime prevention purposes' in December 1990, noting that:

> Whereas at one stage the activities of the Durban City Police were devoted to duties in connection with Traffic Control and the enforcement of the Council's Byelaws, the tendency in recent years was to more comprehensive policing activities.[130]

The city council also agitated to extend the jurisdiction of its force to some surrounding areas to clear up 'the legal implications which could arise with regard to arrest, detention, use of firearms, etc'.[131]

Other city councils have agitated for the establishment of full-blown local police forces, but these moves have been opposed by the SAP on the grounds that it would amount to an admission of the failure of the national force.[132] The wealthy council of Randburg, on the outskirts of Johannesburg, found a way around this in 1992 by paying for a special force to be trained and deployed by the SAP within its municipal boundaries.[133]

Two other largely white formations help the SAP spread its workload. *Neighbourhood Watch* schemes, launched in Randburg in 1984 as a result of a householder's initiative, have mushroomed in recent years as crime has increased. They are almost exclusively middle-class and white – Sebokeng is the only African township where some residents participate in the scheme.[134] Organised by police, councillors and local ratepayers' associations, they involve up to 100,000 whites in suburbs around the country in surveillance and liaison with the police.[135] The activities of Group B reservists have been integrated with the neighbourhood watches,[136] and Neighbourhood Watch encourges its members to join the reservists.[137] In some suburbs self-styled vigilante groups have been set up by alarmed whites – groups such as the Flamingoes, once active in various areas of the Transvaal, Blanke Veiligheid (White Security) in the town of Welkom in the Orange Free State and Brandwag in Brits.[138] A Business Watch scheme is also in operation.

The *Civil Protection* organisation, which used to be called Civil Defence, although not officially linked to the SAP, carries out some policing and control tasks. Initially set up to deal with natural disasters and war, the system was seen as an important component of the state's Total Strategy to mobilise the white population and increase vigilance. The level of organisation varies widely, but in cities like Pretoria a hierarchical network links white neighbourhoods with police and army authorities, and in rural areas the network has been linked into the counter-insurgency effort.[139]

The impact of the mobilisation of white South Africans into police support structures is all the greater because the majority of white South African households have at least one firearm at their disposal. Gun ownership has risen rapidly in recent years as a result of the police failure to stop the increase in violent crime and white fears about the future, and a growing number of blacks are also obtaining arms, legally and illegally. In 1990 the law governing the issuing of firearms licences was tightened up – applicants now have to write an examination and keep weapons in a secure place – but by then nearly 2.9 million firearms had been licensed (and the number of murders carried out with guns had doubled in three years).[140]

RIGHT-WING PARAMILITARIES

Making use of the ready availability of weapons and their links with the police, the army and the private security industry, ultra-right political groups have built up private armies to fight a final battle in defence of white minority rule. Right-wing paramilitaries mushroomed after De Klerk began the process leading to negotiations. There are now more than 100 extremist right-wing organisations, many of them with their own 'military wings' which together can muster several thousand armed militants. Most of the organisations are small crackpot outfits, with less than 50 members, going by names like the World Apartheid Movement, Wit Wolwe (White Wolves) and White Freedom Movement.

The best-established of the paramilitaries, the Wen Kommandos (Victory Commandos) of the Afrikaner Weerstandsbeweging (AWB), claims to have trained 12,000 people, although its organised strength is well below this figure. Its members have been systematically trained and equipped for the 'third Boer war' and organised into paramilitary structures around the country. The AWB also has a security wing, the Iron Guards.[141]

Links between the police and the right-wing militia are extensive. Many of the commanders of the units are ex-policemen (some now active in private security companies). A group called the Pretoria Boer Commando Group, for example, counts amongst its leaders 'quite a few retired defence force and police generals', according to the South African Broadcasting Corporation. The AWB's leader, Eugene Terreblanche, himself an ex-policeman, has proclaimed, 'If there are insufficient police or soldiers, we will defend ourselves, because we are ourselves policemen and soldiers.'[142] Since 1991, when police began to come into conflict with armed right-wingers attempting to attack

National Party functions, the relationship between the extremist groups and the SAP has been strained. The SAP, as an instrument of the government of the day, has confronted some of the paramilitaries, but that is not to say that there are no covert links between the extremists and at least some sections of the police. Sympathy for the ultra-right in the SAP is widespread, and since De Klerk's reforms many have left the force only to join the ranks of the rightist zealots.

Composition and Strength of the SAP

PHYSICAL RESOURCES

During the 1970s the SAP was neglected as resources were poured into the SADF. The police share of state spending, which accounted for over 4 per cent in 1960, had dropped to just over 2 per cent in the early 1980s, compared to around 15 per cent allocated to the SADF. During the 1980s, however, a perceived increase in domestic threats moved the state to redress this imbalance. The police budget was boosted at a much faster rate than the SADF's – its biggest fillip was in 1982/3, when it shot up by 55 per cent compared to the previous financial year.

Under De Klerk the police have been pampered: an increase of over 50 per cent in 1991/2 and 22 per cent in 1992/3 pushed police expenditure to R5,600 million, accounting for five per cent of the state budget.[143] Cuts in the defence budget have considerably narrowed the gap between the resources allocated to the two main arms of the security forces. In the 1980s the defence budget outstripped the police budget by a factor of at least five to one; by 1992/3 it was less than double the size. Actual expenditure on the police by the state is further inflated by policing and law-and-order costs incurred by other government departments, especially on prisons, the justice system and the secret services.

The SAP suffers few equipment shortages, despite the mandatory UN arms embargo which has been in force since 1977 and the steps taken by many nations to prohibit the sale of equipment, such as computers, to the SAP. These measures caused some difficulty, and made police links with other forces more difficult, but were 'too little, too late' and too half-heartedly enforced to seriously affect the SAP's readiness. Although the police still use imported weapons and equipment – for example, vehicles such as Land Rovers and handguns and shotguns – they obtain the bulk of their low-technology goods from one or another of South Africa's recently privatised armaments manufacturers. The manufacture of arms and ammunition is one of the largest industries in the country and some equipment made for the local market, such as the now standard-issue police handgun, the Z88, is exported to other countries. (The arms embargo has had a more marked effect on the South African air force and navy, which depend on high-technology equipment.)[144]

The police are mostly equipped with paramilitary or military weapons, identical to those supplied to the SADF. Standard police weapons include handguns, rifles and shotguns. The new police pistol, the Z88, was specially designed for the force on the basis of the Italian Beretta and is a powerful 9mm parabellum.[145] All regular SAP members are also issued with rifles (unlike handguns, though, these are supposed to be kept in police armouries and issued only for specific duties). The old R1 rifles, South African copies of the Belgian FN, are being replaced by R5s – semi-automatic assault rifles based on the Israeli Galil which fire high-velocity military rounds. While the R5 fires a smaller-calibre bullet than the R1 (5.56mm as opposed to 7.72mm) the bullet tumbles on impact and is if anything more lethal. The same weapon is used by the SADF.[146]

A variety of shotguns are used, some imported and some made locally. The SAP has used them with various grades of shot. Lighter 'birdshot' (usually No. 5 is used) can cause serious injuries, especially if people are shot in the eye.[147] But it is safer than the heavy-duty 'buckshot', some grades of which, such as SSG, can penetrate a sheet of heavy metal at a distance of several metres.[148] For specialised operations and covert tasks, various weapons are employed, including Israeli Uzi sub-machine guns and Eastern bloc AK-47 automatic rifles.

Since the Soweto uprisings, baton rounds, better known as rubber bullets, have been introduced – they are usually fired from shotguns but can also be used with a South African-devised 37mm weapon, the Stopper. At close quarters, rubber bullets can kill, and their use has been banned in many countries.[149]

Teargas is usually fired in canisters from from the Stopper or from cap dischargers which can be attached to the end of an R1 rifle. It is made in abundant quantities in South Africa. While police euphemistically call it 'tearsmoke' in official announcements, the CS gas used is potentially lethal, especially when used on babies or young children and in confined spaces.[150] 'The attitude that teargas is harmless in all circumstances is both incorrect and dangerous,' concluded a South African doctor who made a study of its effects.[151] Teargas can also cause panic amongst crowds: 255 people were reported to be injured in the crush trying to escape from teargas fired into a stadium in Mamelodi, near Pretoria in July 1990.[152]

The quirt, a type of plastic whip, shorter than the more traditional sjambok, is an innovation introduced by the SAP in 1980.[153] Other South African contributions to riot-control are the 'sneeze machine', a device which can be mounted on a Land Rover or similar vehicle and which sprays teargas in all directions; the Slingshot, an hydraulic 'machine gun' which fires baton rounds at up to 170 rounds a minute;[154] and the Striker, a 12-round repeater shotgun.[155] Water cannon are available, but they have not often been used.

The SAP controls a fleet of over 24,000 vehicles, mostly cars and patrol vans (in 1990 no less than 15,000 of these were damaged, a testimony to the notoriously bad driving of the police). It also has over 1,000 armoured vehicles, mostly the ungainly high-bodied Casspirs designed for bush warfare, although these are gradually being replaced by 'bullet-proof urban riot vehicles' such as the specially designed Nonquai, which is regarded as being less aggressive-looking than the Casspir.[156] The force also uses helicopters, which have to be imported (most recently Messerschmitts from Germany).

PERSONNEL: THE MAKE-UP OF THE FORCE

The size of the SAP relative to South Africa's population has been a source of controversy. The police themselves have argued that compared to other countries, South Africa is underpoliced. The then Minister of Law and Order, Adriaan Vlok, claimed in 1988 that South Africa had only 1.94 policemen for every 1,000 people, which he compared to 3.1 for every 1,000 in West Germany. It was also remarked upon that South Africa had no more police than New York City.[157]

Leaving aside the validity of such comparisons, these statistics ignore several unique or unusual features of policing in South Africa – the residential segregation of the country and the virtual abandonment of crime-combating work in the black areas; the contribution of bantustan police; the policing tasks carried out by the army; the role of mine police and other private forces; the control function of the state bureaucracy. In any case, with the radical increase in police numbers in the 1990s, the SAP now has an actual strength approaching 120,000, which gives a ratio of 3.2 policemen to every 1,000 people (working on an estimated total population of 37 million).[158] When the bantustan forces are taken into account this rises to 3.8 to 1,000. A still higher ratio of 4.8 per 1,000 has been cited by Law and Order Minister Hernus Kriel, based on the ratio of operational SAP to population excluding the TBVC states. These figures compare fairly favourably with many countries (in Britain the ratio is about 4 per 1,000 people and it is about 5 to 1,000 in Europe as a whole, but many developing countries have lower ratios).[159] The problem, as has been pointed out elsewhere in this book, is not how few police there are but what they are doing.

A detailed breakdown of the personnel in the SAP was given by Deputy Commissioner Lieutenant-General Mulder van Eyk in 1991. He disclosed that of the 108,000 police then serving, 49,000 were classified as African, 47,000 white, 8,500 coloured and 3,500 Indian.[160] About 5 per cent of the force was female. While black police now far outnumber whites, and the percentage of the force which is black is progressively increasing, the officer corps is almost entirely non-African, and the dominant ethos of the force, its self-image and to some extent its public face, is that of a white, Afrikaner and male force. It also appears to be very young. In 1991, 95 per cent of white recruits undergoing basic training were Afrikaans-speaking and their average age was 19.[161]

Few recruits are drawn from the professional world, and most sign up soon after leaving school. In 1989 and again in 1990, barely 1 per cent of applicants had degrees or diplomas.[162] There is also an exceptionally high turnover of staff – in recent years up to 7 per cent of the force have deserted it annually, and resignations were running at 22 a day in April 1991, although this was unusually high (and assumed to be a protest at De Klerkism). Recruiting the required number of police has always been a problem for the SAP and it is rare for it to reach its authorised personnel levels. These shortfalls have been partly alleviated by the practice of allocating a proportion of white conscripts undergoing their compulsory military service to the SAP. In most years in the 1980s around 1,000 conscripts were allocated to the police, but this shot up to 4,000 in 1989.[163]

Morale in the force is low, although recent salary increases may have led to some improvement. In the late 1980s many police in desperation went to the press or contacted opposition MPs with their complaints. A sergeant who approached a national newspaper in 1989 complained of long hours of work and poor pay which resulted in a rapid turnover of personnel. He also said that young recruits were given little supervision and were left to their own devices on riot duty in the townships:

> The force consists largely of youngsters doing a four-year stint and then getting out....
>
> At our police station there are about 50 white policemen – of these only seven have more than four years' service ....
>
> A typical example is a young policeman who comes out of police college. He's 19, he's had six months' training; after two or three months he's drafted into a riot unit and deployed in a black township for more than a year. He runs amok.
>
> Those policemen in the townships have no proper discipline. They're left to their own devices and I'm certain that superior officers have absolutely no idea what is happening with those policemen in the townships ....
>
> They end up hating blacks and blaming them for their miserable position. I've seen normal young guys come out of the townships complete racists.[164]

Police who stay in the force work their way up the ranks as far as their abilities or opportunities allow, and they are trained either on the job or through police training centres – thus the culture of the force is reinforced continually, with little outside input. The closed nature of the police as an institution is reinforced by the fact that many police live in dormitories or flats provided by the SAP, which are often attached to police stations. Community links are further impaired by the SAP's practice of not deploying police in the areas where they were recruited, and often transferring them to other parts of the country on promotion.[165]

All police forces have a 'cop culture' or a 'canteen culture' – their sense of mission and solidarity, which often entails elements of authoritarianism, aggressiveness, suspicion, resistance to change, sexism and racism. The SAP is no exception. These attitudes are widely prevalent amongst white South African males, and, if attitude surveys are anything to go by, are especially common amongst young Afrikaner males who form the main recruitment pool for the police. Interviews with individual police and the few investigations carried out by the media point to an overwhelming culture of racism, sexism and intolerance amongst white police.[166] Trials of police accused of the torture, killing or assault of black South Africans have repeatedly shown that many white police regard blacks as sub-human. The SAP has shown little enthusiasm for rooting out police found guilty of crimes of violence against blacks and other criminal offences. Statistics for the years between 1970 and 1985, for example, indicate that in a typical year between 200 and 250 police were found guilty of crimes of violence, ranging from assault to murder. Only about 10 per cent of those convicted were eventually discharged from the police and many repeated offenders have been retained in the force.[167]

Afrikaner nationalism has been actively promoted in the SAP, mainly through the cultural organisation Akpol. The police code of honour, which all police were expected to swear to, opened with the phrase 'as a member of the South African Police that serves a nation with a Christian National Foundation'. The vast majority of white police are believed to support right-wing political parties or paramilitary formations – estimates range from 70 to 90 per cent support.[168] And, if anything, attitudes of new recruits appear to be hardening. A security policeman, Lieutenant-Colonel John Horak, who resigned from the force in 1990, said that most of the new recruits at Pretoria police college, where he taught, were supporters of the Afrikaner Weerstandsbeweging. Support for the extreme right was more common amongst young members of the force than older ones, he said.[169]

Right-wing attitudes amongst police are overlaid with a Calvinist belief that the will of God legitimises the law and the state, and that the task of the police is thus God-given – a theme drummed home by the officer corps and government ministers. The then Minister of Justice, Jimmy Kruger, probably went furthest when in 1977 he declared that South African policemen were 'the mandate-holders of God',[170] but the tradition of thanking the Lord for the SAP continues. 'We are grateful in the first place to our Heavenly Father who in His goodness and mercy has made it possible for the Force to meet the great challenges of the times,' typically declared the Deputy Minister of Law and Order, Leon Wessels, when commemorating the force's 75th anniversary.[171]

Most ordinary white police officers share this view: 'children of God' is how they were described to a BBC TV interviewer in 1990.[172]

POLICEWOMEN

After some limited early experimentation, for more than 50 years the SAP steadfastly resisted calls for white women to be allowed to serve in the force. It changed its mind in 1972, in the face of yet another crisis in personnel levels, and much to the shock of most policemen. Although conditions of service and training were similar to those of men (but with less emphasis on military aspects), women officers were assigned specific roles in keeping with their expected social roles. The SAP's Commissioner explained:

> Naturally, Women Police will be employed in specific designated tasks, particularly in cases where female accused and witnesses are involved, but primarily also in criminal cases where the complainants are women.

The Commissioner also justified the recruitment of women on the grounds of 'the alarming increase of social ills such as alcohol abuse, the use of dagga and other drugs',[173] although quite how women police were expected to combat this was not explained.

Black women – first coloureds, then Indians, then Africans, following the usual apartheid hierarchy – were recruited into the force in the mid-1980s, although numbers have remained small. Women are now also allowed to join the reservists.[174] The number of women in the force has been growing slowly, and in 1991 the SAP decided to increase female recruitment: between a quarter and a third of students at white, Indian and Coloured police training colleges in that year were women. But the 1991 intake were trained for only three months, instead of six, and were recruited specifically to replace men in administrative tasks who were being shifted to active policing duties. There are still very few African women recruits.[175]

The SAP likes to emphasise, in the words of an article in the police journal *Servamus*, that policewomen 'have remained ladies amongst men',[176] and the 1990 White Paper on the police explains that they 'receive finishing-off lextures [*sic*] in make-up, deportment and social etiquette'.[177] Otherwise women receive much the same training as men, but they are exempted from counter-insurgency training and are not sent to scenes of violence. Thousands of women also work for the SAP as clerks, typists and in other service roles. Wives of policemen, many of whom live in accommodation provided by the force, are assigned an important role by the SAP and form part of the police sub-culture. A 1990 article in *Servamus* has this advice for them:

> It is true that your husband may be in the front line of the attack on the very fibre of our ordered society, in the heat of the battle, but you must be that quiet, unseen

source of his strength for that battle, from you must flow the strength that he needs to come out of that battle, unscathed and victorious.[178]

BLACK POLICE IN THE SAP

Although most black police in South Africa serve in auxiliary and bantustan formations, the SAP itself is now more than 60 per cent black. With the recruitment of increasing numbers of Africans it is likely that soon the force will reflect fairly accurately the overall racial composition of South Africa. But it will be years, if not decades, before the imbalances in the officer corps are corrected. Whites made up no less than 94.4 per cent of the 4,600 strong officer corps in 1991, Indians 2.3 per cent, coloureds 1.5 per cent and Africans 1.8 per cent (a mere 82 officers). The highest-ranking black officer in the SAP was an Indian brigadier, although in December 1992 two black major-generals were promoted to help lead the newly formed Community Relations Division.[179] Given the overwhelming preponderance of Africans in the South African population, the representation of whites in the officer corps is 244 times as great as that of Africans.[180] Even allowing for the officers in the 'independent' bantustan forces, the dominance of whites is overwhelming.

The SAP claims that conditions of service for blacks are now the same as for whites and that the force is therefore 'non-racial'. In fact, it is extensively segregated, and changes introduced under De Klerk have only scraped the surface. Training is still largely segregated and the legacy of discrimination in pay, training, housing and promotion,[181] which was formally abolished only in 1984, lingers on.

It is only comparatively recently that black police have been given authority over white civilians or their white subordinates in the SAP. Blacks were under instructions – dating from the inception of the force – not to arrest whites, and a white policeman or woman of any rank had authority over a black officer.[182] It was only in 1981 that the Police Act was amended to allow, for the first time, a black officer to give orders to a white subordinate.[183] In practice, even today white police and civilians are seldom subjected to the authority of black police. Black officers are put in charge only of black police facilities in black areas, and this segregation is extended through further subdivision into Indian, coloured and African police facilities.

In recent years the SAP has tried to entrench segregation further by extending a policy of establishing racially exclusive police districts, such as Chatsworth in Durban. However, an attempt in 1991 to set up an Indian district in Phoenix, outside Durban, was resisted by the local community. The leader of the opposition campaign, an ex-police lieutenant and station commander, Mike Reddy, said:

Because the district, or for that matter, the Indian police stations, is manned by

Indians, it would be no doubt short-staffed, have insufficient vehicles, broken-down equipment and old furniture.[184]

In recruiting blacks the SAP has met resistance in some areas, particularly in politicised townships since the Soweto uprisings, but there has seldom been a greater shortfall of black recruits than whites. Facing chronic unemployment, and with few career opportunities, many young blacks have been prepared to join the force, despite its role in the enforcement of apartheid rule. The SAP has also sidestepped community resistance by concentrating its recruitment in rural areas, and by deploying black police in areas remote from their home neighbourhoods.[185] All recruits are carefully screened.

While the 'cop culture' of the white force undoubtedly rubs off on black police, Indian, coloured and African police have developed their own sub-cultures, which reflect the opposing pressures of their communities and the police hierarchy. But black police have many grievances against their white colleagues – in November 1992, for instance, police generals had to placate 300 black police in the Vaal townships, who complained that while their white colleagues were inflaming tensions by harsh and violent policing, they were left to bear the brunt of residents' anger without the protection of the armoured vehicles and automatic weapons available to white police.[186] Attitudes to the democratic struggle vary and are undoubtedly changing. On the one hand, black police have been subjected to official propaganda and have been cut off from their communities by being housed in separate compounds or deployed in areas remote from their homes. The effects of this process was reflected in an interview with one African constable in 1985:

> I know that some people don't like us in Soweto. But we don't care. We are told that we must be hard on them. My seniors tell me black people want to take over the country and run it like a Communist country where we are all going to starve. We are also shown films of people starving in Africa and are told that if we don't stop the children from their nonsense we will all starve.[187]

Under these pressures, and finding themselves isolated by their communities, or even targeted by community groups for physical attack, many black police have become just as cruel and uncaring in their attitude to their communities as their white colleagues. But these same community pressures – including public calls on black police to heed the voice of their struggling brothers and sisters, and attempts by revolutionary organisations to win them over – and the racism of their white colleagues have brought many around to the democratic cause. The acceleration of this process was seen most dramatically in the formation in 1989 of the Police and Prison Officers' Civil Rights Union (POPCRU), whose background and prospects are examined in Chapter 5. Some black police – although probably still a small minority – are now sympathisers with or even members of the ANC. An ANC member, who said that he joined the police nine years previously because it was the only job he could find, explained the apparent contradiction of serving two masters in an interview with the *Weekly Mail* in January 1992:

> [I] never harassed the people, I made them understand that I was a victim of that harassment too. Some people think we are the government; we are government servants. But even black policemen are oppressed.[188]

TRAINING AND CONDITIONS OF SERVICE

On joining the force, recruits often have to wait for some time (occasionally up to two years) for a place in one of the SAP's four basic training institutions, and are employed in menial tasks around police stations. Until they were notionally desegregated in 1992 there were four separate colleges for each population group: Pretoria (whites); Bishop Lavis in Cape Town (coloureds); Wentworth in Durban (Indians) and Hammanskraal near Pretoria (Africans). Pretoria and Hammanskraal, each with room for over 1,000 students, are far larger than the other two.

Researchers from the University of the Witwatersrand who visited the Pretoria institution in 1991 and 1992 found that training is 'dominated by a military approach', and that the college functions like a secondary school, 'with the students being tightly controlled in every aspect of their lives'. Training, which takes six months, consists of academic courses in aspects of the law and police science and administration, English and Afrikaans, as well as practical experience in firearms handling and extensive drilling and physical exercise.[189] The programme is similar at the other basic training colleges, but the training given to black auxiliary forces, the police assistants at Koeberg, and the municipal police at Oudtshoorn in the Cape, is more rudimentary, with even more emphasis on military aspects like drilling.

After basic training, all male SAP recruits are sent for six weeks to the counter-insurgency and riot-control training centres at Maleoskop, Verdrag or Slagboom. Specialised training takes place at several other centres, including the SA Police Dog School at Pretoria and the Mechanical Training Centre at Benoni. Since February 1990, an Advanced Training Centre at Paarl has been providing further training for officers and detectives – unlike the other colleges, it is effectively integrated.[190]

Promotion now depends on candidates passing academic examinations in Police Adminstration. A lieutenant, for example, now requires a National Diploma in the subject. However, many of the higher-ranking officers were promoted before these academic qualifications became necessary. Police can also study part-time for a degree or diploma in policing at the University of South Africa.

Conditions of service are a constant source of complaint, especially amongst black police and auxiliaries. While police receive many perks, notably housing, they can be posted anywhere in the country without any choice and have to endure the arduous conditions of counter-insurgency and riot-control work. They are also expected to work night shifts and overtime with little or no extra pay. A group of police officers who contacted the *Cape Times* in 1989 to complain about conditions said that overtime averaged 80 hours a month, without compensation.[191] Salaries, once far below those for comparable jobs in the private sector (at least for whites in junior ranks) have improved somewhat as a result of De Klerk's initiatives. According to one report, a policeman with five years' experience in 1990 was paid R800, not much more than the cleaners and clerical assistants employed by the police.[192] For black police in auxiliary forces the situation was even worse – pay ranged from R250 to R400 in 1988, and they were denied virtually all the benefits available to other police.[193]

Despite the changes of the 1990s, the influx of black police, the vast increase in available funding, and the public declarations by senior police officers that the force has changed fundamentally, the SAP's composition remains much the same as it was throughout the apartheid era. Its officer corps and its ethos still reflect the dominance of the white Afrikaner male, it is still substantially segregated (indeed, the overall position of black police in relation to white police may have deteriorated because of the increasing numbers involved in auxiliary formations), and it is still equipped and trained for confrontational policing involving the use of force.

NOTES

1 Sachs 1973; Sachs 1975, p 227-39.
2 Corder 1989, p 49; *Star* 24.8.91.
3 Lubowski 1989, p 16.
4 Mandela 1990, p 135.
5 Corder 1989, pp 47-55; Marcus 1986, p 18.
6 Sachs 1973, p 262.
7 Sloth-Nielsen 1990, p 195.
8 Scharf 1989.
9 Scharf 1992, pp 8, 21.
10 *Weekly Mail* 22.11.91.
11 *Financial Mail* 15.2.91.
12 *South* 8.8.91.
13 SAP 1990, p 3.
14 SAP 1990, p 3.
15 *Star* 5.3.83; *Government Gazette* 30.3.83.
16 *Government Gazette* 25.6.80.
17 *Government Gazette* 13.6.79; *Natal Mercury* 5.2.92.
18 *Government Gazette* 16.3.77.

19   *Star* 4.6.84.
20   Omar 1990, p 24.
21   Brewer 1988, p 170.
22   Haysom 1987a, p 10.
23   *BBC Summary of World Broadcasts* 12.5.91.
24   *Daily Dispatch* 8.5.91; *Cape Times* 8.5.91.
25   *Business Day* 17.6.92; *Sunday Times* 21.6.92.
26   *SouthScan* 5.2.93.
27   Jeffery 1991, p 130.
28   *Hansard* 30.3.88.
29   Haysom 1989a, p 145.
30   *Weekly Mail* 8.8.91.
31   *SouthScan* 13.3.92.
32   Hansson 1989, p 56; Nathan & Phillips 1991, pp 7-8; *SouthScan* 25.10.91.
33   *Independent* 24.6.92.
34   *Servamus* December 1988, p 20.
35   SAP 1990, pp 13–4.
36   SouthScan 4.9.92.
37   Rauch & Marais 1992.
38   *Servamus* September 1989.
39   SAP 1990, pp 15–6.
40   Rauch 1991, p 13.
41   *Servamus* September 1989, pp 15–6.
42   SAP 1990, p 21.
43   SAP 1990, pp 34–5.
44   *Servamus* February 1988, p 27; Rauch 1991, p 6.
45   SAP 1990, pp 37–8.
46   Dippenaar 1988, pp 790–2.
47   *Servamus* February 1983, p 24, August 1984, p 40.
48   *Servamus* January 1985, pp 20–3; SAP 1990, pp 25–6.
49   *Citizen* 13.11.81; *Servamus* June 1984, p 34.
50   *Hansard* 6.6.80, p 847.
51   *SouthScan* 15.6.90.
52   *Weekly Mail* 28.8.92.
53   Rauch 1991, pp 3-4.
54   Laurence 1990, p 25.
55   *Servamus* October 1982, p 4.
56   SAP 1990, pp 32–3.
57   *Guardian* 17.1.91.
58   *Daily Telegraph* 2.3.91.
59   *Independent* 14.8.87.
60   For example, Olivia Forsyth, *Daily News* 3.2.89.
61   *Servamus* September 1981, pp 6–10.
62   *Weekly Mail* 5.8.88; Rauch 1991, p 3.
63   Pauw 1991, p 115.
64   Lawyers' Committee 1990, p 10.
65   *Vrye Weekblad* 17.11.89.
66   *War on Peace*, BBC-TV, 2.10.92.
67   *Weekly Mail* 22.1.93.
68   *Sunday Express* 13.12.81.
69   *Rand Daily Mail* 22.6.77; Grundy 1988, p 89.
70   Williams 1992, pp 5, 8.
71   *Weekly Mail* 29.1.93.

72 Coetzee 1984, pp. 38–9; *Resister* February/March 1985, pp 22–3.
73 *Annual Report of the Commissioner of the SAP*, 1990, p 52; *SouthScan* 13.3.92.
74 *Star* 23.3.88.
75 *Servamus*, February 1990, p 40.
76 *Annual Report of the Commissioner of the SAP*, 1990.
77 *Annual Report of the Commissioner of the SAP*, 1990, p 27.
78   *Rand Daily Mail* 16.3.81; *Sunday Express* 31.5.81; *Resister* April/May 1985.
79 *Annual Report of the Commissioner of the SAP*, 1990, p 52.
80 Herbstein & Evenson 1989, pp 61-93; Cawthra 1986, pp 12-25.
81 *Weekly Mail* 4.10.91.
82 *SouthScan* 17.5.91.
83 *Weekly Mail* 10.7.92.
84 Fine 1989; Leap 1990.
85 *Cape Times* 19.8.87.
86 *Servamus*, December 1990, pp 18–9; Rauch 1991, p 8.
87 *Focus*, March/April 1987, p 3.
88 *Cape Times* 11.12.87; *Star* 11.12.87; *Daily News* 11.12.87.
89 *BBC Summary of World Broadcasts* 2.10.89; SAP 1990, pp 41–2.
90 Jeffery 1991, p 90.
91 Cawthra & Navias 1992a.
92 Marais 1992, p 11.
93 *Annual Report of the Commissioner of the SAP* 1990, pp 14–9.
94 Marais 1992, p 5.
95 Marais 1992, p 6.
96 *Star* 4.10.75.
97 *Sowetan* 30.3.82.
98 *Daily Dispatch* 4.5.91.
99 *Daily Dispatch* 8.2.89; Haysom 1983, pp 18–23.
100 *Weekly Mail* 9.8.91.
101 *SouthScan* 11.9.92.
102 *SouthScan* 20.11.92.
103 Africa Watch 1991b; *Rand Daily Mail* 30.12.81.
104 *Rand Daily Mail* 25.1.84, 27.1.84; *Star* 18.6.86.
105 *Annual Report of the Commissioner of the KwaZulu Police* 1990, p 7.
106 Legal Resources Centre 1991, p 12.
107 *SouthScan* 12.7.89.
108 Legal Resources Centre 1991, p 11.
109 *War on Peace*, BBC-TV, 10.3.92.
110 *Star* 10.10.81; *Frontline* October 1982.
111 *Rand Daily Mail* 5.5.80.
112 Scharf 1989, p 222; Scharf 1991b, p 36.
113 Haysom 1983, pp 45–53.
114 *Star* 19.11.90.
115 Haysom 1989d; Haysom 1990; Plasket 1989.
116 Holloway 1989, p 5; *Daily Dispatch* 9.3.90.
117 Grant 1989, p 96.
118 Holloway 1989, pp 33–4.
119 Cawthra 1986, p 86.
120 Scharf 1989, p 212.
121 *Servamus* November 1983.
122 Grant 1989, pp 100-10.
123 *New Nation* 12.7.91.
124 *SouthScan* 1.3.91.

125 *Sunday Tribune* 16.11.89; *Weekly Mail* 24.11.89; *Guardian* 10.7.92.
126 *Daily News* 29.9.82.
127 *Cape Times* 18.9.82; *Sunday Tribune* 24.10.82; *Argus* 6.8.83.
128 *Rand Daily Mail* 25.10.83.
129 *SouthScan* 23.3.90; Laurence 1990, pp 49–52.
130 Cited in Taylor 1992, p 3.
131 Taylor 1992, p 3.
132 *Rand Daily Mail* 4.4.83; *Star* 8.8.87, 17.5.90.
133 Crail 1992.
134 *Weekly Mail* 22.11.91.
135 Rauch 1988.
136 *Annual Report of the Commissioner of the SAP* 1990, p 42.
137 Neille 1992, p 6.
138 *Star* 19.11.90.
139 Scharf 1989, pp 217–8.
140 *Cape Times* 25.5.90.
141 *BBC Summary of World Broadcasts* 21.2.92.
142 *BBC Summary of World Broadcasts* 21.2.92.
143 *Independent* 21.3.91; *SouthScan* 20.3.92.
144 Landgren 1989.
145 *Servamus* December 1988.
146 *Cape Times* 24.1.91; Jeffery 1991, p 48.
147 *Sunday Tribune* 28.12.86.
148 Haysom 1987a, p 3.
149 Haysom 1987b, pp 218–2.
150 *Cape Times* 12.10.89.
151 SACBC 1984, pp 33–4.
152 Jeffery 1991, p 125.
153 *Cape Times* 17.7.80.
154 *Armed Forces March* 1988.
155 *Armed Forces August* 1988.
156 *Cape Times* 4.9.87; *Annual Report of the Commissioner of the SAP* 1990, pp 66–7.
157 *SA Barometer* 2.12.88.
158 In 1991 the SAP told a reseacher that the ratio of police to population in South Africa was 2.65 to 1,000, but this figure excluded the 20,000 bantustan police, and was based on a total of 110,000 SAP members less 14,000 said to be engaged in administrative tasks.
159 *Financial Mail* 19.1.90.
160 Van Eyk 1991, p 1.
161 Policing Research Project 1991.
162 *Annual Report of the Commissioner of the SAP* 1989, p 11 1990, p 11.
163 *BBC Summary of World Broadcasts* 11.10.89.
164 *Sunday Tribune* 20.8.89.
165 Buchner 1992, p 4.
166 For example, *Children of God*, BBC TV, 17.4.91.
167 Foster & Luyt 1986, pp 303–5.
168 *Frontfile* March 1990; *Weekly Mail* 5.4.91.
169 *Independent* 24.6.92.
170 Cited in Pinnock 1980, p 314.
171 Dippenaar 1988, p vii.
172 *Children of God*, BBC-TV, 17.4.91.
173 Cited in Dippenaar 1988, p 429.
174 *Cape Times* 11.12.81; *BBC Summary of World Broadcasts* 19.5.83.

175 Rauch 1992, p 11.
176 *Servamus* November 1986.
177 SAP 1990, p 23.
178 *Servamus* August 1990.
179 Commonwealth Observer Mission 1992, p 43.
180 *Weekly Mail* 18.1.91.
181 Grundy 1983.
182 Sachs 1975, p 234; *Sowetan* 25.1.89.
183 *Citizen* 14.2.81; *Cape Times* 25.3.81.
184 *Daily News* 20.7.91.
185 Grundy 1983, pp 147–8.
186 *SouthScan* 27.11.92.
187 *International Herald Tribune* 3.4.85.
188 *Weekly Mail* 17.1.92.
189 Policing Research Project 1991; Rauch 1992.
190 *Annual Report of the Commissioner of the SAP*, 1990, pp 1–29.
191 *Cape Times* 11.12.89.
192 *Star* 18.5.90.
193 LEAP 1990, p 13.

3

OPERATIONS: FROM THE BUSH WAR TO THE STATE OF EMERGENCY

Counter-insurgency Warfare

Counter-insurgency, guerilla war, bush war, the 'border' war: the SAP was embroiled in conflicts of this nature without a break in Rhodesia, Namibia and South Africa for a quarter of a century. This war against 'terrorism', especially the battle for Namibia, was an overarching concern of the police and shaped its approach to many of its other operations, from the prevention of crime to the suppression of political rebellion.

While the government did not hesitate to send police to Rhodesia in the 1960s and 1970s, the legal basis for the action was questionable (the Police Act authorised operations 'in South Africa' which was taken to mean Southern Africa). But external operations were formally justified by a 1979 amendment which authorised the deployment of police anywhere outside South Africa 'in the event of war or other emergency'; the following year, a further amendment authorised foreign operations relating to any 'police functions'.[1]

THE SAP IN RHODESIA

The war of liberation in Zimbabwe, like many guerilla struggles, was nasty and protracted, its result determined as much by politics as progress on the battlefield, although towards the end the liberation movements were poised for military victory. It was the bloodiest of all anti-colonial struggles in Africa: more than 35,000 Zimbabweans died in the struggle to end white minority rule, following Ian Smith's unilateral declaration of independence from Britain in 1965.[2] Throughout the war South Africa played a prominent part, paying up to half the war costs of the Smith regime and supplying military hardware, expertise and troops.[3] Although there were often differences of strategy between the South African and Rhodesian governments, Pretoria shared a determination to prevent the liberation movements from coming to power. These movements themselves underwent many transformations, eventually emerging as two main forces, ZANU and ZAPU, which were uneasily allied in the Patriotic Front.

Between 1967 – a year after the first shots in the liberation war were fired – and August 1975, militarised units of the SAP provided South Africa's firepower in Rhodesia. Pretoria publicly justified the deployment on the grounds that ANC fighters had been amongst the first group of Zimbabwean combatants which had crossed into Rhodesia from Zambia – their aim was to traverse Rhodesia and set up bases inside South Africa. SAP platoons helped the Rhodesian forces patrol the Zambezi river border and clashed repeatedly with guerillas in the dense bush. There were relatively few SAP deaths, but the police involvement had a profound effect on white South Africa. The state propaganda machine made sure that the SAP's sacrifices were used as part of the psychological campaign to gear up for protracted war. The first South African policeman to be killed, Danie du Toit, a 21-year-old constable who was ambushed by guerillas in July 1968, received what amounted to a state funeral, attended by several members of parliament and the deputy Commissioner of Police.[4]

At the time of the SAP's formal withdrawal in 1975, more Rhodesian police than soldiers were directly involved in the fighting, and the war was still being fought at a relatively low level (it was the large-scale opening of the Mozambique front in 1977 that swamped the Rhodesian forces). Estimates of the strength of the SAP contingent in Rhodesia vary, but authoritative accounts put the total at around 2,000. As Rhodesian army forces on active deployment at the time numbered less than 7,500 men and those of the British South Africa (Rhodesian) Police less than 10,000, the SAP contribution to the Rhodesian war effort was considerable.[5] The withdrawal had been announced at the end of 1974, at a time when the South African Prime Minister, B. J. Vorster, was engaged in a process of 'detente' with African countries in an effort to shore up South Africa's position following the collapse of its Portuguese allies in Mozambique and Angola (the police to be withdrawn were also needed in Namibia). However, the SAP remained involved in the Rhodesian conflict until the Zimbabwean independence elections in 1979, as a part of an extensive, covert South African support operation involving thousands of SADF troops.[6]

The Rhodesian armed forces, aided by a mercenary élite recruited from around the world, adapted counter-insurgency strategies developed in other conflicts, particulary those pioneered by the British in Malaya. The SAP and SADF observed these operations closely, and sometimes participated in them. The Rhodesians made extensive use of black auxiliaries and developed elaborate psychological operations using propaganda and disinformation. As the war progressed, they increasingly resorted to covert and irregular operations, which were mostly carried out by 'special forces', notably the Selous Scouts. The special forces chalked up the most spectacular successes of the war in terms of intelligence and body counts. They developed an expertise in assassinations and the use of poisons – contaminating water supplies and foodstuffs used by guerillas or their supporters and even impregnating guerilla uniforms with poison – and apparently passed these tricks on to the South Africans. Another speciality was 'pseudo operations' whereby security force members disguised themselves as insurgents to gain intelligence or deliberately committed atrocities in the hope of discrediting the guerillas. Cross-border raids on 'terrorist bases' in neighbouring Zambia or Mozambique (often refugee settlements or recruiting stations) were carried out with South African assistance.[7]

Using these tactics, as well as more conventional counter-insurgency methods, the Rhodesian forces killed tens of thousands of guerillas and their supporters. But, as the Americans found out in Vietnam, high body counts were not an indication of impending victory. Indeed, it has been argued that the more insurgents the security forces killed, and the more brutally they killed them, the more alienated the local population grew. By the time they came to cast their votes in the independence elections, the masses of Zimbabwe had no hesitation in condemning Ian Smith and his allies to the scrapheap of history as Robert Mugabe's ZANU swept to power.

The SAP's adventure in the Rhodesian bush was a formative experience, its baptism of fire in modern counter-insurgency warfare. Psychologically, it had a profound effect on the police, who now saw themselves even less as 'bobbies on the beat' than as warriors against terrorism and communism. Many of the security policemen who played a key role in developing the SAP's counter-insurgency strategies, including those accused of involvement in death squads, were based in Rhodesia.[8]

It was in Namibia, however, that the SAP really gained its counter-insurgency credentials. For the police, Namibia provided a testing ground for organisational approaches, battlefield tactics and psychological operations for use in South Africa itself. But it was more than a dry-run for South Africa: it was a struggle in its own right, in which thousands of SAP members were involved over a period of 24 years.

THE WAR IN NAMIBIA

The South African police and army had controlled Namibia since the First World War with little difficulty. Until the 1960s a relatively small contingent was kept in Namibia, and from time to time extra SAP and SADF forces were brought in to put down rebellious sections of the subjugated black population.

Namibia was all but incorporated into South Africa, despite UN rulings that South Africa's occupation of the territory was temporary (in 1966 the UN General Assembly finally revoked South Africa's right to rule Namibia, a decision endorsed three years later by the Security Council). SWAPO took up arms when diplomatic efforts failed to dislodge the white-minority administration. At the beginning the guerillas appeared to be operating against impossible odds and the small groups who crossed the border from Zambia were fairly easily hunted down by the SAP. SWAPO loosely followed classic guerilla insurgency strategy, infiltrating combatants during the rainy season when the bush formed a thick cover, launching hit and run attacks on bases, laying landmines, setting up ambushes, sabotaging communications, pressurising or attacking people collaborating with the South Africans, and working amongst the population with the aim of establishing control of territory in rural areas.[9]

This strategy met with some success in the late 1970s and early 1980s, when SWAPO was on the brink of moving from guerilla warfare to the next phase of mobile warfare in which larger groups of fighters – in SWAPO's case over 100 strong – would seek to engage the enemy.[10] But the movement never really established 'liberated areas' and, in the face of very high personnel losses, it was unable to step up the war further. The conflict was largely restricted to the area known as Ovamboland, a vast flat plain of sand and bush lying just south of the Angolan border, in which up to a third of Namibia's people live.

The opening shots came at Omgulumbashe, a SWAPO base in Ovamboland where combatants had been training local people. A unit from the SAP's Security Branch, acting on intelligence, launched a helicopter raid on the base on 26 August 1966, the results of which are disputed but which certainly precipitated the armed struggle – SWAPO combatants attacked the homes of two white South African officials in Namibia a few weeks later.[11] The SAP responded by rounding up 37 SWAPO leaders in Namibia and taking them to Pretoria where they were ruthlessly tortured.[12] The Terrorism Act was rushed through parliament and made retrospective to 1962, specifically to deal with the Namibians – 20 were sentenced to life imprisonment and most of the remainder received long prison sentences.

The war was a desultory low-level affair for the first few years. It was restricted mainly to the Caprivi Strip, the finger which Namibia extends towards Zambia, as SWAPO fighters found it difficult to infiltrate through Portuguese-controlled Angola. Landmines were increasingly used, often to devastating effect as the police were still using Land Rovers and other vehicles which were not mineproofed. At the end of 1971 the war took a new turn when 20,000 migrant workers from Ovamboland went on strike in Windhoek and other towns in the south of the country. SAP reinforcements were flown in from South Africa to break the strike but the striking workers returned to their homes in the north where they continued to organise and protest. The SAP followed them and it was only a short time before the conflict had escalated into war. SWAPO's fighting ranks were swelled, and it began to open up the Ovamboland front. In the Caprivi, the pressure on the police units mounted – by 1973 SWAPO combatants were using rockets, machine guns and mortars, and the police patrols were proving inadequate in tracking down the growing number of SWAPO fighters.[13]

In January 1972 SADF reinforcements were brought in, and the next year the SADF took control of operations. The police fighting units were withdrawn from northern Namibia – they were needed in Rhodesia and back home in South Africa where the perennial problem of calls on police for a wide range of tasks had exacerbated personnel shortages.[14] However, SAP members remained in Namibia to carry out policing rather than military tasks and they played an important part in a campaign of political repression in 1973 and 1974, breaking up meetings and arresting SWAPO leaders. In Ovamboland, a poorly trained force of 'tribal police' had been set up, as well as a system of 'traditional courts' – many SWAPO supporters were processed through these courts and publicly flogged.[15]

By the end of 1975 the security situation had deteriorated dramatically from Pretoria's point of view: with the collapse of Portuguese authority in Angola, SWAPO combatants had been able to move in strength through south-east Angola into Namibia. Counter-insurgency police units, recalled hastily from Rhodesia, were again sent to northern Namibia. 'We are going to clear Ovamboland. The moment the operation is over we will bring the men back to Pretoria,' declared Minister of Police Kruger.[16] But SAP units were to stay for another 15 years.

The SAP began to recruit local residents into guard units and auxiliary police formations. The auxiliaries, known as special constables or home guards, were recruited on ethnically exclusivist lines and given brief training. Armed with West German G3 automatic rifles, light machine guns, hand grenades and mortars, they were used mostly as bodyguards and militia at the disposal of chiefs and other officials collaborating with the South African occupation.[17] Their behaviour gained them a reputation for indiscipline and lawlessness. An official of the Lutheran World Federation who visited northern Namibia remarked:

> These men are uneducated, unemployed and live by good pay and excitement. Armed bands, often undisciplined, are known for committing atrocities against their own people. South Africa now appears to be replacing some of its own units with Home Guards assembled from all parts of the country and from various tribes.[18]

A string of police bases were established in parts of northern Namibia to train special constables. In 1981, Bert Wandrag, then a brigadier and second in command of the SAP's operations in Namibia, took journalists on a tour of some of the bases, where boys as young as 12 were observed undergoing training (although they had to wait until they turned 16 before being deployed in operations).[19] The special constables were used throughout Namibia, and by 1985 they numbered more than 9,000, a complement greater than that of the regular police.[20] A third of this force was based in Ovamboland.

Although the special constable programme was mainly a response to the exigencies of the counter-insurgency war in the north, it had a political aim as well. In the second half of the 1970s, and for most of the 1980s, South Africa experimented with the possibility of allowing Namibia a homeland-type 'independence' under a client administration. In a process similar to that which took place in the TBVC states, a nominally independent police force, the South-West Africa Police (SWAPOL) was created. SWAPOL officially came into existence in 1981, although at the time virtually its entire command structure was South African and its members were trained at facilities in South Africa[21] – it was only in 1987 that a Namibian police training college was established.[22] To differentiate it from the SAP, new uniforms and rank structures were introduced, but it remained basically an arm of the SAP. The inception of the new force led to a reduction in the number of South African policemen deployed in Namibia, and after 1981 SAP members there (except in counter-insurgency units) were officially on secondment to SWAPOL. In practice, SWAPOL's writ ran only in the south – the war zones, where the homelands of Kaokoland, Ovamboland, Kavango and Caprivi ran up to the Angolan and Zambian borders, were controlled by the SADF and the SAP.

In the Namibian force, many of the SAP's structures were replicated in miniature. SWAPOL remained small – newspaper reports indicated that just before independence it had a strength of only 6,300, of whom nearly half were involved in the front-line counter-insurgency unit Koevoet (this figure presumably excluded special constables).[23] Riot control and the combating of 'urban terrorism' was the responsibility of a Special Task Force, set up in 1977 as a clone of the SAP's unit of the same name. The Special Task Force was responsible for counter-insurgency operations outside the operational areas and if necessary it could draw on other SWAPOL members trained in riot control and formed into a Reaction Force.[24] To an even greater extent than in the SAP, the emphasis on counter-insurgency in SWAPOL left little room for the combating of crime, and gangsterism, murder, rape and other crimes, fuelled by the social dislocation caused by the war, became an endemic problem in Namibia.[25]

The most notorious of Namibia's police units was Koevoet, which was transferred to SWAPOL in 1985, although it effectively remained a combat section of the SAP's Security Branch, which set it up in 1976.[26] Modelled in part on Rhodesia's Selous Scouts, Koevoet was led by about 300 white SAP officers. Its commander, Hans Dreyer, had previously been chief of the Security Branch in Natal and had served with the SAP in Rhodesia. The 3,000 men in Koevoet were mostly recruited in Namibia or Angola, especially from the ranks of the special constables. It also included some 'turned' SWAPO guerillas who played a vital intelligence function, although their numbers were smaller than the SAP liked to claim.[27] Initially, Koevoet's role was restricted mainly to intelligence work, tracking down guerillas and calling in SADF units to eliminate them, but increasingly it took on a combat role. According to South Africa's Minister of Law and Order Louis le Grange :

> the long distances, impassable routes and dense undergrowth made it impossible for the combat units of the security forces to mount their attacks in time, with the result that the terrorists got away. [So] the unit in due course ... began to operate as a combat unit ....[28]

Koevoet was supplied with Casspir armoured vehicles and a variety of weaponry which gave it a formidable advantage of speed and firepower over guerilla groups. From three main bases in northern Namibia, and an array of smaller, often temporary bases, Koevoet units roamed freely through the war zones, tracking guerillas and bursting into homesteads to interrogate the inhabitants. Once contact was made, they laid down a withering stream of machine gun and rifle fire from the relative safety of their Casspirs (although SWAPO fighters scored more than a few hits with Soviet-supplied RPG-7 rockets). Militarily, it was an effective tactic, leading to high body counts and relatively few police deaths, but the reliance on quick information gained through interrogation while in pursuit, and the indiscriminate use of firepower, coupled with a lack of control and supervision over Koevoet, inevitably led to widespread lawlessness. Koevoet took few prisoners and kept no records of its killings (other than a body count) and usually left the bodies of its victims in the bush where they fell – although sometimes they were strapped to the sides of the Casspirs as a warning to local people. 'We are not interested in captures. Killing is the name of the game,' said one Koevoet commander – a policy underlined by the bounties paid to Koevoet members for every body they could claim.[29]

By the time the war ended in Namibia Koevoet had accumulated an appalling record of atrocities, usually involving torture or intimidation. It was Koevoet policy to use 'a measure of violence' in interrogation, said a white Koevoet member in 1986, explaining in court how he had assisted in beating up a suspected guerilla who had died under interrogation and been buried in the bush.[30] Even children were subjected to the Koevoet treatment. In one case brought to court, a 15-year-old boy was found to have been tortured by Koevoet members by having his face held against the hot exhaust of a Casspir – the two policemen responsible were each fined R500.[31]

Koevoet also engaged in pseudo-operations, although not on the scale of the Selous Scouts in Rhodesia. Usually, these were carried out more for vengeance than to obtain information. In one of the worst recorded cases, in March 1982, Koevoet members masquerading as SWAPO combatants rounded up and shot eight people in the village of Oshipanda, near Oshikuku in Ovamboland.

Survivors identified the leader of the gang as a local police commander.[32]

Koevoet's notoriety was well-deserved, but other police and military units also acted in a lawless and intimidatory way. Policing in northern Namibia – and to a lesser extent in other parts of the country – was not so much a matter of maintaining law and order as underpinning a military occupation. The Bar Council of South West Africa, representing all advocates in the territory, once issued a public statement remarking:

> In Namibia, the institutions of the Rule of Law such as the police, the courts, the legal practitioners and the law itself are suspect in the eyes of the overwhelming majority of the people. A large section of the population never had any confidence in the security forces and security laws applicable to this country and probably has less confidence in them today.[33]

The powers given to South African police and soldiers under South African legislation were augmented by martial law proclamations, particularly Proclamation AG9 of 1977, which empowered police and military officers to detain people without trial for renewable 30-day periods. The Terrorism Act, replaced in South Africa in 1982 by the Internal Security Act, remained in force in Namibia.[34] Dusk-to-dawn curfews were imposed on most of the operational areas, and, as one constable put it, 'orders in the war zone [are] to shoot at anything that moves between sundown and sunrise.'[35] A delegation from the Southern African Catholic Bishops' Conference which visited Namibia in 1982 reported:

> The Security Forces stop at nothing to force information out of people. They break into homes, beat up residents, shoot people, steal and kill cattle and often pillage stores and tea rooms.
>
> When the tracks of SWAPO guerillas are discovered by the Security Forces the local people are in danger. Harsh measures are intensified. People are blindfolded, taken from their homes and left beaten up and even dead by the roadside. Women are often raped .... [36]

Detention without trial was one of the mainstays of police and army work in Namibia. The main purpose of detention was interrogation, but many detainees were held long after their interrogation had ended, for punitive reasons. In one notorious case, a group of over 140 Namibian refugees, captured at Kassinga in Angola during a South African raid in 1978 which claimed over 700 lives, were first tortured and then held incommunicado at a secret camp for up to six years.[37] In 1983 the security police revealed that in the previous five years they had detained 2,624 people, 90 per cent of whom had not subsequently been charged: for the same period the army was unable to provide accurate figures, but had records of at least 2,883 detentions, none of which had resulted in court actions.[38] Many detainees were tortured; in many units intimidation and torture were officially condoned as methods of war. For the Security Branch, in particular, there was an assumption that torture led to intelligence and intelligence led to tactical victories.[39]

Many of those detained were never seen again. One who disappeared was Johannes Kakuva, a stock farmer in Kaokoland, who was detained along with seven other men by the Security Branch in 1980. The men were accused of aiding guerillas and held for several months at a police base where they were systematically beaten. The last that was seen of Kakuva was when his body was dumped outside the interrogation building after a session of electric shock treatment and beatings. The case received some international attention, and eventually an official enquiry accepted that the men had been tortured, although a security police captain charged with Kakuva's murder was acquitted when he was finally brought to trial seven years later.[40] There is considerable evidence that police and soldiers summarily executed people after interrogation. The South Africans refused to extend prisoner-of-war status to captured SWAPO combatants, and as early as 1981 a representative of the International Committee of the Red Cross expressed unease at the lack of information about captured guerillas. 'It simply does not happen in any conflict or battle that you have a clash with 200 people and 45 killed and no prisoners or wounded are taken,' he remarked. [41]

Infected by the climate of lawlessness and contemptuous of the local population, police and soldiers were responsible for countless crimes. Rape, sexual assault, robbery, random killings, revenge killings and drunken shooting sprees were everyday events in the war zones. Sometimes the men responsible were prosecuted: often they escaped with lenient prison sentences or small fines.[42] In some cases, Section 103 of the Defence Act, which indemnifies security force members from prosecution, was invoked to stop trials.

Paradoxically, the terror was accompanied by attempts to 'win hearts and minds', although this was more the preserve of the SADF than the SAP, and it was carried out with little enthusiasm in Ovamboland. Nevertheless, many police belonged to 'cultural' organisations like Etango, an Ovamboland-based organisation which held meetings, distributed propaganda and encouraged local people to support the security forces.[43]

As the war dragged on, it increasingly spilled over into Angola, where South African attacks on Namibian refugee camps and SWAPO forward bases escalated into a conventional war. The police played only a minor role in this conflict: even the combat sections such as Koevoet were usually restricted to operating south of the border. But the war in Angola profoundly affected security developments in Namibia: SADF setbacks in Angola proved a turning point, and in December 1988 South Africa agreed to UN-supervised independence elections. Fifty-seven per cent of Namibians voted for SWAPO: support for the movement was most solid in the north, where the security forces had directed most of their efforts.

At independence some sections of Koevoet were stood down, and the rest were withdrawn to South Africa along with most of the remaining seconded SAP members – although some Security Branch members remained behind to serve the new SWAPO government.[44] The new government set about demilitarising the police force and re-establishing it as a community-based service (see Chapter 5).

The SAP and its Namibian offspring, especially Koevoet, played a crucial role in the war for Namibia. The police were responsible for a significant proportion of security force killings (Koevoet alone sometimes claiming up to 80 per cent), which, according to official figures, averaged more than 1,100 a year between 1978 and 1986 (dropping from a high of 2,032 in 1978 to 645 in 1986).[45] Koevoet helped to turn the tide of war against SWAPO, whose operational success, measured in terms of recorded incidents, declined almost every year after 1980.[46] Yet Koevoet and other police units, through their terror, helped to alienate Namibians from the security forces, persuaded young Namibians to leave the country and fight for SWAPO, and contributed to the international pressure on South Africa to leave Namibia. For all their assertions that counter-insurgency war was won or lost in the minds of the population, the South African security forces came more and more to rely on body counts. Operational successes, assessed in terms of kill rates, could not stem political defeat and indeed probably contributed to it.

COUNTER-INSURGENCY WAR IN SOUTH AFRICA

In Namibia, and in Rhodesia, the police were involved in counter-insurgency campaigns fought almost entirely in rural areas. In South Africa the conflict was more intense in the townships than in the bush – the distinctions between counter-insurgency and riot control were blurred. But police continued to patrol border areas until the 1990s when the task was taken over by the army, and in some rural areas, particularly in the bantustans, they were involved together with units of the SADF in clashes with groups of guerillas.

The armed struggle in South Africa was largely the preserve of Umkhonto we Sizwe (MK), launched by Nelson Mandela and other ANC and SACP leaders in 1960. Other armed units, such as the PAC's Azanian People's Liberation Army (APLA) played a very minor role. In the first phase of the conflict, MK concentrated on sabotage, targeting mostly electricity pylons and government buildings and seeking to avoid casualties. The aim was not to seize power but to 'bring the government to its senses', as Nelson Mandela put it, and to demonstrate that a new phase in the struggle had begun. The Security Branch cracked MK's high command through classic police intelligence work, as discussed in Chapter 1, and it was left to the ANC's exiles to begin the slow process of building up a guerilla army and attempting to infiltrate small groups of fighters into the country. Acting on intelligence, and often following the progress of guerillas as they moved through neighbouring states, the police were able to pick them off. The SAP also patrolled the borders and rural areas, and police mobile units, equipped for counter-insurgency as well as riot control, were stationed in various parts of the country.[47]

In 'Strategy and Tactics', a policy document adopted at its crucial 1969 Morogoro conference in Tanzania, the ANC saw eventual victory through the spread of guerilla warfare from the rural areas: 'the main physical environment of such a struggle in the initial period is outside the enemy strongholds in the cities.'[48] In practice, the ANC's military campaign was moribund, and it was not until the Soweto uprisings in 1976, when thousands of new recruits fled South Africa to join MK, that guerilla actions were resumed on a significant scale. Soweto had refocused attention on urban areas: sabotage operations became the stock-in-trade of ANC guerillas. The ANC decided to use its limited resources for 'armed propaganda' which would provide the sparks for more generalised guerilla warfare later. Trained saboteurs and combatants, now operating from bases in Angola, were infiltrated through the 'forward areas' – Botswana, Lesotho, Swaziland and Mozambique.

Police border patrols were stepped up immediately after the Soweto uprising, and they soon came into contact with guerillas moving into the country.[49] In 1977, the Minister of Police announced that a further 10 SAP companies (around 1,400 men) would be equipped for counter-insurgency duties.[50] Permanent police bases were established along the Botswana, Mozambique and Swaziland borders, from where vehicle and foot patrols were carried out. Bases were also established along the Lesotho border – eventually there were 27 of these, usually of platoon size.[51] Police operations in rural areas were closely integrated with those of the army. Under the 'area defence' strategy, it was envisaged that the whole country would be covered with a network of early-warning and first-response units which could call up heavier-armed reaction units after contact with guerillas.[52]

The police relied on patrols and roadblocks to try to halt the influx of guerillas and weapons, and on intelligence and detective work to track down fighters already in the country. Captured guerillas were interrogated and often tortured. Some were dragooned into SAP service as Askaris, and used to track down their comrades. Others were put on trial. A wave of executions of captured combatants followed the hanging of a young MK fighter, Solomon Mahlangu, in 1979 – 28 people were executed for guerilla actions or political resistance between 1979 and 1991.[53] Although the ANC undertook in 1980 to abide by the Geneva Conventions on the conduct of war, which included an undertaking to treat captured enemy soldiers as prisoners-of-war, the South African authorities did not reciprocate. There are strong arguments that it acted in violation of international law by executing MK combatants.[54] The security forces also carried out what can be considered summary executions of alleged guerillas, killing them rather than attempting to arrest them, or executing them after capture. (see 'Hit Squads and Assassinations' later in this chapter).

As well as trying to eliminate guerillas inside the country, the security forces targeted the 'forward areas' and rear bases. Political, military and economic pressures were brought to bear on neighbouring states, until by the mid-1980s none of the countries which share borders with South Africa were prepared to tolerate guerilla activity. MK combatants were forced to operate underground. The SADF and the Security Branch attempted to assassinate or kidnap suspected guerilla commanders in these areas and to destroy alleged transit facilities through airborne attacks or sabotage. Their intelligence was often out of date or inaccurate, their methods less than surgical, and they killed many innocent refugees and foreign nationals as well as MK members.[55]

In the early 1980s MK scored some spectacular sabotage successes in its campaign of 'armed propaganda', notably in its attacks on the Sasol oil-from-coal plants and South Africa's first nuclear power station. All the time the movement was trying to raise the guerilla war to a higher plane. In 1979 guerillas for the first time took the initiative in provoking contact with the security forces, attacking a police station with automatic weapons and grenades; such attacks became a regular feature of the war. Later, MK attempted to set up bases in rural areas in South Africa, in preparation for the next phase of the struggle, 'people's war'. Arms would be cached and combatants entering the country from the 'forward areas' would act as an 'officer corps', training others and thus widening the scope of the war. A few such bases were established – for example, in 1985 the Minister of Law and Order announced that police had arrested 27 guerillas who had been trained at a secret base in northern Natal.[56]

Many MK fighters were caught; the attrition rate was very high. The SAP had good intelligence through the effective infiltration of MK by the Security Branch and the extraction of operational information through the interrogation and torture of captured guerillas. A network of police spies, extending up to senior commander level, was discovered in MK ranks in 1981. The success of the infiltration operations engendered a climate of suspicion, encouraged by the Security Branch through disinformation campaigns, which further weakened MK's operational abilities.[57] (The ANC managed to return the favour, however: in 1986 two black security policemen appeared in court, charged with furthering the aims of the movement, and they were not the only policemen discovered to be secretly working for the ANC or its armed wing.)[58]

The nationwide uprising which began in September 1984 upset all the SAP's calculations. A wave of political violence swept the country. Between September 1984 and July 1986, almost 1,000 businesses, 1,272 schools, 3,902 private homes, 937 police homes and thousands of vehicles were destroyed or

MK actions did not much exceed 300.[60] But it became difficult to separate popular actions from planned MK actions, and the movement encouraged the young militants to stay in South Africa and use whatever means possible to carry out acts of political violence, rather than leave the country for formal military training. In 1985 the ANC declared that 'people's war' was incipient – it aimed to establish mass combat units drawn from popular organisations. It also said that it would no longer seek to avoid loss of life and that all police and soldiers would be targeted for attack.[61] Firearms and grenades were increasingly used by demonstrators in conflicts with police, and many attacks were carried out by largely untrained youths. There were at least 30 shoot-outs with police in 1986, and by 1989 nearly a third of all guerilla actions were directed at the SAP.[62] MK for the first time also turned to landmine warfare in border and other rural areas, with the aim of stretching security force operations and activating rural resistance.[63]

While the police were put under great pressure by the level of mass resistance, and armed actions topped 200 in 1986, they were still relatively successful in hunting down MK operatives inside South Africa. MK's networks remained heavily infiltrated by spies and the police concentrated on destroying the movement's 'machinery' in the forward areas. Operations from Lesotho were all but knocked out by a military coup fomented there by Pretoria in January 1986; and the key Swaziland structures were torn apart by police agents.[64]

Security Branch agents aimed to cause maximum disruption to MK operations, through disinformation campaigns, the sabotage of equipment and the poisoning and assassination of MK's operatives. The options available to them in this covert war were set out frankly in 1977 by Helmoed Romer-Heitman, a South African security expert:

[The security forces] should attempt to infiltrate the insurgency and/or subvert them or its members ... other operations can include the sabotage/doctoring of dis-covered arms or supply caches. The resultant difficulties will sap confidence and morale as well as creating distrust between the insurgency and its suppliers. Such operations should not however be overdone so as to avoid creating suspicion. They could range from doctored foodstuffs ... and tampering with medical supplies to the placement of instant detonation fuses in e.g. every 10th hand-grenade etc. The preference here would be to the affliction of illness or injury, not death, the former having the added advantage of sapping morale and straining logistics. The intelligence services can also create some havoc by the supplying of false information, particularly the type designed to create mistrust. Thus the leader of an insurgency could be made to appear to be a police informer, by for instance paying him more or less secretly, or less subtly by rewarding him publicly ....

Further, some extra operations may prove beneficial in eliminating key members of the insurgency and sowing suspicion. Needless to say such operations would need to be suitably disguised and the necessity for them carefully weighed .... [65]

In the second half of the 1980s in particular, an inordinately large number of guerillas were killed or maimed when grenades and limpet mines exploded in their hands or their weapons failed to work. While some of these incidents no doubt were attributable to inadequate training or inferior equipment, in at least some cases the ANC believed there was SAP involvement. In one well-publicised incident, in May 1985 several student activists who had been given grenades by men they thought were members of MK were killed or maimed when the weapons exploded in their hands. A member of the group said in an affidavit that police who afterwards visited his home had known a code-name he had given only to the 'MK men', and he had also seen the men talking to known policemen.[66]

The police clearly enjoyed some successes in countering the armed struggle and disrupting the functioning of MK, often by extra-legal methods. In 1986 General Coetzee asserted that there were only three unsolved bomb attacks in South Africa and that the police had infiltrated the ANC 'from top to bottom'. But Coetzee went too far in claiming that the SAP's counter-insurgency record was 'the best in the world' – guerilla actions increased virtually every year in the 1980s, eventually reaching the rate of more than one a day.[67]

In the second half of the 1980s, and into the new decade, guerilla struggles merged with mass struggles. This accorded with the ANC's new characterisation of its struggle as:

> a protracted people's war in which partial and general uprisings would play an important role. Led by the ANC underground, mass and armed actions were to dovetail and merge in a process leading to the seizure of power, in which the armed element would occupy a crucial place.[68]

In August 1990, however, the ANC formally suspended its armed struggle in order to seek a negotiated end to apartheid. The SAP's counter-insurgency role theoretically came to an end – although the PAC remained committed to revolutionary violence it had virtually no operational capability. Nevertheless,, as we shall see, the methods of counter-insurgency, particularly the disruptive activities pioneered by the Security Branch, would continue to be used by the SAP.

Troops and Police in the Townships

THE LEGACY OF SOWETO

In the period of partial or complete emergency rule, from July 1985 to June 1990, the police spearheaded security force operations aimed at suppressing popular resistance and restoring state control. In this campaign, several thousand people were killed and tens of thousands detained. Hundreds of political trials resulted from police arrests.

Police operations during the period of emergency rule developed out of their experiences in the Soweto uprising and its aftermath. In the reassessment of operational tactics following the carnage of Soweto, the SAP came to the belated realisation that new equipment and methods of crowd control would have to be adopted. Even the official Cillie commission of inquiry into the uprising, which was widely dismissed as a whitewash, concluded that the police were 'completely unprepared' in terms of 'manpower, equipment and mental attitude'.[69]

There was some resistance to change. Major-General Bert Wandrag, then Deputy Commissioner in charge of riot control, declared as late as 1985 that the lesson of Soweto was that too little force was used. This, he declared, 'has a negative effect in that police members tend to act passively at the outbreak of a riot. This results in the rioters gaining confidence and acting in an increasingly impudent and militant way.'[70] Even the introduction of protective equipment was resisted – visors, shields and helmets not only reduce police casualties but also make the resort to force less necessary. The Minister of Police, Jimmy Kruger, told parliament with his usual tactlessness why in his view the SAP did not want modern equipment:

> To have our police running around like knights of the Middle Ages, heavily armoured with coats-of-mail and visors, and goodness knows what else – policemen in such garb pursuing fleet-footed little Bantu all over the veld – is something I can hardly imagine. Not only would it be ridiculous, it is also completely unnecessary. In any case, a police officer will hardly be able to handle his rifle if he is also wearing a heavy flak jacket and a face guard.[71]

Nevertheless, plastic shields were issued to the police within a couple of months of the onset of the uprisings[72] and more protective equipment and less-lethal weaponry was issued in the following years.

This didn't mean that police were less ready to fall back on shotguns, pistols and rifles, apparently with official approval. In 1980, when South Africa was rocked by a series of industrial strikes and a school students' boycott, the police soon abandoned teargas in favour of firearms, with resultant killings in various parts of the country.[73] At the height of the protests, in June, the police commissioner, General Geldenhuys, issued a statement saying that police would 'shoot to kill' arsonists and rioters. After a public outcry, the phrase was changed to 'shoot with live ammunition people who looted etc', and later entirely withdrawn on the grounds that it was 'an unfortunate choice of words'.[74]

The *Cape Times*, a mainstream white-readership newspaper, asked in an anguished editorial after children had been shot by police in the township of Elsies River:

> it is difficult to understand why the police, in the light of the fiasco of 1976 and

their unpreparedness at that time, have still not learnt how to suppress juvenile stone-throwing without resorting to gunfire ....

It is known that the South African police, in the light of 1976, are now equipped with the appropriate protective equipment. Why, then, was it not used?[75]

Another tactical change since 1976 was the more widespread use of army units in a policing role. It was argued that conflict could best be avoided by a demonstration of overpowering force, and that one reason the police had shot so many people in the 1976–7 uprisings was that they were often outnumbered. The deployment of the army was also a symptom of the rising influence of the SADF.

The use of the army in a pre-emptive show of force was demonstrated in 1981 when police and soldiers carried out what the SAP called 'the biggest security operation ever seen in the country' in the expectation of protests against celebrations to mark the twentieth anniversary of the declaration of the South African republic.[76] Police/army operational collaboration was becoming common by then, although usually the army's role was restricted to sealing off townships while the SAP carried out searches.

Conflict between police and township residents increased during the 1980s. Often clashes arose as a result of popular protest marches and demonstrations, many of a spontaneous nature, in which students, residents and workers vented their grievances. Events of late August and September 1984 proved a watershed, unleashing much more generalised conflict which by early 1985 had spread until it was virtually civil war. Crowds attacked targets they associated with apartheid – the beerhalls, run by local authorities as money-spinners and seen by many as a symbol of oppression or degradation; the homes or businesses of local councillors, the often corrupt front men for 'the system', as the entire structure of administration became known; and the homes of suspected informers or policemen.

In many cases, violence resulted from police action itself. On countless occasions relatively peaceful demonstrations were attacked by police on the grounds that they were illegal (all outdoor demonstrations had been banned since 1976). That police actions have tended to aggravate or provoke unrest rather than dampen it was borne out by a study of 657 incidents involving 'collective action' (demonstrations, attacks by crowds and so on) in the Pretoria–Witwatersrand–Vaal (PWV) area between 1970 and 1984. The study concluded that the mere presence of police at a demonstration or other crowd action increased the subsequent rate of collective action by 68 per cent. And when police opened fire on protesters, the incidence of subsequent mass action more than doubled.[77]

CROWD CONTROL

Controlling large, militant crowds is any police officer's nightmare, and the potential for violence is always close to the surface. Careful forward planning, in which action is coordinated and there is a gradual but discernible escalation of force or threat of force, with clear stages, is essential to the relatively peaceful dispersal of crowds. This is recognised in Section 48 of the Internal Security Act of 1982, which details police powers in the dispersal of crowds. The Act authorises an officer of the rank of warrant-officer or above to order a gathering to disperse, and to use force if the crowd does not obey. However, the force used 'shall not be greater than is necessary'. Firearms should only be used if other means have proved ineffective or there is actual or imminent violence, and they should be used 'with all reasonable caution'.[78]

The phased use of force is also endorsed in SAP operational instructions and standing orders. In September 1984, just before the outbreak of township protests, Major-General Wandrag sent a telex to his divisional commissioners setting out procedures for the dispersal of crowds. Teargas should be used first if a crowd failed to disperse, he said, followed by sjamboks and rubber bullets. The next stage was the use of shotguns – bird-shot and then buck-shot. Only as a last resort, and if police were trapped, should they resort to their rifles.[79]

By international norms, the SAP's approach as outlined by Major-General Wandrag was tough, and it paid little attention to the prospects for negotiating an end to the confrontation or using a show of superior force to persuade a crowd of the hopelessness of their position. Explaining his instruction, Wandrag also later argued that he did not approve of warning shots before opening fire. The bullet used in the warning shot could injure someone some distance away when it came down to earth, he argued, and could also incite rather than deter a crowd.[80] Furthermore, he later qualified his approach to the phased use of force by arguing that 'European' models of crowd control were not suitable for South Africa. In the first place, the police were usually outnumbered. Secondly, climatic and geographic factors intervened. The design of townships, with their large open spaces, gave rioters more room to manoeuvre in and police could easily be surrounded. South Africa's warm, often windy weather made teargas and water-cannon less effective, and full protective gear uncomfortable.[81] Similar conclusions were reached in a 1985 article in the official SAP journal *Servamus*, which concluded:

> In present circumstances there are probably only two ways in which the number of fatal casualties can be reduced: either the rioters must exercise firmer control over their own activities … or the police will have to act far more strongly earlier in the proceedings ….[82]

While General Wandrag and other police commanders only half-heartedly endorsed the concept of minimum and phased force in crowd control, police on the ground adopted even more aggressive tactics during the emergency years, with profoundly destabilising effects on communities.

FROM THE VAAL TRIANGLE TO LANGA

The SAP's reluctance to use minimum force was demonstrated repeatedly in the first months of the 1984–6 uprising. The immediate causes of the uprising were: residents' resistance to the imposition of local authorities, which were supposed to extract all the money needed to administer the townships from residents themselves; the continuing grievances over education (nearly a quarter of a million children were boycotting classes by the end of 1984); and, to a lesser extent, the exclusion of Africans from the new tricameral parliamentary system. The uprising was sparked in the townships of Sharpeville and Sebokeng in the Vaal Triangle, near the industrial cities of Vereeniging and Vanderbijlpark, when rents were increased.[83] On 3 September residents stayed away from work and held protest marches which the SAP tried to prevent through a show of force. Residents reported that police opened fire without provocation, not only on crowds but also on individuals in the streets. They also accused them of looting shops and damaging property.[84] The shootings led to funerals, which inevitably became the focus for further political protests – the police regarded these as illegal gatherings and attacked mourners.

The violence rapidly spread to other townships in the PWV area. Much of the police action resembled unjustified provocation or revenge rather than crowd control; it was punitive rather than preventive. Their aim appeared to be to humiliate and strike fear into residents: this they may have succeeded in doing, but their actions also led to popular outrage which manifested itself in further protests and an increasing number of attacks on policemen and officials.[85]

Daily police patrols and swoops on gatherings were supplemented by occasional shows of force – selected townships, or sections of them, were sealed off by the army while police carried out house-to-house searches. One of the largest operations, which set the pattern for future tactics, was Operation Palmiet, when 7,000 police and soldiers besieged Sebokeng and other townships in the Vaal Triangle (see Chapter 1).[86]

Conflict continued in the PWV into 1985, and there were sporadic clashes in other parts of the country as the political temperature rose. In the highly politicised townships of the Eastern Cape, a stonghold of the ANC, over 70 people were killed during a stay-away organised over the weekend of 16–18 March.[87] Then on 21 March – 25 years to the day after the Sharpeville massacre – police opened fire on a crowd making its way to a funeral just outside the Eastern Cape township of Langa, near Uitenhage, killing more than 20. The massacre provided the spark that set the Eastern Cape alight and the next weekend the homes of 17 local policemen were firebombed.[88] Like Sharpeville before it, Langa did not have merely local effects: violence exploded across the country, and internationally a battery of criticism was levelled at the

SAP. The government was obliged to appoint an inquiry into the Langa incident, headed by Justice Kannemeyer.

The evidence put before Kannemeyer showed that in the days leading up to the Langa massacre, clashes between police and residents in the Eastern Cape had been intensifying. In February 1985 police headquarters in Pretoria wired all units authorising them to use buckshot, instead of lighter birdshot, in shotguns. On 15 March the local police stopped using birdshot, teargas and rubber bullets. They went on patrol equipped only with shotguns loaded with buckshot and R1 rifles with live ammunition. On 19 March Deputy Commissioner General De Witt sent out an instruction to all divisions, stating: 'When acid or petrol bombs are thrown at police or private vehicles and/or buildings an attempt must be made under all circumstances to eliminate the suspects.'[89]

As a result of the progressive escalation of lethal force by police in the Eastern Cape, several residents of Uitenhage townships were killed. A funeral for six of the dead was planned for 17 March, a Sunday, but after submissions by a Security Branch officer, Captain André Goosen, weekend funerals were banned by the local magistrate. The burial was rearranged for Thursday 21 March, but Captain Goosen then persuaded the magistrate to reverse his original order, and require that funerals could be held only on a Sunday. On the evening of 20 March police vehicles equipped with loudspeakers drove around Langa informing residents that the funeral had been banned. Not surprisingly, the residents went ahead the next day and the scene was set for the confrontation.[90]

The police were evidently itching for a showdown. Shortly before the massacre, officers in Casspirs taunted the crowd, urging them to attack. 'Where are the stones? Throw them, throw, throw!' one white policeman was reported as shouting, but the crowd maintained its discipline.[91] The route the crowd followed took it through white Uitenhage, and the police were determined to stop it. But they were grossly unprepared – a mere 15 policemen in two Casspirs against a crowd variously estimated at between 500 (according to some residents) and 4,000 (the police figure). The police concerned were equipped only with rifles and shotguns loaded with SSG, a form of buckshot. After one warning shot, they opened fire. Of the 20 killed, 17 were shot in the back.[92]

THE PARTIAL STATE OF EMERGENCY 1985

The Langa massacre was the most notorious incident of the 1984–6 uprising, exemplifying the worst aspects of the SAP's attitude to crowd control. After Langa, rioting and protests spread throughout South Africa with a new intensity. On 20 July 1985, a State of Emergency was imposed in 36 magisterial districts, mostly in the Eastern Cape and PWV. Troops and police poured into the townships. Temporary joint bases were set up in football stadiums or at the entrances to townships and joint forces of policemen and troops patrolled the township, usually in Casspirs. Information on their activities was restricted by the emergency regulations: the main source of information came from the daily 'unrest reports' issued by the SAP, which lacked detail and reflected the SAP's interpretation of events.

The severity of the uprising, particularly in the Eastern Cape, took the police by surprise and it is clear that the security forces lacked an overall plan of action, at least in the initial stages of the uprising. Often they would simply drive around in the Casspirs looking for trouble. There was an atmosphere of war; little control was exercised over police patrols and their actions rapidly degenerated into indiscriminate violence. A policeman who resigned from the force in 1990 recounted his experiences in 1985:

[We] were driven to Uitenhage sports stadium. On our arrival it was dark already. A temporary camp had been erected in the parking area. It consisted of a couple of caravans, army tents, a police vehicle parking space, an army field hospital, armoury tent, a helicopter pad, a mess and an officers' briefing tent. It was really unorganised....

About 4am the following morning we were woken up and ordered to fall in to the parade ground area. All the drivers, me included, were told to choose a vehicle. Two other members of the platoon were to go to the armoury and collect ammunition, R1s and 37mm rubber bullet/combination tearsmoke stop guns, as much as we wanted. We had about 50 rounds each of shotgun, 200 rounds for R1s, sufficient tearsmoke and rubber bullets to start a small war....

Our first patrol was into the township of KwaNobuhle. It was bad. There were road barricades burning, houses burning, large crowds of people, male and female and kids included, throwing stones at police vehicles. There was a lot of gunshots. It sounded as if a small war going on. For 18 hours a day, every day, we patrolled through this war. Sometimes we worked five days a week, sometimes we worked six days a week, sometimes we worked seven days a week ....

The persons in my Casspir retaliated with shotgun fire, teargas grenades and rubber bullets.... We had no particular instructions so it was really chaotic. If there was a fire we would go to it to see what was going on otherwise we would travel in a convoy of four Casspirs up one street, turn, go down the next.[93]

The overwhelming impression of police operations in the first months of the emergency is that many police relished the atmosphere of war and welcomed the opportunity to 'teach the blacks a lesson'. A young soldier deployed with police wrote:

We come across a *bakkie* [pick-up] loaded with children and youths who show us the clenched fist salute. The cops go into action: the bakkie is overtaken and forced to stop, the pile of black bodies spill off in all directions as the cops tumble out of the back the Casspir in pursuit. Shortly they return in triumph with their catch: a boy of about ten who they are hitting and slapping as they drag him into the vehicle where they continue to slap and punch him ....

The funeral is over. We head towards the returning crowd which seems to be starting to break up. Knots of people form on street corners singing and shouting their defiance ... A sudden hail of stones is just what they've been waiting for. 'Yahoo, let's go!' and we launch into a hurtling, lurching circuit, past streams of panicking, running people, pumping gas and rubber bullets. It's over in a couple of minutes: the cops have reached for their shotguns for the second round but the crowd has dispersed. The whole thing had the atmosphere of sport: kaffir baiting, beating and hunting.[94]

Many cases were recorded where police deliberately encouraged youths to attack them so they could retaliate, or laid ambushes. In these incidents, the aim, as in war, was to kill and injure the enemy by whatever means available, rather than to contain violence and restore law and order. In Bongweni township, near Colesburg, for example, police laid an ambush for militant youths by hiding in a house and opening fire when they rushed past, killing four of them. In another incident in the same township, they detained a youth and then assaulted him on top of an armoured vehicle, provoking onlookers to throw stones at them – they then opened fire on the gathering crowd.[95]

In October emergency rule was extended to eight districts in the Western Cape, after two months of protests and a school boycott.[96] In the Cape Town suburb of Athlone, police staged one of their most notorious provocations – the so-called 'Trojan Horse' incident, which was captured by an American camera crew and seen by millions around the world on TV. The operation, which was planned by the Special Task Force of the railways police, involved police armed with shotguns hiding in crates on the back of a railways truck. As a government vehicle, the truck was thought to be a likely target of attack. When youths threw stones at it, the police jumped out of the crates and fired 39 rounds from pump-action shotguns, killing three of the youths – the youngest only 11. The parents of two of the dead brought a private prosecution against the 12 policemen and one army officer involved, but all were acquitted.[97]

The Trojan Horse incident gained notoriety, but it was not the first incident of its kind, nor the last. The tactic was pioneered in 1976 in Soweto, when police hiding on the floor of unmarked civilian vehicles would cruise the township, opening fire when stones were thrown.[98] In November 1986 a similar event occurred in Soweto when armed men, who eyewitnesses said wore police uniforms, commandeered a bus and careered around shooting at people.[99]

Another incident in a Cape Town suburb in 1985, which resulted in the prosecution of two policemen for murder and attempted murder, shed some light on the SAP's policy of deliberately killing people suspected of coordinating resistance. Armed with shotguns, Constable Ernest Villet and Warrant-Officer Paulus Kruger hid behind a fence near a road junction where barricades had been erected earlier in the day. According to Kruger, they had been instructed by the head of the Bellville riot unit, Captain Ockert van Schalwyk, to form 'a surprise party' and to 'shoot at ringleaders'. They had also received orders from the Bellville district commandant, Brigadier Martinus Mans, to 'eliminate' rioters. That evening a group of residents gathered at the junction, apparently out of curiosity. Another policeman fired teargas at them and, as they ran, Kruger and Villet jumped out and opened fire, killing schoolgirl Sarah van Wyk and injuring a 15-year-old girl and two young women. As one of the women lay moaning on the ground, Kruger threatened her: 'Lie still or I'll shoot you dead!' Captain van Schalwyk arrived in a Casspir and congratulated the men on their 'good work'. They filled in a false report on the incident, saying they had been attacked by a stone-throwing crowd who had tried to erect burning barricades – the report was signed by Brigadier Mans, although he admitted in court he knew it was false. Kruger and Villet were eventually acquitted of the charges against them on the grounds that they had carried out lawful orders.[100]

This was just one incident amongst many. Between September 1984 and the end of 1985, over 1,000 people were killed in political conflict, at least half of them by the SAP.[101] Police themselves increasingly became targets as residents retaliated. In 1984, no politically motivated attacks on police homes and installations were recorded, other than by MK guerillas. By August 1985, seven police had been killed, 270 injured and 300 made homeless.[102] Nearly a thousand police homes – virtually all of them the houses of black police in townships – had been destroyed by June 1986.[103] Black police and their families were forced to leave many townships and were housed in tented camps or in other temporary accommodation. Later, more permanent camps were set up.[104]

In Alexandra, one of Johannesburg's oldest townships, the homes of black police were attacked in February 1986 and about 100 police families were forced to leave. The attacks happened during the so-called 'six-day war' which followed a police assault on the funeral of a youth activist killed by a private security guard. This was a period of violent confrontations, mass funerals (one was attended by 70,000 people), stay-aways, meetings and marches to demand better housing, the resignation of town councillors and the withdrawal of troops and police.[105] The police abandoned normal patrolling, saying it was impossible because people hated them and attacked them, and comrades – activists from the mass organisations – took over, running 'people's courts' and carrying out their own policing. The comrades were apparently more successful than the SAP had ever been in combating crime, and some residents reported that they felt safe for the first time.[106] However, on the night of 22

April, a group of vigilantes – at one stage 200 strong – roamed the streets of Alexandra, attacking the homes of comrades and shooting residents at random. They were almost certainly the exiled black policemen – many residents reported that they wore police clothes, and the SAP incident book on the night reported that black police were preparing to march into the township. Police armoured vehicles in the vicinity of the attacks did not intervene (and some residents reported that they had actively assisted in the attacks) and no culprits were ever identified.[107] Residents fought back, however – a mass meeting agreed to establish self-defence units, and gunmen with AK47s opened fire on police when they confronted a crowd shortly after the night of terror.[108]

Similar events took place in Kagiso, a township near Krugersdorp. Residents were subjected to night-time raids during March by balaclava-wearing men who shot, teargassed and assaulted people indiscriminately. The raids started after two white policemen had been killed in the township, and eyewitnesses said the attackers were mostly white and wore police uniforms.[109]

In March 1986 the emergency was lifted (see Chapter 1), but police operations against popular protests continued. In April, for instance, the township of Lamontville outside Durban was subjected to a four-day 'swamping' operation by 700 police and soldiers, who drove around in armoured vehicles while a light aircraft circulated overhead broadcasting propaganda messages through loudspeakers.[110]

THE NATIONAL STATE OF EMERGENCY 1986-90

The State of Emergency was reimposed over the whole country (except the TBVC states) four days before mass protests scheduled for the commemoration of the Soweto uprisings on 16 June.

Police and army operations during the national State of Emergency, which lasted until 1990, took place under a veil of secrecy which was only occasionally lifted. Reporting on any security force operations was banned and amongst the extensive powers the Commissioner of Police and his regional subordinates were given was the ability to ban or restrict newspapers and other publications.[111] The pattern of the earlier emergency was maintained, with mass detentions, occasional cordon-and-search operations and daily patrols which often resulted in clashes. But the repression was much more severe: the aim was to destroy the popular and democratic organisations which had emerged since the late 1970s and taken control of many townships.

As the crisis deepened, the mass movements adopted new and more militant tactics. Barricades were thrown up in townships and ditches dug across streets to stop armoured vehicles entering; warning systems involving lookouts at street corners were set up; youths armed with petrol bombs, stones and whatever weapons they could lay their hands on drew police and army patrols into ambushes; strikes, boycotts and other forms of mass protest became the order of the day. The police, if anything, appeared to be even less disciplined and more violent than before, especially in the first few months of the State of Emergency. Some townships were subjected to security operations comparable to an occupation or a seige. At Zweletemba, near Worcester in the Western Cape, for example, an army camp was set up at the township's entrance, roadblocks were established, parts of the township were sealed off with razor wire, and towers were erected from which searchlights were played across the houses at night to ensure no one was breaking the dusk-to-dawn curfew.[112]

The police spent much of their time detaining people. In August the government released a list of 9,000 people who had been held in detention for more than 30 days (they did not release details for people detained for shorter periods).[113] The 9,000 long-term detainees were mostly activists and officials from the popular organisations the government was determined to destroy – police raided offices and scoured townships for 'leaders' and 'agitators', acting on Security Branch records or information extracted from the summary interrogation of people picked up in the streets. Those detained for shorter periods were usually suspected of involvement in protests or of having useful information, or were held simply to intimidate them and their colleagues. To prevent the mass organisations holding meetings police occupied halls and churches and even sealed off areas where funerals were due to be held.[114]

Cordon-and-search operations, following the pattern set by Operation Palmiet, were carried out in many townships. Police and soldiers also besieged schools: after two years or more of stop-start boycotts, the student movement committed itself to a return to classes with the hopelessly optimistic notion of implementing an alternative 'people's education'. When pupils returned from their holidays in July 1986, they found that many schools had been sealed off by police and army units. The security forces tried to issue identity cards to students, and in some schools even stationed themselves in or outside classrooms to monitor lessons and administer corporal punishment, using sjamboks on 'unruly' students. At other schools pupils were prevented from leaving schools during lunchbreaks by police.[115]

Demonstrations and marches were broken up ruthlessly. Sometimes the police were vastly outnumbered and appeared to panic; on other occasions the shootings seemed to be calculated. In one incident, at Kabokweni near White River in the Eastern Transvaal, a 15-year-old boy was killed and 80 children injured when police opened fire on a crowd of 3,000 schoolchildren outside a magistrate's court. A majority of the victims – 50 – were shot in the back.[116] The children had come to support eight classmates on trial for public violence and were in a militant mood. A lawyer representing the eight accused tried to negotiate with them, and at the request of the captain in charge of a small contingent of police guarding the courtroom he asked for leaders to be selected from the crowd. Six leaders joined the lawyer at the front of the crowd, but the police opened fire before discussions could take place. In a statement released to the press, the lawyer, Laurence Tonkin, said:

I feel it my duty to make the following observations:
- The crowd was not uncontrollable.
- I heard no order to disperse whatever.
- I neither saw nor experienced any teargas being fired.
- I saw nothing to justify the view that the shooting was the last resort available to the police.

It is true that the crowd was very angry. I was frightened and the police also looked frightened to me. There was, however, no apparent justification for the shooting.[117]

In another incident, in Mamelodi near Pretoria, police opened fire on a crowd protesting at high rents and the activities of the police and troops occupying the township. At least 12 people, including old age pensioners, were killed and many were injured. Police admitted at the inquest into the killing that the crowd was unarmed and had not thrown stones or attacked them. However, they had refused to disperse when ordered to, which one police officer described as an 'essential sign of aggression'.[118]

In some townships, especially in the Eastern Cape, violent conflict was endemic for much of 1986 and into 1987. Police became progressively more brutalised and lawless as they spent months in constant clashes with residents, with little control exercised over their operations. This was nowhere clearer than in the operations of a police unit in Cradock on 25 and 26 July 1986, which resulted in the trial on charges of murder and assault of two members of the Port Elizabeth reaction unit, Warrant-Officer Leon de Villiers and Constable David Goosen. While it is to the SAP's credit that the men were brought to book, the trial provided a horrifying insight into the attitudes of some policemen and the way in which they were allowed relatively free rein to carry out gratuitously violent attacks on township residents.

The unit of 10 men, commanded by De Villiers, was dispatched in a Casspir to the small town of Cradock on 25 July, with instructions to monitor a funeral to be held the next day. The men drank heavily that night, and in the early hours of the morning, hearing a radio report of stonings in the township, they decided to leave the police camp and go on an unofficial patrol. They took an oath of 'blood brotherhood' by cutting their wrists and mixing the blood, and then, armed with a knife, a shovel, an axe and a shotgun they entered the township in their Casspir. They grabbed the first man they saw, and Constable Goosen killed him with the knife. They attempted various other assaults and the foray ended with another constable firing a shotgun at an 'unknown target'.[119]

After a few hours sleep, the men drove off to monitor the funeral. Other police units in the townships were involved in clashes with residents, and De

Villiers' unit detained several township residents whom they assaulted in the Casspir by holding plastic bags over their heads, beating them and half-strangling them with a fanbelt.[120] The ostensible aim of the torture was to extract information, but in cross-examination in court it became clear that there was little chance of the police obtaining anything useful. One of the victims, who was given the plastic bag and fanbelt treatment, said that he had not even been asked any questions. The following exchange took place between the court assessor and Constable Neveling:

What did you hope to achieve by [the detentions]?

You never know until you try. It's pure luck if you get anything.

And if the person does not want to talk?

You make them talk.

How?

As we did, assaults, plastic bags and so on.

But how did you expect to [obtain any information] when you did not even have anyone who could speak Xhosa?

If you take them far enough, they talk Afrikaans.[121]

After being 'panelbeaten' as the policemen called it, those detained were released. But one, Wheanut Stuurman, who was detained for wearing a Cradock Youth Association T-shirt, was judged to be too badly beaten to be freed. De Villiers ordered that he should be 'taken out', and they drove to the bank of a local river where Goosen shot him through the back of the head with a pistol. They threw his body onto a sandbank and drove off again on patrol, firing their shotguns and rifles at youths.[122] Goosen and De Villiers were tried with murder and sentenced to death. But the sentences were commuted to life imprisonment and in July 1991 the two were released under an amnesty for political prisoners.[123]

Many other events of a similar nature – although perhaps not quite as pathological – came to light in other court cases arising from police actions during the State of Emergency. The introduction of municipal police and special constables or *kitskonstabels* (see Chapter 2) led to a rash of beatings, shootings, acts of intimidation and sexual assaults. The special constables ravaged the communities they were supposedly protecting, drawing complaints and protests from residents wherever they were deployed. In 1987, 569 complaints were laid by the public against the municipal police and 349 against the special constables, ranging from theft to murder.[124] The Minister of Law and Order admitted at the end of 1987 that special constables had carried out 95 crimes involving the use of firearms.[125] An account of their behaviour in one township, Eluxolweni, near Hofmeyr in the Eastern Cape, was given in an affidavit by one resident:

> In April [1987], the special constables were introduced to our township. They just seemed to appear from nowhere – no one ever told or called us together to tell us who they were, what they were supposed to do....
>
> They are always aggressive, abusive, provocative and intimidating towards many of the residents. They are literally always looking for confrontation, loitering in the streets or walking around in bands of four or five, sometimes even more. Whether on or off duty, they are more often than not drunk, whether in or out of uniforms. They walk around looking for something to do....
>
> When they are drunk, it seems to be their first instinct to use their guns to point, to threaten, as a club, to shoot....[126]

Given that they had only six weeks training before deployment, and many had only a vague idea of what policing entailed, the Special Constables could only have functioned effectively with close supervision from regular police. But they were usually left to their own devices, while the regular force patrolled in armoured vehicles and devoted their attentions to combating unrest. Far from acting as 'bobbies on the beat' – as the Deputy Minister of Law and Order described them – the special constables struck fear into the hearts of residents. A survey in the township of Bhongolethu (Oudtshoorn) by the Institute of Criminology at the University of Cape Town found that 80 per cent of those interviewed had a negative view of the special constables, and only 2 per cent a positive view. Nearly two-thirds had personally witnessed special constables beating people.[127]

Police repression was most intense in 1986 and the first half of 1987. By 1988 the security forces had gained a firmer grip on the townships, and, although the mass movements were still functioning in a semi-underground way, the alternative structures of 'people's power' which flowered briefly had been all but eradicated. The number of detentions and shootings by the security forces fell off, and police opted for more pro-active methods: banning and restricting meetings and sealing off the venues rather than trying to break them up while they were in progress; restricting individuals and banning organisations. They continued to maintain a high profile in the townships, however, with day-to-day patrols in armoured vehicles and sporadic cordon-and-search 'crime sweeps'.[128]

Conflict spread to the bantustans. In Venda popular protests against the local administration in 1988–9 were met by bantustan police wielding sjamboks and firing teargas.[129] Extra-legal operations became common – in many bombing and arson attacks on offices, and assassinations of officials, there were strong indications of police involvement. One monitoring group counted 165 incendiary attacks and 15 bombings on offices of anti-apartheid organisations between 1985 and 1989.[130] In 1987 the headquarters and some of the Congress of South African Trade Unions were bombed; in the following year the headquarters of the South African Council of Churches in Johannesburg was blown up by a massive bomb and the offices of the Southern African Catholic Bishops' Conference were destroyed in an arson attack.[131]

By 1989, troops and police were maintaining their firm presence in the townships, but were less active than before. By April only 150 people remained in detention under the emergency regulations, although the police had imposed restriction orders on many of those released from detention, obliging them to report to police stations or to remain in certain areas.[132] The anti-apartheid movement initiated a campaign to defy the emergency regulations, holding massive protest marches in the major cities. Initially the police responded to these in their traditional manner, wading in with shotguns and sjamboks and arresting 2,000 people (although most were released shortly afterwards).[133]

Police violence intensified in September, when there were countrywide protests against parliamentary elections – they reportedly killed up to 30 protesters and wounded 200 in several incidents, mostly in Cape Town suburbs. Eyewitnesses said police fired randomly with shotguns at people standing near barricades, which had been put up in some coloured suburbs.[134] Many of those injured were children – doctors at Cape Town hospital reported that they had treated at least ten children, including a three-year-old, and the children had been shot 'everywhere ... heads, limbs, trunks'. But police backed down from confrontation when the mayor of Cape Town and other prominent figures undertook to lead another protest demonstration, and mass demonstrations were afterwards authorised in South Africa's other cities.[135] This opened a new phase in crowd control, which is examined in the next chapter.

Detention and Interrogation

Over the years, the SAP has been responsible for detaining or arresting tens of thousands of people for political reasons and interrogating many of them. The laws empowering the police to detain people were progressively strengthened over 30 years until 1990 when the De Klerk reforms for the first time reduced their powers (see Chapter 4). The Human Rights Commission estimated that 75,000 people had been detained without trial by 1989, 52,000 of them in the previous five years.[136] The State of Emergency provided the basis for mass detentions on an unprecedented scale: although the army was responsible for some detentions during the emergency, the vast majority were carried out by the police.[137]

Interrogation does not necessarily follow detention. Many of those held under the emergency regulations were subjected to only cursory interrogation, or none at all. The police used their powers of detention to remove people from society – perhaps also the sheer numbers in detention made systematic interrogation prohibitively time-consuming. Police interrogators have had three main aims, apart from sheer intimidation. When detainees have been suspected of involvement with guerilla or underground organisations, the police have sought to extract operational information, allowing them to crack down on organisations and detain other members. Secondly, interrogation has been used to generate confessions and other information for use in possible prosecutions in the thousands of political trials for which the police have been required to provide evidence. The final aim has been to add to the vast bank of background information (some of it computerised) held by the Security Branch.[138]

Interrogation and torture have become virtually synonymous in South Africa. Many of those detained in the 1960s reported being tortured, and in 1963 Solwandle 'Looksmart' Ngudle became the first person to die in detention under the new laws. The death of Steve Biko in police custody in 1977 resulted in an international outcry. Regarded as the founder of the black consciousness movement, Biko died of brain damage after being kept for more than 20 days in police cells, manacled and naked, and being interrogated at the headquarters of the Port Elizabeth security police.[139] While there is some evidence that the publicity following the Biko case led to a slight let-up in torture, by the early 1980s its use was again widespread. In 1982 a detainees' support group submitted to the Minister of Law and Order more than 70 statements from people who said they had been tortured in police custody.[140] The declaration of the State of Emergency in 1985 led to wide-scale torture. Dr Wendy Orr, a district surgeon inspecting detainees, made an urgent appeal to the courts, backed by affidavits, to stop the police torturing detainees.[141]

A detailed study of the treatment of detainees was carried out in 1985 by researchers at the University of Cape Town, who arranged for 176 ex-detainees in various parts of the country to be interviewed. Eighty-three per cent of them said they had been tortured physically and all reported psychological coercion. Nearly a fifth had been subjected to interrogation sessions lasting more than eight hours, and 60 per cent had faced six or more sessions of intensive interrogation. Africans were much more likely to be physically tortured than whites. The study also found strong regional variations – torture was most common in the Eastern Cape.[142]

It has been argued that the conditions of detention – incommunicado solitary confinement – can themselves amount to torture: many detainees have reported the symptoms of sensory deprivation after long spells alone in cells.[143] This apart, the police have over the years devised an assortment of torture methods ranging from simple beating to sophisticated psychological pressure, and some security policemen have evidently made careers out of their ability to extract information from detainees. In more important cases, torture has often been employed for long periods by alternating teams of interrogators.[144]

Methods of torture reported over the years are a testimony both to the inventiveness and the moral degradation of the SAP's interrogation squads. They include beating and assaults with fists, sticks, whips, hosepipes and various implements; being forced to squat or stand for hours; electric shocks to various parts of the body (usually administered from an adapted crank-operated telephone or generator); sleep deprivation and prolonged interrogation; being kept naked or denied food or toilet facilities; choking and strangulation; hooding and suffocation; immersion of the head in a bucket of water; crushing of toes or fingers; burning; being forced to drink petrol; attacks on genitals; being threatened with execution; threats to family members; suspension from walls or in mid-air; use of animals (dogs, spiders, snakes); and the administration of drugs. A variety of psychological methods have also been used, some of which the police have readily admitted to. These have included the alternation of 'good guy' and 'bad guy' interrogators, a practice the SAP disarmingly refers to as 'Mutt and Jeff'; the presentation of misleading information (usually of the we-know-everything or a colleague is dead/has confessed variety); and the threat of prolonged or indefinite detention.[145]

Torture is not restricted to political cases. Systematic abuse appears to be institutionalised at certain police stations. For every case of torture of political detainees, there is a similar story for criminal offenders, although most are unreported. In one case which reached the courts, three young policemen were found guilty in November 1990 of killing George Ndaba, who had died while they assaulted and interrogated him. They had thrown his body onto a busy highway to give the impression that he had been the victim of a hit-and-run accident.[146] At the trial of five policemen from a police station at Port Shepstone on Natal's south coast, who were accused of murdering a criminal suspect by suffocation, a police captain told the court that it was an 'everyday occurrence' to place a bag over a suspect's head during interrogation (he claimed it was to protect the identity of the police).[147] The most dramatic indication of routine torture by police came in June 1992, when the country's leading pathologist said he had evidence of police killing nearly 200 people in custody (see the next chapter).

Police chiefs and government spokesmen have dismissed virtually all reports of torture as fabrication by revolutionary elements intent on undermining the reputation of the force. Little has been done to bring torturers to book or to implement procedures which would make it more difficult for police interrogators to use violence. Very few police have been charged or convicted for abuse of detainees – the more than 70 deaths in detention have resulted in only one conviction of a police officer, Sergeant Harms van As, who served six years in jail after shooting Paris Malatji through the head during interrogation.[148] The official response to the deaths of detainees has usually been along the lines that communists are trained to commit suicide if captured,[149] while Jimmy Kruger, Minister of Law and Order at the time, explained Steve Biko's death by declaring sarcastically that it was the 'democratic right' of detainees to starve themselves to death.[150] Nevertheless, the government responded to international pressure in 1978 by appointing two inspectors of detainees, and the Internal Security Act of 1982 stipulated that a magistrate and a district surgeon should visit detainees every two weeks. A 'code of conduct' governing detentions was introduced in 1983, but, as subsequent events showed, these measures had little effect and if anything police inquisitors increased their rule of terror over detainees.[151] Torture continues to be associated with detention and arrest today.[152]

Vigilante Violence

'Indirect' policing through the use of vigilante groups, a long-standing strategy of the SAP, took a more bloody turn during the State of Emergency. As the SAP moved away from 'formal' repression through crowd control and detentions and towards 'informal' methods of containment after 1987, it came to rely more and more on these vigilante groups. By October 1988, the police were responsible for less than 10 per cent of unrest-related deaths – the bulk could be ascribed to vigilante and counter-vigilante actions.[153]

Vigilante actions flared in many areas after the emergency was imposed. In Thabong, near Welkom in the Orange Free State, a group of migrant labourers patrolled the streets, rounding on militant youths. Their intervention was not spontaneous: it had been organised by the town councillors, with the apparent approval of the local police. Some youths reported being abducted and taken to the headquarters of the local town council; there, in a room dubbed Room 29 after section 29 of the Internal Security Act, they were stripped naked and flogged. Others were beaten and killed.[154] In the tiny homeland of Kwandebele, local officials and businessmen organised vigilante groups known as Mbokodo to wage war against residents of the Moutse area, who were refusing to recognise the bantustan authorities. Youths reported being forced by threats of beatings to join the vigilantes.[155] In the Mapetla and Phiri areas of Soweto, and in Tembisa on the East Rand, vigilante groups attacked residents at the end of 1986.[156] In Leandra, also on the Rand, where the Leandra Action Committee had mobilised residents against the town council, vigilantes hacked the leader of the committee to death and harassed its members, forcing it to disband.[157]

KwaNobuhle, a township near Uitenhage, was subjected to a 12-hour vigilante attack on 4 January 1987, when a mob led by leaders of the Ama-Afrika movement destroyed the homes of anti-apartheid activists while police stood by and watched.[158] Ama-Afrika attacks continued later in 1987. The leader of the organisation, a self-styled reverend, Mzandile Maqina, espoused 'Africanist' ideas associated with the PAC or the black consciousness movement – at the time the clashes were put down to divisions between ANC supporters and Africanists. In fact, Maqina sat on a committee of the Joint Management Committee, part of the state's National Security Management System, and was funded and supported by the Security Branch.[159]

One of the ugliest vigilante operations was the destruction of the homes of 70,000 people living in squatter camps outside Cape Town in May 1986.[160] For ten years the squatters, who had defied the pass laws and moved to Cape Town to seek work, resisted government efforts to move them. As their tin, cardboard and plastic homes were demolished, they rebuilt them, their dogged resistance gaining international recognition. But the squatter leader in the Old Crossroads settlement, Johnson Nxgobongwana, turned his back on the UDF and other militant anti-apartheid organisations. His followers became known as *witdoeke* for the white headbands they wore. Other settlements became progressively more militant and the police alleged that residents there allowed the ANC to cache arms and carry out attacks on them.

Between 17 and 23 May, in a series of operations, *witdoeke* armed with axes, knives and other weapons attacked and destroyed the settlements known as Nyanga Bush, Nyanga Extension and Portland Cement. According to eyewitnesses, police in armoured vehicles escorted the *witdoeke* and assisted the attacks by firing teargas and shotguns at residents resisting them or trying to save their possessions. The *witdoeke* also threatened to attack residents of another settlement, KTC. On the basis of affidavits from witnesses to the other attacks, the KTC residents obtained an temporary interdict from the Cape Town Supreme Court directing the Ministers of Law and Order and of Defence to ensure that the SAP and SADF did not help in any attack on KTC and would take steps to prevent one.

On 9, 10 and 11 June thousands of *witdoeke* swept down on KTC and torched it. Over a hundred police (three riot squad platoons) in dozens of vans and Casspirs were present during the attack but did nothing to prevent it. Eyewitnesses, including ministers of religion, doctors and local residents, reported that police appeared to be on friendly terms with the *witdoeke*, escorted them on their forays and even transported them. Not one person was arrested for the attack on KTC.

Some 3,000 residents of KTC subsequently instituted claims for damages against the Minister of Law and Order totalling R5 million (the case was eventually settled out of court, when, without admitting liability, the state paid R2 million in compensation). In court, police commanders explained away video and photographic evidence showing their men ignoring the attacks by claiming that they were distracted by other incidents. Major Dolf Odendaal, the commander of the regional riot squad, described the attack as a 'faction fight' which was impossible to stop. The SAP's task was mainly restricted to monitoring, he said, and the use of teargas or shotguns would have merely provoked the *witdoeke* into more violent action. But other police testified that the *witdoeke* usually cooperated with the SAP and obeyed their instructions. The police did not make any plans at the end of each day to prevent a recurrence of the violence, and they kept hardly any records of the attacks they 'monitored'.

While KTC was the most devastating – and clinically executed – vigilante operation of the 1980s, many townships continued to be plagued by vigilante groups of various types, especially gangs with names like Champions, Eagles, Sharp, A-Team and Black Cats.[161] The links between the police and some of these groups were exposed in the 1990s. But after 1987 the main source of vigilante-type violence and counter-violence was the conflict involving the KwaZulu homeland organisation, Inkatha. During the 1980s this was focused on the KwaZulu/Natal area.

THE NATAL CONFLICT

Under Chief Mangosuthu Buthelezi, the Zulu nationalist movement Inkatha rose to dominance during the 1970s through its control of housing, schools, and administrative structures in the KwaZulu bantustan. But its command of Natal's urban townships was sufficiently insecure for Inkatha to feel threatened by the growth of the UDF and COSATU in the first half of the 1980s.[162] Although there were occasional clashes, it was only towards the end of 1987 that political competition between Inkatha supporters and followers of the ANC-aligned mass movements degenerated into widespread violence. The immediate cause of the violence appears to have been the efforts of local Inkatha strongmen – later known as warlords – to establish control over residents of the sprawling townships and villages of the Edendale valley to the west of Pietermaritzburg. The conflict escalated rapidly. Inkatha warlords pressed their subjects into joining large 'armies', which, equipped with pangas (machetes), knobkerries, assegais, guns and other weapons, waged a struggle for territorial control against formations of comrades equipped with improvised weapons. By 1989 the strife had spread to other parts of Natal, including the city of Durban and the coastal settlements spreading north and south of it. It has the scale and horror of a civil war: more than 50,000 and perhaps up to 100,000 made homeless, countless thousands maimed and injured, at least 5,000 dead.[163]

While the often brutally violent nature of the conflict has much to do with the poverty, alienation and desperation of the black population in Natal, the SAP and its bantustan offshoot, the KwaZulu Police, must shoulder much of the blame for the spread of the carnage. International observers who have monitored police actions in Natal have been devastating in their criticisms, pointing to the manifest police bias in support of Inkatha, their secret role in funding and aiding the movement, and their failure to clamp down on warlords and others responsible for coordinating campaigns of attrition.[164]

The failure of the police to investigate and prosecute alleged murderers and planners of violence, especially from the Inkatha side, has created a climate in which people feel they have no option but to rely on their own resources to protect themselves or exact retribution.[165] It has also given warlords the impression that they are free to operate as they wish. A delegation from the International Commission of Jurists which visited Natal in 1990 found that police investigating the violence had on average over 100 murder dockets to investigate. With that workload it was impossible for the police to carry out more than rudimentary enquiries: one of the Natal attorney-general's deputies told the ICJ delegation that investigating more than one murder docket at a time was unrealistic.[166]

Even where killings and attacks were investigated, the police usually failed to prosecute Inkatha offenders. In one case, although an inquest found that named Inkatha leaders had been responsible for killing COSATU shop stewards in Mpophomeni in 1986, they were not charged. In another case, a member of the Inkatha Central Committee, David Ntombela, was found by a magistrate at an inquest to have been unlawfully responsible for the death of a woman, but he was not charged. Warlords taken into custody were released on bail shortly afterwards, and the police also failed to protect witnesses, or people applying for court interdicts against Inkatha.[167] One observer, John Aitchison of the University of Natal, who has monitored the conflict since its inception, has estimated that only five per cent of the approximately 5,000 political murders in Natal since 1987 have led to trials.[168] Having carried out its own investigations, COSATU concluded that 'it is our sincere belief that five or six vigorous prosecutions in 1987 would have saved the lives of 1,000 people, and indicated to the warlords and others that the taking of lives would not be tolerated.'[169]

In their day-to-day operations, the police were widely accused of siding with Inkatha. While UDF areas were searched rigorously for weapons, Inkatha fighters were allowed to bear arms openly. As a result the UDF activists were drastically outgunned – UDF deaths outnumbered those of Inkatha by seven to one in the period January 1987 to March 1988. UDF supporters were also targeted for detention: in the two years after July 1987, for every one Inkatha adherent detained, more than 50 UDF supporters were rounded up. Mass arrests of youths living in UDF areas took place in 1988, which police claimed was to combat crime, but few were charged with any offences. In any case, violent criminal gangs such as the Amasinyoras, which have flourished in the climate of lawlessness, are usually aligned with Inkatha. Police even detained UDF negotiators trying to work towards a peace agreement with Inkatha in 1987–8.[170] In some of their raids on UDF areas, police were accompanied by Inkatha officials who pointed out comrades, and residents also reported that the police handed over some comrades to Inkatha to be 'disciplined' or killed.[171]

Inkatha attacks on UDF supporters were actively aided by the police on many occasions. In Mpumalanga, where more than 1,000 homes had been destroyed in 1989, Inkatha launched a devastating attack on 27 November that year, reportedly with the support of the regular SAP, the KZP and special constables who had been brought into the township some months earlier (and many of whom were recruited directly by Inkatha leaders). Residents said that police accompanied and transported the vigilantes during the raid, shot at people resisting and stole property.[172] In another incident, the details of which came to light in a rare prosecution of the police officers involved three years later, an SAP officer, Brian Mitchell, led a team of four special constables in an attack on a house in Trust Feeds in which Inkatha supporters were mourning one of their dead. Eleven people were gunned down. The local UDF-linked residents' association was blamed for the massacre and its supporters were driven out of the area. The court prosecuting Mitchell and his men found that the attack was the *coup de grâce* in a police campaign to destroy the residents' association and deliver the area to Inkatha.[173]

Such was the extent of police bias that residents in some areas bucked the UDF's national demand for 'troops out of the townships' and publicly welcomed SADF units when they were brought in; they also expressed their preference for the SAP over the KZP. Given the links between Inkatha, the bantustan administration and the KZP, it is hardly surprising that the KZP should be perceived by many residents of Natal as little more than a private militia. KwaZulu is in effect a one-party statelet, as no parties other than Inkatha sit in the homeland assembly. Chief Buthelezi is at once the President of Inkatha, the Chief Minister of KwaZulu and the Minister of Police (see Chapter 2). In a study of how local people perceived police actions, more than 70 per cent said that the police were partial in their handling of the violence (and only 14 per cent claimed that they were impartial). The performance of the KZP rated much lower than that of the SAP – over half of those who responded classified its performance as 'very poor'.[174]

Secretly, the security forces also trained and funded Inkatha. After 1986 the Security Branch funded Inkatha's trade union wing, the United Workers Union of South Africa (UWUSA) which was set up to counter COSATU, and in 1989–90 the police transferred secret funds to Inkatha's account to pay for two political rallies. Several hundred Inkatha members were taken for training by the SADF to a counter-insurgency base in occupied Namibia, and later transferred to a covert training facility in northern Natal, which was funded by Military Intelligence. The trained men were dispatched to various KZP bases, and there is evidence that they were involved in assassinations of UDF supporters and became part of the loose network of security force hit squads.

Hit Squads and Assassinations

As the Security Branch and the SADF's Special Forces stepped up their raids on the ANC in neighbouring states in the 1980s, assassinations of exiled ANC officials and supporters became common. Joe Gqabi, the movement's representative in Zimbabwe, was killed by a car bomb in Harare in 1981; the next year Ruth First, a well-known writer and Communist Party member, was killed when she opened a letter bomb in Maputo, Mozambique; ANC activist Jeanette Schoon and her daughter were blown up by a parcel bomb in Angola in 1984; Cassius Make, a member of the movement's executive committee, and two colleagues were gunned down in Swaziland in 1987; Dulcie September, an ANC diplomat, was shot dead in Paris.[175]

Assassinations were also carried out in South Africa. Several incidents suggested that police were deliberately trying to kill suspected ANC combatants and supporters rather than arrest them. In March 1986 police acting on intelligence surprised seven alleged guerillas in Guguletu township near Cape Town. They made no attempt to arrest them, and, according to eyewitnesses, shot them dead while they tried to surrender – one man was shot by at least six policemen. An inquest magistrate found that the police acted legitimately. The authorities then prosecuted Tony Weaver, a local journalist who reported the eyewitness accounts, arguing that he had infringed the Police Act by repeating untrue allegations. But they lost the case and were forced to re-open the inquest, although the magistrate still concluded that the police had acted legitimately 'in combating terrorism'.[176]

In Chesterville, near Durban, a few years later, three Askaris opened fire on a shack in which six youths suspected of links with MK were meeting, firing more than 90 bullets and killing four of them. They claimed they had heard a shot. Although the inquest magistrate found that the shot had not come from the shack, he concluded that the police had acted in 'reasonable defence'.[177] In another incident, police deliberately drove a Casspir over a shack in which an alleged guerilla and two 'sympathisers' were hiding, crushing all of them to death.[178]

In the Transkei, more than one incident had the appearance of a summary execution. Batandwa Ndondo, a former student leader, was killed in September 1985 by a group of men who arrived at his home in a white panel van and were identified by eyewitnesses as police. He was taken away in the van and shot eight times; then his body was taken to the local police station. The President of the Transkei administration said later: 'Many people are asking why Mr Ndondo was killed. He is the one who came from Lesotho ... and exploded a bomb in Umtata.'[179] In another incident in the Transkei in 1988, police driving in an unmarked vehicle with false number plates and armed with an AK-47 rifle, an Uzi sub-machine gun, a machine gun and two pistols killed three men pointed out to them by an informer.[180]

Evidence began to mount that the security forces were applying the covert tactics they used to disorganise the ANC's underground guerilla force against activists working in legal anti-apartheid organisations in South Africa. By 1990, well over 100 anti-apartheid activists had been killed in circumstances which pointed to political assassination, but prosecutions had been instituted in only two cases.[181] In one of these, two men allegedly intent on robbery were found guilty of murdering Dr Abu-Baker Asvat, known as 'the people's doctor', in his Soweto surgery – but suspicions that it was a political execution remained.[182] In the other case, six senior Ciskei policemen (including two with the rank of major-general) were convicted and imprisoned for murdering Eric Mntonga, a director of the Institute for a Democratic Alternative for South Africa (IDASA). It transpired that Mntonga had died as a result of torture while in detention. He was detained on 24 July 1987 and interrogated at the Mdantsane police station, where torture was routine. In the course of being suffocated with a rubber tube, he was killed. The next day the police dumped his body by the roadside after stabbing it repeatedly in the chest to make it appear as if he had been robbed and assaulted. As well as the stab wounds, and injuries to his head, Mntonga had 25 other injuries to his body.[183]

In another infamous incident the mutilated and burnt bodies of four prominent UDF leaders in the Eastern Cape, Matthew Goniwe, Fort Calata, Sicelo Mhlawuli and Sparrow Mkhonto, were found near Port Elizabeth on 27 June 1985. The four were killed on their way back from a meeting to discuss how to protect community leaders, following the disappearance of three members of the Port Elizabeth Black Civic Organisation, who were apparently abducted by white men in uniform.[184]

Goniwe and his colleagues were respected leaders of the community, and their killing further inflamed already volatile emotions in the area. The police tried to blame black consciousness factions for the killings, and an inquest concluded that they were killed by 'persons unknown', but many South Africans were convinced that the police were responsible. Seven years later evidence emerged to implicate the security forces, when a secret communication between the local Joint Management Committee and the national State Security Council was uncovered recommending the assassination of Goniwe and Calata. Other information indicated that the killings were authorised by the Chief of Staff of Intelligence in the SADF, Lieutenant-General CP van der Westhuizen. The newspaper which published the information, the *New Nation*, said that it also had information pointing to the assassination by the security forces of three other anti-apartheid activists.[185] The killings were apparently part of a plan hatched by Military Intelligence and detailed in leaked documents to create a greater Xhosaland from the Ciskei and Transkei bantustans. The plan would also entail the assassination of the Ciskei's President Lennox Sebe, regarded by Pretoria as an 'embarrassment', and the launch of a Xhosa Resistance Movement which the Military Intelligence documents argued 'must in nature – and even extent – be similar to Inkatha, and must together with our security forces form a counter-revolutionary front'. After the assassination of Goniwe, the plan apparently had to be abandoned because General Holomisa seized power in the Transkei and turned against Pretoria.[186]

The confessions from Death Row of ex-security policeman Butana Almond Nofomela, in October 1989, set in motion a chain of events which eventually shed a little light on some of the assassinations and other 'dirty tricks' employed against anti-apartheid organisations. Nofomela, an Askari and a member of the C1 unit of the Security Branch based at Vlakplaas (see Chapter 2) said he had been involved in eight killings in South Africa and neighbouring states. Griffiths Mxenge, a human rights lawyer practising in Durban, had been amongst their victims. Nofomela and three of his colleagues, acting on the instructions of C1 commander Captain Dirk Coetzee, had abducted Mxenge on the night of 19 November 1981 and taken him to a football stadium.

> We then started assaulting him with kicks and punches, until he fell to the ground. We then all stabbed him several times. He immediately died and we carried on butchering his body. In accordance with our instructions from Captain Coetzee, we removed Mxenge's items of value like money and a watch in order to simulate a robbery.[187]

Later, when asked why he had only arrested one person in eight years, he said: 'I don't arrest anyone. I kidnap or assassinate them.'[188]

Nofomela's revelations were followed by those of his commander, Dirk Coetzee, who, fearing he would be made a scapegoat and plagued by his conscience, fled the country and sought the protection of the ANC. Another member of the Vlakplaas unit, David Tshikalanga, backed up Coetzee and Nofomela's accounts. Between the three of them, they provided details of several murders and other incidents which they said were carried out by C1. These included killing Ace Moema, a captured member of MK; setting fire to the cars of anti-apartheid activists in the town of Barkly East to intimidate them; luring three young activists from Krugersdorp into an abandoned mine where they were killed with a hand grenade; and abducting, interrogating and shooting Japie Maponya, a security guard whose brother was suspected of involvement with guerillas. They also gave details of raids into neighbouring countries, to kill or kidnap ANC and PAC members.[189]

Coetzee explained how the head of the SAP's forensics section, Lieutenant-General Lothar Neethling, had provided him with poison to kill anti-apartheid activists. This was not the first time the police were accused of poisoning people. In 1977 the children of Donald Woods, then editor of the East London *Daily Dispatch*, which had campaigned to expose the police role in Steve Biko's death, received T-shirts impregnated with a burning substance. It turned out that the chemical was widely used in police forensics, and two security police officers were reported to have intercepted the parcel at the post office.[190] Then, in October 1981, a leader of the Port Elizabeth branch of the militant Congress of South African Students (COSAS), Sipiwe Mtimkulu, had to be admitted to hospital after losing his ability to walk after five months in police detention. He had been poisoned with thallium, a rat poison, and he said the police had given him tablets in the last month of his detention. He began proceedings against the SAP, suing them for damages for torture and poisoning. But he mysteriously disappeared with a friend from a hospital where he was seeking treatment. His wheelchair and his friend's car were found later near the Lesotho border: the two men have never been seen again. According to Dirk Coetzee, the security police had decided to kill him when he sued them, and were responsible for his disappearance.[191] Another target of poisoners was Frank Chikane, the current secretary-general of the South African Council of Churches, who fell seriously ill when his clothing was impregnated with poison.[192]

The activities of C1 were overshadowed by revelations of a hitherto secret SADF unit, the Civil Cooperation Bureau, exposed in the course of police investigations into the murder of David Webster. An anti-apartheid activist who was researching death squads, Webster was gunned down outside his home in Johannesburg on 1 May 1989. Activists suspected the police, but the SAP brigadier investigating the case, Florence Mostert, instead fingered the SADF: '[A] secret organisation exists in the country, with members from all levels of society, which strives to terrorise left-wing radicals with the aid of violence and intimidation.'[193] As details of the extent of CCB operations unravelled – it had a budget of R28 million in 1989, directly employed 139 agents and had carried out more than 200 'projects'[184] – pressure mounted for the government to come clean.

In January 1990 Justice Louis Harms was appointed to investigate 'certain unsolved murders'. But his brief was severely restricted. He examined only cases in South Africa (excluding the TBVC states), while the vast majority of alleged assassinations took place outside the country's borders. Furthermore, the counsel to the commission, advocate Tim McNally, had already at the government's request conducted an investigation into Dirk Coetzee's allegations and concluded that they were untrue. Much of the evidence disappeared; many senior police and army members refused to say anything on the grounds that they could incriminate themselves, and Harms failed to call several key witnesses. In the end, he indicted the CCB:

> The CCB arrogated to itself the power to try, to sentence and to punish people without the persons knowing the allegations against them or having had the opportunity to defend themselves.[195]

However, Harms let the SAP off the hook: he concluded that there was no proof that a police hit squad existed, and concurred with SAP claims that Vlakplaas had a legitimate role in tracking down guerillas. A human rights organisation commented:

> If the sole job of the SAP unit at Vlakplaas was to identify and arrest suspected insurgents the organisation achieved very little of what it was supposed to do. On the most generous interpretation of the police's own testimony only 20 arrests were made in approximately six years.[196]

Harms's findings were discredited by another judge when a defamation case brought by Lieutenant-General Lothar Neethling against newspapers which had reported Coetzee's account of his role in poisonings backfired. Justice Kriegler concluded that Neethling had misled the court and the Harms commission. In all probability, he found, the police had carried out political murders and poisonings, and Coetzee had been telling the truth about the SAP's hit squads.[197] It is symptomatic of the rot in the SAP and the government of the day that these findings – that senior police were poisoners, that SAP death squads carried out assassinations, that police officers had misled the Harms commission and destroyed evidence – were shrugged off by the authorities and did not result in any prosecutions.

NOTES

1   Grundy 1983, pp 141–2; *Rand Daily Mail* 11.3.80.
2   Sparks 1990, p 249.
3   IDAF 1980, p 65; *Focus* no 26, January/February 1980, p 11 Cilliers 1985, p 33.
4   Dippenaar 1988, pp 353–491.
5   Martin & Johnson 1981, pp 161, 170; Cilliers 1985, pp 24; 30.
6   Anti-Apartheid Movement 1979, p 36; Grundy 1983, p 139; *Focus* no 26, January/February 1980, pp 11–2.
7   Anti-Apartheid Movement 1979; Cilliers 1985; Martin & Johnson 1981; Ellis & Sechaba 1992, p 97.
8   Ellis & Sechaba 1992, p 98.
9   SWAPO 1981, pp 259–63; *Resister* no 47, January 1987.
10 *Resister* no 20, July 1982.

11   Katjavivi 1988, p 60.
12   Katjavivi 1988, pp 61–2; Shityuwete 1990, pp 139–45.
13   IDAF 1980, p 54.
14   SWAPO 1981, pp 201–5; IDAF 1982, p 9, Dippenaar 1988, p 454–5.
15   SWAPO 1981, pp 210—2.
16   *Guardian* 5.12.75.
17   IDAF 1982, pp 26–7.
18   *Lutheran World Information* no 20, 1979.
19   *Citizen* 2.2.81; IDAF 1982, p 33.
20   *Armed Forces* February 1985.
21   *Windhoek Advertiser* 1.4.81.
22   *Republikein* 11.1.87.
23   *Times of Namibia* 3.2.89.
24   *Armed Forces* April 1985.
25   Nathan 1990, p 21.
26   *Windhoek Advertiser* 2.5.85.
27   Herbstein & Evenson 1989, pp 70–1.
28   Cited in Herbstein & Evenson 1989, p 67.
29   *Focus*, no 61, November/December 1985, p 11; Cawthra 1986, p 210–1; Herbstein & Evenson 1989, p 76.
30   *Windhoek Observer* 28.6.86.
31   *Namibian* 18.7.88.
32   *Windhoek Advertiser* 2.7.82; *Windhoek Observer* 28.8.82.
33   Cited in Weaver 1987, p 252.
34   Ruppel 1987, pp 229–32.
35   *Windhoek Observer* 4.1.88.
36   SACBC 1982.
37   IDAF 1989, p 62.
38   *Focus* no 86, January/February 1987, p 10.
39   SACBC 1982, p 21; Weaver 1987, p 250.
40   *Focus* no 74, January/February 1988.
41   *Star* 18.8.81.
42   Cawthra 1986, p 210.
43   *Focus* no. 73, November/December 1987, p 4.
44   *UN Security Council Document S/20883*; *New York Times* 15.1.89 Nathan 1990, p 26.
45   *ISSUP Bulletin* no 4, 1987.
46   *ISSUP Bulletin* no 4, 1987.
47   IDAF 1980, p 67.
48   ANC 1979, pp 9–10.
49   Dippenaar 1988, p 521.
50   *Hansard* 28.2.77.
51   Cawthra 1986, p 227.
52   Cawthra 1986, pp 228–33.
53   IDAF 1991, p 70.
54   Suter 1980, p 12.
55   Hanlon 1986.
56   *Focus* no 58, May/June 1985, p 6.
57   Ellis & Sechaba 1992, pp 116–8.
58   *Weekly Mail* 14.11.86.
59   *Star* 12.8.86.
60   Calculation based on press reports.
61   *Message of the National Executive of the ANC* 8.1.85; *BBC Summary of World Broadcasts*

4.7.85; *Weekly Mail* 11.7.85.

62   *Indicator SA* vol 5, no 2, 1988; *Annual Report of the Commissioner of the SAP*, 1989, p 52.

63   *IDAF Briefing Paper* no 22, March 1987.

64   Ellis & Sechaba 1992, pp 168–71.

65   *Militia* vol 7, no 4, 1977.

66   Seekings 1989, pp 14–5.

67   *Daily Dispatch* 15.9.86.

68   ANC 1991, p 14.

69   Cited in Jeffery 1991, p 27.

70   Wandrag 1985, p 10.

71   *Hansard* 22.7.76.

72   Brooks & Brickhill 1980, p 249.

73   *Cape Times* 17.6.80; *Rand Daily Mail* 21.6.80; *Sunday Telegraph* 22.6.80.

74   *Times* 19.6.80; *Daily Telegraph* 21.6.80.

75   *Cape Times* 30.5.80.

76   *Focus* no 35, July/August 1981.

77   Olivier 1991, pp 6–7.

78   Internal Security Act, 1982, sections 48 and 49.

79   *Star* 30.4.85; Baynham 1987, p 115; *Cape Times* 24.10.89.

80   *Cape Times* 24.10.90.

81   Baynham 1987, p 116.

82   *Servamus* September 1985, p 31.

83   Murray 1987, pp 247–8.

84   SACBC 1984, pp 6–7, 18–21.

85   SACBC 1984.

86   Cawthra 1986, pp 244–6.

87   Murray 1987, p 249.

88   *Sunday Times* 16.6.85.

89   *Daily Dispatch* 11.4.85; Haysom 1987a, p 3.

90   *Daily Dispatch* 12.6.85.

91   *Cape Times* 12.8.85.

92   *Daily Dispatch* 12.6.86; *Cape Times* 12.6.86.

93   Affidavit of Petrus Horn, 3.1.1990. The authorities questioned the veracity of Horn's affidavit, but his description of operations in the Eastern Cape townships at this time corresponds closely with those given in interviews with the author by national servicemen serving in the same area.

94   Affidavit released by End Conscription Campaign, August 1985.

95   *Star* 4.8.85; *Sowetan* 9.9.85, 11.9.85.

96   For an account of some of the police operations in the Western Cape at this time see Van Eck 1989.

97   *Cape Times* 18.10.85, 24.10.89; *Times* 12.12.89.

98   *Cape Times* 31.5.80.

99   *Sunday Star* 30.11.86.

100 *Cape Times* 5.8.87, 6.8.87, 26.8.87, 27.8.87, 13.9.87 16.9.87.

101 *Weekly Mail* 10.1.86; *Indicator SA* vol 4, no 4, Autumn/Winter 1987.

102 *Sowetan* 12.8.85.

103 Seekings 1989, p 10.

104 *Servamus* March 1986, pp 32–3.

105 Black Lawyers' Association 1986.

106 Seekings 1989, pp 11–3.

107 *Sunday Star* 8.6.86; Black Lawyers' Association, 1986 pp 1–10; Seekings 1989, pp 18–20.

108 *Cape Times* 24.4.86.

109 *Sunday Star* 15.3.87.
110 *Weekly Mail* 18.4.86; *Sunday Tribune* 27.4.86.
111 *Focus* no 69, March/April 1987.
112 *Cape Times* 15.8.86; *Guardian* 21.8.86.
113 *IDAF Briefing Paper* no 22, March 1987, p 3.
114 *Star* 23.4.86; *Daily Dispatch* 5.6.86.
115 *Resister* no 46, October/November 1986, pp 11–4.
116 *Financial Times* 12.3.86; *Star* 18.3.86.
117 *Star* 15.3.86.
118 *Star* 20.6.88, 21.6.88, 27.6.88.
119 *Guardian* 19.10.87; *South* 29.10.87.
120 *Weekly Mail* 30.10.87.
121 *Eastern Province Herald* 31.10.87.
122 *Weekly Mail* 11.12.87.
123 *Weekly Mail* 8.5.92.
124 *Hansard* 13.4.88.
125 *Weekly Mail* 18.12.87.
126 Cited in Fine 1989, p 58.
127 Fine 1989, pp 58–77.
128 Webster & Friedman 1989.
129 *Focus* no 79, November/December 1988, p 5.
130 Findings of the Independent Board of Inquiry into Informal Repression, cited in Lawyers' Committee 1991, p 8.
131 *South* 1.9.88; *Daily Telegraph* 13.10.88.
132 Webster & Friedman 1989, p 3.
133 IDAF 1990, pp 34–5.
134 *Observer* 10.9.89.
135 *Financial Mail* 15.9.89.
136 *Star* 8.12.89.
137 Foster & Sandler 1985, pp 3-8.
138 See for example Hope 1989, p 13.
139 Bernstein 1978.
140 Lawyers' Committee 1983, p 5.
141 Pauw 1991, pp 100–1.
142 Foster & Sandler 1985.
143 *Rand Daily Mail* 13.6.80; Foster & Sandler 1985, p 6.
144 Amnesty International 1978; Lawyers' Committee 1983.
145 Lawyers' Committee 1983, *Amnesty International File on Torture: South Africa*, nd; Hope 1989; various issues of *Focus* 1975–91.
146 *Citizen* 6.11.90.
147 Affidavit of Petrus Horn, 3.1.90; *Daily News* 14.12.89 15.12.89.
148 Pauw 1991, p 105.
149 Lawyers' Committee 1983, p 3.
150 Bernstein 1978, p 20.
151 Lawyers' Committee 1983, pp 17–22.
152 *Amnesty International Report*, 1992, p 235.
153 Haysom 1989d, p 63.
154 *Sowetan* 3.6.85, 9.6.85.
155 CIIR 1988, pp 7–8.
156 *Guardian* 20.12.86; *Sowetan* 15.1.87.
157 Haysom 1989d, p 71.
158 CIIR 1988, pp 7–8; Haysom 1989d, pp 189–90.

159 *Eastern Province Herald* 16.7.87; *South* 23.7.87; *Weekly Mail* 13.11.87.

160 This account of the Crossroads events relies on court records and other material from the Legal Resource Centre, Cape Town.

161 *Focus* no 75, March/April 1988, p 1.

162 Mzala 1988.

163 Aitchison 1990, p 1; Kentridge 1990; *IDAF Information, Notes and Briefings*, no 90/4, 1990; Africa Watch 1991a, pp 7, 28–33; Aitchison 1991, p 8.

164 For example, Africa Watch 1990a; ICJ 1990; Amnesty International 1992b.

165 Marais 1991, pp 15–17.

166 ICJ 1990.

167 *IDAF Information, Notes and Briefings*, no 90/4, 1990.

168 Aitchison 1991, p 8.

169 COSATU 1989, p 2.

170 Africa Watch 1991, p 30.

171 *IDAF Information, Notes and Briefings*, no 90/4, 1990, p 4 Douglas 1990; Amnesty International 1992b, p 41.

172 Africa Watch 1991a, pp 39–40.

173 ICJ 1992, pp 3–4.

174 Jagwanth (nd).

175 Pauw 1991, pp 270–86.

176 *Focus* no 71, July/August 1987, p 8.

177 *Weekly Mail* 2.2.90; Laurence 1990, p 18.

178 Pauw 1991, p 111.

179 *Daily Dispatch* 26.9.85, 17.9.85, 28.9.85; Laurence 1990.

180 *SouthScan* 26.8.89.

181 Lawyers' Committee 1990, p i.

182 Lawyer's Committee 1990, p 6.

183 *Daily Dispatch* 9.2.89, 11.2.89; *Focus* no 82, May–June 1989 p 4.

184 *Sowetan* 25.8.87; *City Press* 27.9.87; *Eastern Province Herald* 16.2.89; *Focus* no 83, July/August 1989, p 5.

185 *New Nation* 30.4.92; *Guardian* 9.5.92; *Independent* 9.5.92.

186 *Guardian* 20.3.93.

187 Affidavit of Almond Butana Nofomela, cited in Lawyers Committee 1991, p 11.

188 *Sunday Telegraph* 11.3.90.

189 *Report of the Harms Commission of Inquiry*, Pauw 1991.

190 Pauw 1991, pp 118–9.

191 *Focus* no 39, March/April 1982, p 9, no 44, January/February 1983, p 8; Pauw 199, pp 56–7.

192 *Weekly Mail* 9.6.89; *Sunday Star* 21.6.89.

193 *Weekly Mail* 26.1.90.

194 *Guardian* 16.2.90; *Sunday Star* 11.3.90; HRC 1990b.

195 *Report of the Harms Commission of Inquiry*.

196 IBIIR 1991b, p 29.

197 Amnesty International 1992b, p 20; Pauw 1991, pp 246–9.

OPERATIONS: THE DE KLERK ERA

By the time De Klerk legalised opposition organisations on 2 February 1990, thus fundamentally changing the tasks of the SAP, the state's attitude to political opposition had already changed. Rallies and protest marches had been allowed, and the police were instructed to keep a low profile. De Klerk promised to widen the scope for political dissent; he would 'take the police out of the political battlefield' to ease the process of negotiating an end to apartheid. But many aspects of police operations remained controversial, or became even more sinister.

From the beginning of 1991, with some notable exceptions, methods of crowd control showed some improvement. Detention without trial became an exception rather than the rule: the number of people held under security legislation had fallen to single figures by 1992. But these improvements were offset by continuing covert activities and by police partiality towards Inkatha, which, combined with their manifest failure to clamp down on vigilante attacks, contributed to the political violence which reached unprecedented levels under De Klerk. In 1991, 2,582 deaths were monitored by the Human Rights Commission, 78 per cent of them the result of clashes involving groups which could be defined as vigilantes.[1] By June 1992, 10 people were dying every day in political violence:[2] the death toll by the end of the year stood at nearly 3,500.[3] Militaristic police 'crime sweeps' involving joint operations with the army continued, and in the Bophuthatswana bantustan, it was business as usual as far as the local police were concerned. Torture – whether in political or criminal cases, and the distinction between the two became increasingly difficult to make – remained common, as was attested by one of South Africa's leading pathologists, Dr Jonathan Gluckman (see 'Detention and other methods of control').

Managing Political Opposition

CONTROLLING CROWDS

Since the end of March 1991, when a blanket ban on open-air gatherings was allowed to lapse for the first time in 15 years, political demonstrations have been legal without specific authorisation from a magistrate. But organisers still have to apply for permission to the local authority, and police can ask for magistrates to ban specific gatherings. As many demonstrations arise spontaneously, or the organisers neglect or refuse to seek permission, the police are still empowered, at their discretion, to disperse 'illegal' gatherings.[4] Many areas, including some of South Africa's biggest townships, have also been declared 'unrest areas', where all open-air gatherings are automatically illegal. The result has been continuing conflict between police and crowds.

As people took advantage of the new climate following the unbanning of the ANC in February 1990, thousands of public protests took place. According to police statistics, there were more than 8,500 'gatherings', of which only 853 were authorised and more than 7,000 were classed as 'spontaneous' and illegal.[5]

Most demonstrations passed off without incident; usually conflict arose when the police attempted to break them up on the grounds of illegality. Some of these clashes were never reported in the press; others received only small mentions. A careful sifting of the press, however, revealed that the pattern of conflict established during the State of Emergency was far from over. Take the Eastern Cape. In this area alone, between 2 February and the end of June 1990, police fired teargas or used rubber bullets or shotguns against marchers and demonstrators on 14 occasions. The incidents included one in which Ciskei police killed three people celebrating Nelson Mandela's release from prison, the dispersal of striking workers with teargas, and the breaking up of youth organisation marches. In the Orange Free State and the Transvaal, there were even more clashes between police and demonstrators.[6] By the end of the year 323 people had been killed by the police and 3,390 injured, according to the Human Rights Commission.[7] The police said there were more incidents of 'unrest' in 1990 than in any previous year except 1985, and more than double the number in 1989.[8]

One incident, in Sebokeng on 26 March 1990, received widespread publicity and resulted in a government enquiry which strongly criticised the police. A crowd, which some estimates put as high as 50,000, marched on the local police station and handed over a petition about poor housing and education and the behaviour of the police. As happened at Langa five years before, an outnumbered, ill-prepared police unit attempted to stop the march. 'Volunteers', apparently keen to get a bit of the action, joined the original police line. They included a contingent of 35 municipal police, some plainclothes Security Branch members armed with shotguns loaded with lethal SSG buckshot, members of the local SAP stock-theft unit similarly equipped and even a 'private citizen' armed with a pistol. The crowd was militant but not aggressive, and a few stones were thrown. Constable van Rhyn started the shooting 'accidentally', he claimed, by firing off a round of teargas (he then fired off two more, presumably not by accident). The others in the police line immediately opened fire. One municipal policeman claimed that he had used lethal ammunition from his shotgun first, and softer birdshot later, because he had 'forgotten that the first bullet is the last to come out when I fire a shot'. Five demonstrators were killed and at least 161 wounded – 84 were shot from behind (some reports put the number of wounded as high as 300).[9]

The Sebokeng shootings, coming so soon after De Klerk's promise of free political activity, caused an outrage. A commission of inquiry headed by Justice Goldstone was appointed to investigate, and concluded that the police had acted unjustifiably. The judge also said he was 'disturbed at the callous attitude' of some of the police who 'displayed an attitude of unconcern at the lethal nature of their ammunition and the consequence of its use.'[10] Despite the judge's findings, none of the police involved were prosecuted.[11] However, the SAP did double the length of the counter-insurgency training and riot control courses given to all trainees and appeared to take on board some of Goldstone's criticisms and recommendations.

Six months later there was another massacre in Sebokeng, this time by the army. Forty-two people were killed when troops opened fire on a peaceful crowd which sat down in an act of passive resistance when ordered to disperse. The soldiers shot off 162 live rounds and kept on firing for 22 seconds, even though the crowd panicked and ran away at the first shot. Ironically, the local SAP commander had given them explicit orders not to shoot.[12]

The circumstances of many of the confrontations between crowds and police are disputed – invariably, the police and their victims give contradictory accounts. But it is evident that many showdowns could have been avoided if marches had not been declared illegal, and casualties would have been kept down if police had not resorted so quickly to lethal or potentially lethal weapons. In August 1990, for instance, eyewitnesses reported that police opened fire with the usual combination of teargas, rubber bullets and shotguns on a section of a 20,000 strong crowd marching through the Cape Town township of Khayelitsha demanding the resignation of town councillors. A local member of parliament, Jan van Eck, said that the crowd had been attacked for no reason, but police claimed there had been stone throwing.[13] A few days later, a week of rioting erupted in Port Elizabeth's Coloured townships during protests against rent increases and the tricameral parliament. Again, the violence appeared to be set off by a police attack on a protest march. ANC officials said most of the deaths had been caused by 'indiscriminate shooting' by the SAP.[14]

There were many reports of police killings during 1990, especially in small towns in rural areas. In Rammulotsi in the Orange Free State, four youths, including a 14-year-old, were gunned down.[15] In Thabong (Welkom), 12 people were killed in violent clashes.[16] A baby was killed when police fired shotguns into his home in Ikageng near Potchefstroom. In Maokeng near Kroonstad, in an apparent replay of the infamous Trojan Horse incident, police hiding under a tarpaulin in the back of a private hire truck drove into the township and opened fire when youths attacked them, killing two minors.[17] In Barkly East, in the Eastern Cape, the vice-president of the local ANC branch was killed when police fired on protesters during a consumer boycott.[18] At the same time, however, major protest marches passed off without incident. In December, for instance, ANC marshals maintained order as thousands marched through the streets of South Africa's cities in support of the ANC's negotiating demands, while riot police kept a discreet distance.[19]

The peace-keeping efforts of churches, civic organisations, business groups and political organisations, as well as SAP efforts to clean up its act after the inquest into the first Sebokeng massacre, led to a reduction in casualties after November 1990. As the mass protest campaigns ran out of energy in 1991, direct confrontations between police and residents became fewer still, although vigilante-related clashes led to a further increase in bloodshed. Of the 2,582 political killings recorded that year by the Human Rights Commission, only 4 per cent (100) were blamed on the security forces (although the police killed many more in 'non-political' circumstances).[20] There was also an increase in arrests, which the Human Rights Commission took as an indication of a move away from the use of force.[21] But police continued to shoot demonstrators, and the ANC's return to mass protests in mid-1992 led to several incidents in which police opened fire on crowds.[22]

There was seldom agreement on the reasons for violence. A bloody clash at Daveyton on the East Rand on 24 March 1991 elicited different accounts. Police claimed ANC supporters holding an illegal meeting turned on them, singling out a white policeman and killing him. They were forced to retaliate, killing 11 of the protesters. The ANC said that township residents had gathered to discuss how to defend themselves from Inkatha attacks. A joint SADF–SAP patrol arrived and ordered them to disperse within ten minutes. While they were discussing what to do, the security forces opened fire with teargas, rubber bullets and live ammunition. As the residents fled they were cut off by another group of police and they were forced to break a way through, killing the policeman.[23]

The SAP explained the continuing 'mistakes' in crowd control largely in terms of insufficiently experienced and outnumbered police panicking. A police regional commissioner was quoted in one report as saying:

> It is a horrible feeling to face a large crowd (say, 50,000) knowing that you are one of 30 policemen. In the beginning you are very scared. You don't know what will happen. . . .
>
> If there are 20, 100 or even 120 policemen facing a crowd of 50,000 people, they must fear for their lives. They are human beings, kids, in school last year.[24]

The SAP's solution was to build up the Internal Stability Units, forces of more experienced policemen especially trained and equipped for riot and crowd control (see Chapter 2). But, at least on some occasions, the new units behaved in much the same way as the old riot squads. At the end of March 1992, for example, at least 100 residents of Alexandra were injured when Internal Stability police fired teargas and birdshot at crowds demonstrating against political violence. The demonstrations were regarded as illegal because Alexandra had been declared an Unrest Area.[25]

No doubt the exact circumstances in which police have resorted to violence on so many occasions will never be resolved. On the one hand, it is clear that the ANC's suspension of armed struggle did not mean that all the tens of thousands of black South Africans accustomed to regarding the police as their immediate enemies suddenly turned to non-violent means of resistance. The PAC continued to agitate for attacks on police, and some of its supporters were reported to have adopted the slogan 'kill a cop a day'.[26] The police claim that in 1990 alone they were attacked with petrol bombs on 787 occasions and, in the first nine months of that year, were shot at 855 times,[27] although attacks dropped off somewhat in 1992.[28] Whether these statistics are a reliable indicator or not – many of the incidents are likely to have taken place in criminal rather than political contexts – it is evident that many South Africans still regard the police as legitimate targets. But it is also clear that the SAP's approach to crowd control has not changed as much as its public pronouncements would suggest. Much needs to be done to improve SAP crowd control techniques: some of the steps taken under the De Klerk regime, together with proposals put forward by anti-apartheid forces, are examined in the next chapter.

'CRIME SWEEPS'

Another of the tactics of the State of Emergency – the joint police–army cordon-and-search operation, or 'routine crime sweep' as the SAP describes it – has been used extensively in the 1990s. The names given to some of the operations – Thunderbolt, Iron Fist, Operation Sentry – and the scale they were conducted on are more suggestive of military campaigns than policing actions.

The approach has been that of a blitzkrieg and some of the operations lasted only hours. In Operation Watchdog, which was carried out in various parts of the country in June 1990, especially in the Eastern Cape, more than 43,000 arrests were made.[29] The operation drew in the police air wing, which carried out aerial reconnaissance.[30] Operation Sentry, launched in January 1991 as a long-term anti-crime initiative which entailed putting 'bobbies on the beat', fizzled out in 48 hours and observers concluded that its main target was anti-apartheid activists rather than criminals.[31] For Thunderbolt, in February 1991, more than 30,000 policemen, reservists, troops and traffic authorities were marshalled. In some areas, police carried out house-to-house searches, and residents accused them of indiscriminate shooting.[32] Thunderbolt led to the arrest of more than 11,000 people in less than ten hours, although most faced minor charges such as illegal possession of dagga (marijuana) and alcohol-related offences.[33] Another joint army–police blitz in February 1992 netted 13,000 arrests over two days.[34]

BOPHUTHATSWANA AND CISKEI

In Bophuthatswana, the local police – backed by the SAP – appeared to be largely unaffected by changes in the rest of South Africa. The authorities resisted releasing political prisoners, political meetings remained banned (except with the permission of the Minister of Law and Order, who is also the President, Lucas Mangope), and police aggressively harassed anyone opposing the Mangope regime. The local security laws, modelled on Pretoria's Internal Security Act, were strengthened in March 1991 to make meetings and demonstrations effectively illegal. Gatherings were repeatedly dispersed by force: many were killed. For a year, after March 1990, a local State of Emergency was in force, which empowered police officers and soldiers to detain people for five months without trial: over 800 were detained in 1990 and 1991 under the emergency regulations or other security laws.[35] Many of detainees reported that they had been tortured, including a group of high school students who said they had been shocked with an electric cattle prodder.[36]

Some organisations, such as the women's anti-apartheid group the Black Sash, remained banned in the homeland, and in September 1991 a new law was introduced preventing trade unions based in other parts of South Africa from operating in Bophuthatswana.[37] Although the ANC was not banned, it was unable to function openly because of police harassment. Pro-Mangope vigilantes were also active in some areas, especially in the village of Braklaagte, just outside the homeland's border, where residents refused to be incorporated into the bantustan.[38]

The Ciskei regime of Brigadier Oupa Gqozo, under the control of the SADF's intelligence section, also used its police and army against the ANC. Apart from making it an offence punishable by up to five years to criticise him (he reportedly wanted the death sentence but was persuaded otherwise), Gqozo attempted to drive the ANC out of Ciskei and assert its independence. The showdown came during the ANC's campaign of mass action in September 1992. The ANC planned a mass march across the Ciskei 'border' to underline their belief that it formed part of South Africa. Military Intelligence headquarters reportedly sent a signal to Gqozo's army chief, instructing him to use force to crush the demonstration. When a group broke away from the main ANC march, they fell into what appeared to be a carefully laid trap: a corridor in the lines of Ciskei soldiers led through high grass where soldiers with machine-guns were waiting. They opened fire in sustained bursts, killing at least 28 people: the worst massacre in South Africa's history since Sharpeville. Just before the attack, the SAP contingent escorting the marchers pulled back, fuelling the accusations of a set-up.[39] The massacre set in train a string of killings and counter-killings as residents turned on local police and military personnel. Brigadier Gqozo's rule became increasing erratic and reactive as he came increasingly to rely on cronies or ex-South African police or military personnel operating as freelance security experts.[40]

TACKLING THE RIGHT WING

During the 1980s the police turned a blind eye to the activities of extreme right-wing groups, but the cosy relationship was subjected to severe strains in the De Klerk era. In a process perhaps similar to that which occurred at the outbreak of the Second World War, police who mostly sympathised with the cause of the right-wing extremists (if not their actions) came into conflict with them when the government ordered them to clamp down on illegal actions. The position of the extreme right was not helped by its inability to decide whether to threaten the SAP or infiltrate it. But the conflicts over public demonstrations almost certainly did not end covert links between some SAP members and ultra-rightists intent on wrecking negotiations or taking revenge on the ANC.

Police opened fire on white right-wing demonstrators for the first time in many decades in May 1991, when they stopped AWB supporters from driving a group of squatters off land they had settled on at Goedgevonden near Ventersdorp. Although a relatively minor incident – only four people were injured – it sent shock-waves through the Afrikaner political establishment.[41] A more serious confrontation, known as the 'Battle of Ventersdorp', took place three months later when 2,000 armed AWB supporters took on an equal number of police guarding a hall where President de Klerk was due to speak. Both sides appeared to be quick to resort to their weapons and a gun battle ensued in which 48 people were injured and an AWB supporter was shot dead. Without a hint of irony, the AWB accused the police of being too quick to resort to lethal force and deliberately shooting to kill. The police said they had been shot at first.[42] Whatever the truth, for the police it marked an important psychological break with the extreme right, even if it had to take place in the usual SAP way – the fusillade against a demonstrating crowd.

DETENTIONS AND MASS ARRESTS

Despite the unbanning of political organisations in 1990, and the lifting of the State of Emergency a few months later, detention without trial was widely used that year by the police as a way of dealing with political opposition. At least 1,671 people were detained – double the number in 1989, when the government was under pressure from hunger-strikers in detention and had been forced to release most detainees. More than 600 of these were held in Bophuthatswana under local security legislation, and a further 94 fell victim to Ciskei's security laws; most of the remainder were detained under the State of Emergency regulations, the Unrest Areas provisions and Section 29 of the Internal Security Act. Detainees continued to report being tortured: three people died in detention, and six in police custody in politically related circumstances.[43]

Amendments to the Internal Security Act in mid-1991, which restricted police rights to hold people without trial (see Chapter 2), led to a substantial reduction in the number of people detained that year. Although 1,093 were detained, many were released after only a few days.[44] It was clear that the SAP was no longer using detention without trial as a major element in the control and management of political dissent. Another weapon once widely used by the SAP and the government, the banning and restriction of political opponents, has also fallen into disuse. No individuals or organisations have been banned or restricted in South Africa since the amendments to the Internal Security Act in June 1991.

The SAP has not, however, been shy to use its powers of arrest under civil law to stop demonstrations and protests. Between July 1990 and June 1991, for instance, over 8,000 arrests were made during political protests and clashes.[45] Many of those arrested were held on minor charges and released shortly afterwards, but the number of people charged with arson and public violence increased.[46] In one incident, in April 1991, an entire village in the Ciskei was rounded up: more than 400 inhabitants of Cancele, ranging in age from eight to 82, were arrested.[47]

Over 1,500 political prisoners were released in the early 1990s through administrative measures or in terms of indemnity agreements reached between the ANC and the government, but wrangles over the definition of a political prisoner soured the process. The Human Rights Commission accused the authorities of acting in a 'confused, inconsistent and ad hoc manner'.[48] The government was happy to release police and right-wingers imprisoned for murder, including notorious offenders like Villet and Goosen (see Chapter 3), but it refused to recognise some MK combatants as political prisoners, and others who had been sentenced for public violence and other offences remained in jail. By the end of April 1992, according to the Human Rights Commission, 250 political prisoners still remained incarcerated, six of them on death row.[49] Political trials have also continued, with charges being laid for offences like murder, public violence, damage to property, illegal possession of arms and – increasingly – intimidation. During 1992, over 4,000 people were accused in 220 separate trials arising out of political conflict, although many of these arose from incidents which had taken place years earlier, and charges were withdrawn against three-quarters of them.[50]

Police have continued to torture and assault people taken into their custody. In July 1991 Amnesty International told a UN investigation:

> During the last 18 months Amnesty International has received detailed and credible reports of assault and torture, in some cases leading to deaths, of detainees in police custody, particularly at the following police stations: Welverdiend (western Transvaal), Protea (Soweto), Brixton (Johannesburg) and at various police stations in ... Bophuthatswana.[51]

Later, Amnesty published a detailed report of an investigation into reports of torture, deaths in custody and extrajudicial executions carried out by police at the Khutsong, Carletonville, Welverdiend and other police stations in the Western Transvaal in 1990 and 1991. They found that anti-apartheid activists had been assaulted and tortured and witnesses to the events had been killed. After Eugene Mbulwawa, a 15-year-old, had died from his treatment in police custody, three of the people who witnessed the police assaults on him themselves died in 'suspicious circumstances'. The SAP appointed a team of internal investigators, but people who co-operated with it were harassed by the police. Some were arrested and charged with offences which did not stand up in court.[52]

There have been several other reports of torture or summary execution, in both political and non-political cases, suggesting that the old police methods persist.[53] More than 120 detainees died in suspicious circumstances in 1992, according to Amnesty International.[54] South Africa's top pathologist, Jonathan Gluckman, told the press in July 1992 that he had evidence that over 90 per cent of deaths in police custody were caused by police assaulting, torturing and shooting people. He had written three times to De Klerk urging him to stop the SAP's 'barbarism', but when nothing had happened, and after a 19-year-old boy had been found dead 12 hours after being arrested by police, he had gone to the press. 'I get sick at heart. It goes on and on ... I don't think the government knows how to stop it,' he said, adding that he regarded most of the 200 deaths he had files on as 'straightforward murder by the police'.[55]

The government responded by trying to cast doubt on Dr Gluckman's integrity. His office was bugged and he received death threats. But he subsequently revealed further details of torture and summary execution, and similar claims were made by a world-renowned forensic expert Professor Michael Simpson.[56] Later the *Weekly Mail* newspaper published reports about a 'truth room' at the Brixton Murder and Robbery Squad headquarters in Johannesburg.[57]

In October 1992 the government agreed for the first time to allow the International Committee of the Red Cross access to detainees in police custody, although its reports and recommendations would be kept confidential. Detailing tortures carried out by police in early 1993, in evidence to the UN Commission on Human Rights, Amnesty International concluded that:

> Unless and until the government takes adequate steps to demonstrate publicly and unequivocally that all members of the security forces who are involved directly and indirectly in torture, extrajudicial executions and other human rights violations will be brought to justice the current climate of fear, frustration and high loss of life will continue.[58]

This continuing 'formal' repression has been overshadowed by the SAP's involvement in 'informal', vigilante-linked violence, which by mid-1992 had brought South Africa back again to the very brink of civil war. The dividing lines were not as clearly drawn as in the past: police vs people had turned into Inkatha vs ANC – but the baleful influence of the SAP was still strong.

Inkatha-linked Violence

THE TRANSVAAL ERUPTS

The hopes that the onset of negotiations would lead to peace were shattered in late July 1990, when violence unexpectedly exploded in the townships around Johannesburg. Perhaps not coincidentally, the killing began in earnest just at the time the ANC suspended its armed struggle. The new season of violence also coincided with attempts by Inkatha to transform itself from a bantustan-based Zulu cultural movement into a national political party, the Inkatha Freedom Party (IFP).[59] Despite the best efforts of political organisations, and the signing of a detailed National Peace Accord (see Chapter 5), the slaughter has continued, although it began to moderate towards the end of 1992. Unlike the violence in Natal, which has remained at a fairly consistent level resulting in about 100 deaths a month, the Transvaal carnage has increased dramatically at key moments in the negotiations process.

All the main monitoring groups agree that the violence peaked when the first formal agreement in the negotiations process, the Pretoria Minute, was signed; when the ANC held its first legal conference inside the country; when the National Peace Accord was signed; and when a white referendum was held in March 1992 to endorse De Klerk's commitment to negotiations.[60] In contrast, the violence tended to die off when De Klerk was launching political initiatives, such as visiting European capitals, opening parliament and sponsoring his own peace summit.[61] This has led some observers to conclude that the violence can be turned on and off, like a tap.

There are signs of planning and control behind the violence. And the evidence that the police have played an active part in this evil is strong.[62] Although the ANC is not blameless, Inkatha has been the main aggressor. The most detailed survey of the conflict, which analysed 338 incidents of violence from 22 July 1990, when the killing began, to 1 May 1991, showed that Inkatha was reported as being responsible for instigating two-thirds of them, ten times more than the ANC which was responsible for starting only 6 per cent of clashes. The SAP came in second, with the media identifying it as the aggressor in 18 per cent of cases. While the survey was based on press reports, it was careful to include the Afrikaans as well as English press, and newspapers aimed at whites as well as blacks, and found that the reports differed little when ascribing blame to any of the parties to the conflict.[63] Other detailed studies, by local as well as overseas institutions, have also concluded that Inkatha has been mainly to blame.[64]

The pattern of the killings in the Transvaal was established in the first month; with some variations it continued through 1991 and 1992 with fluctuating degrees of ferocity. The focal points of the violence are the bleak all-male hostels housing migrant workers – many of them Zulus from Natal owing at least nominal allegiance to Inkatha – which are dotted around black residential areas. Conditions there are sometimes worse than in prisons, and the men are isolated: resentment against the wider community festers, especially as the hostel dwellers often are ignored by the rest of the community and regarded as outsiders. Regimentation, communal conditions, and – until recently – ethnic exclusivity have bred conformity and a reliance on collective solidarity, although some hostel dwellers have resisted being drawn into the violence,[65] and by early 1993 some 30 hostels were participating in a cross-party peace intiative started by residents themselves.

It took active intervention to turn the hostels into bases for Inkatha attacks. Non-Inkatha supporters were forced out, and in some cases Buthelezi's supporters from Natal were bussed in. Residents of the Alexandra hostels, for instance, were chased off in March 1991 and their places taken by unemployed men brought in from KwaShange in Natal. Violence erupted not long afterwards. There have also been many reports of police instigating violence amongst hostel residents or helping to arm them. In one case, a white policeman was reported to have visited a hostel and told Zulu workers there that the ANC intended to attack them. He handed them weapons and ordered: 'Go out and attack. You're a proud Zulu nation.'[66]

With the hostels transformed into what one human rights group has termed 'fortresses of fear', the scene was set for attacks by residents on local ANC strongholds, especially squatter camps, where traditionally the ANC's writ has run strong. Areas quickly became polarised politically, being regarded as Inkatha or ANC territory. The speed with which townships where people had lived in relative peace for years were turned into battlegrounds surprised many observers, but the seeds of conflict were there waiting to be watered with blood, and since at least 1976 the SAP had realised the potential of turning sections of black communities against their compatriots, when they encouraged hostel dwellers to attack Soweto residents.[67]

Inkatha was clearly threatened by the unbanning of the ANC and the beginning of ANC–government negotiations. While Buthelezi had donned the mantle of leader of South Africa's blacks, no opinion poll put support for Inkatha nationally at higher than 10 per cent, and some rated it a lot lower. Buthelezi had also built support by claiming that he was the true inheritor of the tradition of the ANC of the 1950s, before it had turned to armed struggle. An unbanned ANC would be able to challenge Inkatha and mobilise in its constituencies; already its base had been eroded in Natal by the UDF and COSATU. Furthermore, Inkatha's standing in negotiations and any democratic elections would be limited by its narrow ethnic and regional base. Violence has ensured that Inkatha cannot be sidelined in the process leading to peace. The other political beneficiaries have been the hardliners in the Conservative Party and ultra-right groups opposed to negotiations: many of them are to be found in the SAP.[68]

An ANC national campaign at the beginning of July 1990, calling for the dissolution of the bantustans, including KwaZulu, and the disbanding of the KZP, raised the political temperature. On 22 July Inkatha held a mass rally at a stadium in Sebokeng attended by thousands of armed men. According to local residents, after the rally the Inkatha members descended on hostels accommodating migrant workers who did not support the organisation, attacking and killing many of them. The trade union federation COSATU, which had been monitoring the situation, said that the attack had been planned; getting wind of it, COSATU had informed the police, but they had failed to take any pre-emptive action. The hostel residents retaliated by expelling Inkatha supporters; Inkatha then launched further attacks in early August. The conflict spread to Soweto, Tokoza, Katlehong and other townships around Johannesburg. In just ten days in mid-August, 500 people were killed.[69]

A month after the initial explosion of the violence on the Witwatersrand, the government finally responded to ANC and other calls for action, but opted to revert to the old habits of the State of Emergency period. Instead of announcing a national emergency, the government declared 19 magisterial districts in and around Johannesburg Unrest Areas – subject, in effect, to the same regulations they had endured for the previous six years.[70] Amongst other things, police were empowered to disperse gatherings by force, detain and interrogate people, enter and search properties without a warrant, control the movement of people, and enforce curfews and other restrictions.

The clampdown was followed in September by Operation Iron Fist. Razor wire was rolled out to surround squatter camps and hostels, Casspirs equipped with machine guns went on patrol, troops were moved in and curfews imposed.[71] 'Mr Mandela wants an iron fist. We will give him an iron fist,' declared the local Police Commissioner, Major-General Erasmus. But Mandela and the ANC criticised the police for unilaterally introducing the new measures and condemned the SAP's readiness to resort to lethal force.[72] Some of the mass movements, such as the South African Youth Congress (SAYCO), called on residents to defy the restrictions.[73] There were reports that the police had jumped the gun in announcing the operation and that their gung-ho attitude had embarrassed the cabinet, some of whom had misgivings about the harshness of the measures.[74]

Operation Iron Fist, and similar repressive measures such as the imposition of curfews, failed to staunch the flow of blood. As the conflict intensified and spread to new areas, more and more evidence of police partiality towards Inkatha emerged. Police did not disarm Inkatha fighters, even when they had been involved in killings or when local people had received information that they were going to attack. The SAP explained this failure by arguing either that it did not have the resources, or that Zulu men supporting Inkatha (but apparently nobody else) had a right to carry 'cultural weapons'. Even when police promised, after residents' protests, not to allow Inkatha supporters to carry weapons to mass rallies, they failed to enforce the restrictions.[75] It was often only after months of pressure on the police that they moved into hostels from which Inkatha had carried out raids and confiscated weapons; on several occasions, the weapons were later returned. When they handed back confiscated weapons to Inkatha in Alexandra in April 1991, police said that as the items were not linked to specific crimes and were 'private possessions', they had to be returned.[76] A similar explanation justified the return of more than 2,000 clubs and spears and other weapons to Inkatha's Johannesburg headquarters in June 1992, after police for once had insisted that Inkatha supporters *en route* to a mass rally hand over their weapons.[77] After persistent ANC pressure for tighter security at hostels, De Klerk formally agreed with Nelson Mandela in September 1992 that 28 hostels at the centre of violence would be fenced and the residents disarmed, but progress continued to be slow.[78]

As the violence has progressed, both Inkatha and their opponents have become more heavily armed. AK-47s, many smuggled in from Mozambique, where they are readily available on the black market, were reportedly being cached in Inkatha-controlled hostels 'by the truckload' during 1990.[79] When the ANC provided the police with details of some of these caches, it took the force a week to act on the information – by which time those hiding the weapons had been forewarned.[80]

Given the attitude of De Klerk and his ministers to weapons carried by Inkatha supporters, it is not surprising that the SAP has been reluctant to disarm them. Zulus, De Klerk repeatedly claimed, had a 'traditional' right to carry 'cultural' weapons such as assegais and knobkerries. In fact, the carrying of such weapons has been banned in Natal and KwaZulu for 100 years, and it was only in August 1990 that the law was amended to allow such weapons to be carried in public. After wavering for months, in May 1991 the government finally buckled to public pressure and undertook to ban 'cultural' weapons – but only in Unrest Areas.[81] Later it agreed to prohibit the carrying of all weapons at public occasions (although there would be some exemptions, to be spelt out by the Goldstone Commission) but by early 1993 the police were still not enforcing the ban.[82]

Time and again, residents attacked by Inkatha have reported active police involvement in transporting the raiders and sometimes supporting them by teargassing and shooting at people resisting the onslaughts. While the SAP has dismissed these reports, they are so consistent and so numerous – and have been confirmed by so many journalists and other eyewitnesses – that their truth cannot be in doubt. In July 1991 a human rights organisation, the Independent Board of Inquiry into Informal Repression, published a report which listed dozens of cases where police had transported Inkatha fighters, escorted them on their forays, used teargas or other weapons on people they were attacking, or stood by and watched while the Inkatha men carried out their operations.[83] In one incident, in Phola Park, a squatter settlement at the centre of some of the worst conflict, a TV news crew videotaped police standing by and watching an Inkatha attack, intervening only when someone in the opposing ANC faction opened fire with an automatic weapon. The video also showed police apparently abandoning two wounded men to be killed by Inkatha supporters.[84]

Many victims of Inkatha attacks reported that white men, sometimes 'blacked up' in disguise, or wearing balaclavas, accompanied Inkatha on its raids: residents were convinced that they were police. When the Swanieville squatter camp was attacked in May 1991, victims reported that whites in camouflage uniform, and armed with guns, helped the hundreds of Inkatha supporters who razed the settlement and killed 29 people. Police in armoured vehicles reportedly transported some of the raiders and shot at people trying to escape. After the carnage, police claimed they had been taken 'completely by surprise' although the attackers marched some 10 kilometres across open ground from their hostel in Kagiso. The day before the offensive the Minister of Law and Order had declared Swanieville an Unrest Area and slapped a curfew on it, even though there was no violence at the time. The police mounted an internal inquiry into the event, which concluded that there was no evidence of police involvement.[85]

After an assault on Phola Park in September 1990, more than 100 witnesses signed affidavits saying that Inkatha supporters were led by armed whites wearing balaclavas. The whites reportedly used incendiary devices to raze shacks while Inkatha supporters armed with grenades, guns and 'cultural' weapons went on the rampage. Police who arrived in armoured vehicles failed to intervene, but the next day they raided the squatter settlement looking for weapons.[86]

While there were many massacres in the Transvaal conflict, none had as much impact as the killings carried out on the night of 17 June 1992 in Boipatong, when at least 42 people, including children and a baby, were massacred. Local people had erected barricades as a defence against Inkatha attacks, which people believed were imminent, and the police had been tipped off. SAP units entered the area that night in armoured vehicles and cleared the barricades, firing teargas and rubber bullets at comrades defending them. An hour later, Inkatha fighters from the nearby KwaMadala hostel arrived and went from house to house, breaking in and hacking and stabbing anyone they found. Some of the invaders were brought in by the police in the back of their Casspirs, residents said, and they also reported that armed white men in balaclavas had gunned down people trying to escape the attack.[87] The KwaMadala hostel was the centre of several violent incidents – in one case a police warrant-officer was alleged to have taken part in planning anti-ANC attacks, and the SADF had recruited some of its residents as part-time soldiers. Local people had repeatedly called for it to be closed down.[88]

Coming at a time when the negotiations were critically balanced and the ANC had launched a campaign of mass action, the killings received wide publicity. For once, President De Klerk was led to a public expression of regret at the deaths – but when he tried to inspect the scene of the massacre he was driven out of the township by angry residents still mourning their dead. In the process, a line of police opened fire on the unarmed protesters. Once again, police actions had precipitated a political crisis: the ANC temporarily pulled out of negotiations in protest.[89] While an official enquiry into the massacre did not find any evidence of active police involvement, it did roundly criticise the force failing to prevent the killings and to plan for an outbreak of violence, and reproached it for shoddy investigation.[90] The investigation was hampered by the fact that crucial police recordings of radio communications on the night of the massacre were erased: according to some experts who examined them, the erasure was deliberate.[91]

Attacks on commuters on trains have been a distinctive and ugly feature of the Transvaal violence. The first such incident took place shortly after the outbreak of violence on 26 July. Like most of the subsequent massacres, it was a premeditated, carefully planned operation carried out against victims selected at random and with no known political affiliation: the only possible purpose of the assault was to spread havoc and fear. Again, COSATU knew from informants beforehand of the planned attack. Through its lawyers it urgently requested the SAP to take pre-emptive action. But when a group of 300 armed Inkatha supporters gathered on the platform of Inhlanzane station in Soweto, eyewitnesses reported that police stood by passively. The Inkatha fighters then randomly attacked commuters alighting from a train, killing two and injuring many. Only then did the police move in, firing teargas which reportedly merely added to the confusion.[92]

Another train massacre took place on 23 September. While a raiding party moved systematically through a commuter train, randomly slashing, stabbing and shooting people in the ten minutes between Johannesburg's Jeppe and Benrose stations, another group waited on the platform at Benrose. When people tried to escape as the train pulled into the station, they were trapped. Twenty-six people were killed and 130 injured.[93] Pallo Jordan, the ANC's director of information, commented:

> The massacre was organised with military precision.... Now that needs a mind with some military training and someone who can plan this degree of precision.... We are implying that there must have been involvement from people who know about these things, who are trained in these matters.... Obviously it is not just a group of migrant workers from the hostels who were doing this.[94]

Jordan's suspicions were apparently borne out a year later when Felix Ndimene, a defector from the SADF's No 5 Reconnaissance Regiment, one of the Special Force units based at Phalaborwa in the North-Eastern Transvaal, gave details of how the unit had been involved in the train massacres. Ndimene said that when the ANC and other organisations were unbanned their commanding officers had told them that 'we would now have to fight a different kind of war'. His unit had been deployed in several train attacks, armed with AK-47s and pangas, and had also carried out random attacks in Natal, he said.[95]

By the beginning of 1992, the death toll on the trains had reached at least 112, with over 500 injured. Almost all the attacks took place at peak hours on the Soweto-Johannesburg line, often just before or after a breakthrough in the national peace negotiations.[96] While the police reported that 'several suspects' had been arrested, not one person had been convicted in connection with the attacks.[97] The SAP response to the massacres was roundly criticised. In June 1991 a police spokesman, Colonel Tienie Halgryn, strongly denied that the attacks could have been orchestrated by forces intent on destabilising political negotiations, but he admitted that the police themselves had no leads or theories. Later, another police spokesman claimed that it was 'too dangerous' to put police on the trains. After two Catholic priests had said that they had seen police standing by and watching as a force of about 20 men armed with pangas and axes boarded a train on 21 January 1992, the police claimed there was nothing they could do: it was not an offence to carry such weapons on trains. But at the end of that month the Commissioner at last issued a statement banning weapons on trains.[98]

Large-scale searches for weapons – which were welcomed by commuters – began only after 13 months of persistent killings. The International Commission of Jurists, which witnessed one of the occasional SADF showpiece operations at stations in March 1992, commented:

> If the Government had used soldiers at stations to search people in July 1990 after the first attacks over 100 lives would have been saved and one of the most serious manifestations of violence would have been nipped in the bud. We do not understand why the Government has failed to act.[99]

By the end of 1992, the police had made over 100 arrests in connection with train killings, but there had still been only one successful prosecution. Investigating the train killings, the Goldstone Commission linked them to the hostels, criticising the police failure to secure hostels and also noting that the failure to secure convictions meant that 'the deterrent effect of the prosecution of criminals is thus rendered ineffective'.[100]

NATAL: NO END IN SIGHT

While the savagery of the violence in the Transvaal deflected attention from Natal, the conflict between Inkatha and the ANC continued unabated there. The De Klerk government's public commitment to peace appeared to have little effect on the cycle of violence in Natal, and the behaviour of the police worsened. Communal violence reached new depths of horror in the Pietermaritzburg area only a few months after De Klerk had declared a new dawn in South Africa at the beginning of 1990. The trigger for the killing was an Inkatha rally in Durban which the government had paid for at the behest of the SAP. Major Louis Botha of the Durban Security Branch, who persuaded the government to bankroll the rally, wrote to his chief in Pretoria:

> The perception is created and enforced that virtually all blacks (and many whites, Indians and coloureds) support the ANC/MDM/UDF alliance....
>
> As a counter-measure to this one-sided propaganda and these gatherings, the Chief Minister [Buthelezi] is currently busy planning a mass Inkatha gathering at King's Park, Durban, on 1990-03-25....
>
> This Region [of the SAP] feels that it is vitally important that we make a financial contribution.... It is of cardinal importance that enough people be at King's Park to support the Chief Minister and show everyone that he does have a strong base.[101]

When the Inkatha supporters returned from the rally (which was not as well attended as hoped), they immediately came into conflict with local comrades.

In what became known as the Seven Days' War, Inkatha warrior parties up to 2,000 strong invaded non-Inkatha areas around Pietermaritzburg, burning, looting and killing. Police showed their usual bias, and reportedly helped in some of the attacks. At least 80 people were killed and thousands fled from their homes. No one was prosecuted.[102]

The conflict also spread to other areas of Natal. Bruntville, the township serving the white town of Mooi River, was torn apart during 1991. Community leaders, through their lawyers, repeatedly made urgent representations to the government to ensure the police helped to keep the peace, but the force did little to disarm the Inkatha supporters and failed to stop their attacks. Instead it concentrated its efforts on ANC supporters, allegedly torturing some of them at the local police station with hoods and electrical equipment.[103] The events in Mooi River were investigated by a commission set up in terms of the National Peace Accord (see Chapter 5), chaired by Justice Goldstone who had earlier investigated the Sebokeng massacre. Goldstone found that the police had failed to plan for the escalation of violence, or to increase the number of police available; on the advice of government officials, they had decided not to impound 'cultural' weapons. The commission also condemned the strong-arm police tactics used against township residents, which included night raids without search warrants. It concluded that the police were biased towards Inkatha.[104]

The De Klerk regime did little to inhibit the pro-Inkatha activities of the KwaZulu Police, who played a more active part in spreading the violence during the period in which he claimed he was depoliticising the police. In KwaMakutha, scene of earlier conflict, residents were granted a Supreme Court injunction in 1990 restraining local KZP members from assaulting and threatening them, following a number of attacks, but this did not stop the harassment. Such was the severity of the KZP onslaught that two local SAP members supported the application. One, a sergeant, said:

> The KZP in KwaMakutha have shown themselves to be a completely partial force who seem to be incapable of maintaining law and order.... Through their conduct in attacking and shooting residents at random and for no apparent reason, they have shown themselves to be highly reckless and a real danger to the livelihood and well-being of local residents.[105]

Then, in February 1992, the KZP escorted armed Inkatha supporters who attacked ANC-supporting residents of the hostel and township of Esikhawini on Natal's north coast. Only when hostel residents retaliated did the security forces intervene, and according to an eyewitness joined the Inkatha fighters in shooting at the hostel dwellers. The Inkatha supporters then turned their attention on the township, looting and burning homes, while the police moved into the hostel, rounding up 200 of the residents. They did not arrest any of the

Inkatha members who carried out the assault.[106] A similar attack took place a few weeks later when the KZP assisted hundreds of Inkatha supporters in an attack on the so-called Uganda squatter settlement near Umlazi outside Durban. Eighteen people, most of them women and children, were massacred.[107]

After a visit to South Africa in September 1990, the International Commission of Jurists concluded that 'the KwaZulu police are perceived to be partial by the vast majority of the population.... In some places their conduct has been violent and cruel.' When the ICJ returned again in March 1992, they found that 'the misconduct of the KwaZulu police has become more blatant since we were last in Natal. The massacre at the Uganda squatter camp says it all.'[108] They called for policing in KwaZulu/Natal to be brought under unified command.

As if the failure to prosecute Inkatha and KZP members was not enough to inflame the situation, the government used the 1991 amnesty for political prisoners to release some of the few who had been imprisoned. An outcry greeted the news that Khetani Richard Shange, an Inkatha member and KZP detective, described by a judge as a 'beast in policeman's clothing' had been freed after serving only nine months of a 27-year sentence for murderous attacks on ANC supporters. It was disclosed that the government had decided at ministerial level only a month after he had been sentenced to treat him as a political prisoner and release him. Minister of Correctional Services Adriaan Vlok later conceded that he did not qualify as a political prisoner, and claimed he had been released as a result of a computer error.[109]

Where the bloodletting has died down in Natal, as it has in some areas, the reduction in conflict has not usually been the result of effective policing: the violence has simply burnt itself out and the communities had been so thoroughly polarised that there has been little scope left for territorial contest. But in a few areas the SAP has broken its mould and helped in the process of establishing local Inkatha–ANC peace accords (see Chapter 5).

The 'Third Force'

The Harms Commission, appointed by De Klerk to investigate the evidence that the police and defence force were involved in covert assassination squads (Chapter 3), failed to settle the issue. It was not only that the commission's report was deficient, or that the De Klerk government displayed a paralysis of will in cleaning up its security forces. Assassinations, sophisticated bombings, vehicles with armed gunmen stalking the townships, armed white men in balaclavas involved in the Inkatha killings – all these were taken as evidence that official or semi-official hit squads in the security forces continued their operations. The mysterious role of whites in fomenting the violence led Nelson Mandela and other ANC leaders to raise the spectre of a 'third force'.[110]

The conflict in the Transvaal townships was repeatedly fuelled by groups of armed men, white as well as black, carrying out random killings. Sometimes the assassins travelled in vehicles, some of which had false number plates. In September 1990, for example, four gunmen in a white mini-bus randomly fired on pedestrians in central Johannesburg.[111] Shortly before the incident, three whites armed with AK-47 automatic rifles had been discovered by ambulancemen driving around Soweto in a vehicle disguised as an ambulance, with false number plates. When questioned, they claimed they were acting under the instructions of a senior police officer.[112] In Tokoza in September 1991, at the funeral of civic leader Sam Ntuli, himself assassinated, gunmen in six vehicles mounted a coordinated attack on mourners in which at least 18 people were killed.[113] 'It is our considered opinion that these killers are professionals, forming part of a squad acting on instruction,' the ANC said in a statement. A few weeks earlier, another coordinated attack by gunmen on a crowd of marchers – this time Inkatha supporters – had taken place in neighbouring Katlehong. Observers suggested it pointed to a Machiavellian attempt to stir up animosities between the two organisations.[114]

The random killings were accompanied by carefully targeted assassinations of ANC and community leaders – often those, like Sam Ntuli, who were involved in peace negotiations. These increased dramatically under the De Klerk government. The Human Rights Commission, which carefully monitors political killings, published a list of 119 people apparently assassinated between January 1990 and April 1992. The organisation commented:

> during the era of Total Strategy, from 1985 to 1989 ... HRC records reflect 45 assassinations, five disappearances and 160 attempted assassinations of anti-apartheid activists.
>
> However even these startling figures pale into relative insignificance against the record of the nineties, the era of reform/destabilisation. During the short 28 months from January 1990 to April 1992, HRC records show a total of 119 political assassinations, over five times the rate of such murders during the emergency years. Nor is there any reason to believe that the origin of these assassinations, or at least a great preponderance of them, was any different from that in the eighties. Over 100 of these victims are clearly identifiable as belonging to the anti-apartheid camp....[115]

In March 1991 the ANC reported that its activists in Alexandra were being tailed and threatened by gunmen. 'We have to ask the question how this can take place in a township that Pretoria has declared an Unrest Area and saturated with police and soldiers,' said Popo Molefe, an ANC leader living in Alexandra.[116] Returning exiles and other ANC officials reported that they were being harassed and threatened, and for their safety many were obliged to move around constantly, seldom sleeping in the same house twice.[117]

A prominent victim of assassination was Chief Mhlabunzima Maphumulo, former president of the Congress of Traditional Leaders, an ANC-aligned chiefs' organisation, who was active in trying to make peace between Inkatha and the ANC in Natal. Sipho Madlala, an ex-member of the SADF's intelligence section, confessed that he had been part of a joint police-army hit squad which had carried out the murder in February 1991.[118] The local Security Branch had provided the 9 mm revolvers for the killing and each of the hit squad members had received a R5,000 bounty, he said.[119] But Madlala's evidence was rejected by a magistrate at the inquest into Chief Maphumulo's death, and he concluded that his death had been brought about by 'persons unknown'.[120]

Nevertheless, the evidence pointing to continued security police involvement in assassinations is strong. The same security policeman identified by Madlala as authorising Chief Maphumulo's death had bought 24 revolvers in a Pietermaritzburg gun shop a couple of years earlier and some of the weapons were later used in political killings carried out by Inkatha. Toti Zulu, a bodyguard of an Inkatha politician, used one of them to gun down the Reverend Victor Afrikander, a priest working for peace between the warring parties.[121]

Some killings were linked to the hundreds of Inkatha members who had been trained by the SADF in the Caprivi Strip in Namibia and at a secret base in Northern Natal (see previous chapter) and who had been issued with false KZP identifications and sent to various KwaZulu police stations. The police strenuously denied that the trained men were involved with hit squads, but some of them were later arrested on murder charges.[122] A few even turned up in faraway Wesselton, near Ermelo in the Northern Transvaal, where they helped a local gang, the Black Cats, in a murderous campaign against the ANC. The Black Cats were not the only gang that, apparently under police tutelage, turned their attention from ordinary crime to attacks on ANC activists. In Tembisa, for instance, local ANC officials complained that a gang called the Toasters had killed seven supporters of the movement.[123]

Some assassinations, using sophisticated explosive devices, had all the characteristics of those carried out by police and army hit squads. Michael Lapsley, an Anglican priest living in Zimbabwe and a known ANC supporter, was maimed by a parcel bomb sent to him shortly after De Klerk declared his season of peace.[124] Nick Cruise, a Durban computer consultant working for an agency which the Security Branch claimed had links with the ANC, was blown up by a bomb in a computer sent to him from Johannesburg in October 1991. In a bizarre sequel to the killing, two right-wingers were arrested by the police, but jumped bail to Britain and claimed that the Security Branch had carried out the bombing and were intent on framing them. Their claims might have been dismissed, but other factors unearthed in a British TV investigation pointed to security force involvement.[125]

Tiny but deadly explosives hidden in the headset of a personal stereo sent through the mail to Bheki Mlangeni, a Johannesburg lawyer, killed him instantly in February 1991. Mlangeni had been investigating the security police's Vlakplaas operations and was in close contact with Dirk Coetzee – in fact, the parcel was destined for Coetzee, then staying in Zambia, but had been returned to Mlangeni when Coetzee failed to pick it up, as Mlangeni's business address had been written on the back.[126]

In 1992, reporters from the *Weekly Mail*, the newspaper which had earlier exposed the Security Branch's role in funding Inkatha, unearthed a secret network of police bases covering the whole country, set up in 1988 by the Security Branch and then transferred to the Crime Intelligence Service. In the Southern Transvaal region, the reporters found that the network involved at least four different bases, usually private houses, and more than 30 vehicles. The properties and vehicles were fraudulently registered and dummy companies had been set up to cover tracks. The SAP tried to stop the *Mail* publishing the story and claimed that it was a legitimate operation aimed at tracking down illegal weapons. The newspaper found two men who claimed to have been abducted by the police, taken to one or another of the secret bases and pressurised to carry out covert operations, including assassinating ANC leaders,[127] although the Goldstone Commission later found no truth in their allegations.[128]

The Goldstone Commission did, however, confirm the existence of a secret operational centre run by Military Intelligence and known as the Directorate of Covert Collections. One of its projects was a plan to enmesh ex-Umkhonto we Sizwe members in criminal activities, including prostitution and drug-dealing. The task force, which had access to the SAP's computer records, was headed by Ferdi Barnard, a former policeman who had been sentenced to 20 years imprisonment for murder in 1984, but had been released four years later and recruited into the SADF's Civil Cooperation Bureau. A prime suspect in the assassination of anti-apartheid activist David Webster (although the inquest found that there was insufficient evidence to identify the killer) Barnard was only one of at least 48 members of the operational centre.[129]

The search to identify units in the security structures which might be operating their own agendas of destabilisation has pointed to Military Intelligence, the Reconnaissance Commandos of the SADF and to a lesser extent the Security Branch (Crime Intelligence Service) of the SAP. But it would be a mistake to pin the label on one or two units alone. The events of the 1990s have shown that there are individuals and groups within and without the security forces with both the inclination and the capacity to carry out political assassinations, random violence and 'dirty tricks'. Some of these activities enjoy official approval – although it is not clear how high up the authorisation goes. After the Boipatong massacre in June 1992, the ANC stopped giving President de Klerk the benefit of the doubt. Even if he did not authorise the covert activities, argued Mandela, they suited his political purposes. In a statement issued when the ANC called a halt to negotiations, it declared that the De Klerk regime was pursuing a strategy 'which embraces negotiations, together with systematic covert actions, including murder, involving its security forces and surrogates'.[130]

Fighting Crime

When De Klerk promised that under his premiership the police would no longer have a political role, he said they would instead take up the neglected battle against crime. But crime has increased dramatically in the 1990s, even if many of the reasons for this lie outside the remit of the police. An increase in crime, or least in recorded offences, appears to be an ineluctable feature of many societies in the late twentieth century. But the rise of crime in South Africa is at least in part due to apartheid and its policing system. It is also, as the SAP is the first to argue, partly a by-product of political struggles and counter-struggles which have destroyed local networks of social control.

Crime statistics are notoriously unreliable, but they do indicate that South Africa is one of the most violent, crime-ridden countries in the world, and that the problem is growing. Claimed police clear-up rates for solving reported crimes are not too bad by world standards, although they have showed a steady decline to an overall rate of 53 per cent in 1990 (with a slight improvement in the first few months of 1992).[131] But these statistics are misleading because the majority of crimes, especially in black areas, are not reported. The Commonwealth Observer Mission which visited South Africa in 1992–3 reported that its members 'were told frequently by the residents of townships that, because of widespread distrust of the SAP, even the most heinous crimes were often not reported.'[132] Nevertheless, reported statistics for more serious crimes, such as rape, murder and assault, have increased fairly rapidly since the mid-1980s, although the increase is not as significant as the somewhat hysterical reaction of many white South Africans would suggest – many countries, such as Britain, have faced similar rates of increase in the 1980s and 1990s. Some of the increases, for example the 28 per cent rise in murders between 1989 and 1990, must also be attributable to political rather than criminal violence, although the dividing line between the two is increasingly difficult to discern.

Personal insecurity is a fact of life in South Africa, especially in the townships. The increases in reported offences under De Klerk's rule have come on top of an already high rate of crime. The situation was not helped by the release in 1990 and 1991 of more than 60,000 prisoners in a sweeping government amnesty; many of those released undoubtedly returned to crime. The releases were carried out in the name of the agreement with the ANC to free political prisoners: three-quarters of all convicts were freed before the expiry of their sentences. The Human Rights Commission accused the government of releasing prisoners to try to blur the distinction between criminal and political offenders;[133] pressure on the grossly overcrowded prisons provided another motive.

The underlying cause of the acute problems of violence and crime in South Africa is of course apartheid. The system debased the law and its institutions through racist legislation like the pass laws. Migrant labour destroyed families and forced men to live in single-sex hostels isolated from the rest of the community; millions of South Africans were denied opportunities to improve their lives solely on the grounds of the colour of their skin. Apartheid also condemned the vast majority of South Africa's population to poverty, to life in townships denied the entertainments and facilities of a modern city, and to second-rate jobs where many were treated little better than chattels.

Formal apartheid has ended, but for most South Africans living conditions remain the same, and the legacy of decades of malevolent social engineering will endure. Life is harder than before for many: in the second half of the 1980s and into the 1990s population growth has outstripped economic growth and per capita GDP has declined. At least half the workforce is unemployed – with virtually no welfare system, crime is often the only alternative for the unemployed. Since 1976 the schooling system has been riven by almost continuous conflict and boycotts have become endemic. Tens of thousands of young people abandoned – or were forced out of – the education system. Many of them sacrificed their education and potential careers in the interests of the struggle, but now they are a 'lost generation', with little prospect of employment. The average age of a person committing in an offence in South Africa in 1990 was 17, down from 22 two years earlier.[134]

Poverty itself does not necessarily induce crime, although it helps: relative deprivation and crises in expectations are more potent factors. In South Africa in the 1990s, the promises of an end to apartheid and the anticipation of a black-majority government have raised expectations of access to the honey-pots for millions of people, especially youngsters. Their expectations are unlikely to be met, and crime provides the temptation of a quick fix.

The problems induced by poverty and alienation from the structures of authority are reinforced by a culture of violence. The structural violence of apartheid and the harshness of policing resonate in the violence of the liberation movement. The armed struggle – although the ANC has suspended it – enjoys widespread legitimacy: for many people the first response to state violence is revolutionary violence. In a memorandum to President de Klerk in May 1992, the South African Council of Churches wrote:

> Our country has never known real peace since the introduction of white minority rule culminating in the system of apartheid.
>
> Besides the violence inherent in the structural injustices of apartheid, and the consequent poor socio-economic infrastructure for black communities emanating from this, political resistance and the resultant State repression have left a legacy of a society steeped in a political culture of violence. Violence is viewed as a means of achieving political goals. [135]

While the ANC has been responsible and cautious in its sponsorship of violence as a political strategy – to a fault, some South Africans think – there is no doubt that many people have learnt the lesson that force must be met with force. The actions of Inkatha have only sharpened this perception. MK units on the ground have at times responded less to the counsel of their leadership than the emotions of their grassroots supporters. The desire for revenge and the instant solution of violence, given the failure of the policing and justice systems, is strong.

But perhaps the most significant factor behind the rise of violent crime has been the collapse – or destruction – of authority. While the revolutionaries attempted to annihilate the Uncle Toms and the structures of apartheid administration, the police removed from society (as they liked to put it) community leaders who enjoyed widespread support, through detentions, bannings, trials and assassinations. Under De Klerk, anti-apartheid leaders have still been harassed, and the threat from vigilantes and Inkatha has prevented them from playing their full leadership role. The active encouragement given to vigilantes and to some street gangs by the police has further deepened the crisis. The result has been a breakdown of authority, augmented by the collapse of the education system and the weakened influence of family, religious and other traditional institutions since young people took matters into their own hands in 1976.

While the police have repeatedly promised to crack the problem of crime, they have manifestly failed to do so. Historically, increases in the resources available to the SAP have had little effect on the rate of crime – no doubt because most of the new resources have been earmarked for political purposes[136] – and the 1990s have been no different. The promises of 'community policing' made by top police officials and government ministers have not been translated into action. Foot patrols have been re-instituted in central parts of some cities (they were phased out in the early 1970s) and 'flying squad' services to black townships have been improved.[137] But the police have continued to show a visceral preference for paramilitary style solutions to the problem – the crime sweeps coordinated with the army are a classic example.

The SAP's anti-crime campaigns have focused mainly on the problem of illegal weapons, especially those held by the ANC. When the ANC suspended its armed struggle it envisaged that it would reach agreements with the government for the control of its arms caches in the country. But in 1991 the Minister of Law and Order unilaterally introduced a system of cash rewards for information about weapons, and the SAP set up special units, composed partly of ex-Security Branch members, responsible for tracking down unlicensed firearms.[138] The proliferation of weapons was also used as the reason for the proposed strengthening of detention without trial in mid-1992 (see Chapter 2). That the ANC was the principal target of these moves was made clear in repeated verbal swipes by police and government spokesmen. Explaining new anti-crime measures at the end of 1990, for example, the SAP's spokesperson, Captain Craig Kotze, declared that clamping down on illegal weapons was a major priority. 'Certain organisations have been stockpiling these weapons for a long time, which is why they proliferate at such an incredible rate in the townships,' he said.[139] (By 1993, however, the focus had shifted to the PAC, which was accused of random attacks on whites.)[140]

The police were also accused of political bias – and ineptitude – in tackling a 'taxi war' which erupted in Cape Town. A long-running conflict between two associations vying for control of the lucrative minibus routes between the city centre and outlying townships and squatter areas flared into violence in 1991. One of the associations was identified with the ANC, and the police were repeatedly accused of intervening in support of the rival organisation. They were said to be acting like a 'third force' and deliberately prolonging the conflict by colluding in violent attacks and the assassination of community leaders attempting to mediate in the conflict.[141] By the beginning of 1992, monitoring groups in Cape Town had collected 83 affidavits testifying to police complicity or inaction in attacks on supporters of the ANC-aligned taxi association.[142] According to a local ANC spokesperson, Willie Hofmeyr:

> The police appear unwilling to intervene and stop attacks on communities and are seen by the community as supporting one side in the taxi war.... Until the SAP starts to play an impartial role in the present conflict, there is little hope of peace.[143]

In the 1990s, the dividing lines between politics and crime have become even more blurred than in previous decades. And the police appear to be applying much the same methods they have used in the past. As the Johannesburg newspaper *Business Day* commented in June 1992 when the government proposed new measures to restrict civil liberties:

> Now the ANC is unbanned [repressive] powers become essential to combat a crime wave.... The method stays the same, but where it used to be subversives who had no civil rights, now it is criminals. It is a slippery slope....[144]

This slipperly slope led to the remobilisation of military reserves for policing and internal security duties in March 1993, when President de Klerk responded to a series of apparently random attacks on whites by announcing a military call-up and declaring himself in favour of lifting the moratorium on the death penalty, a move subsequently endorsed by the tricameral parliament.[145]

Notes

1 HRC 1992, p 18.
2 *Guardian* 16.6.92.
3 *Business Day* 20.1.93.
4 Jeffery 1991, pp 120–1.
5 Jeffery 1991, p 33.
6 Author's survey of the press.
7 HRC 1991, p 15.
8 Simpson *et al.* 1991, p 8.
9 *Weekly Mail* 25.5.90, 1.6.90, 15.6.90, 7.9.90.
10 *Report of the Commission of Enquiry into the Incidents in Sebokeng, Boipatong, Lekoa, Sharpeville and Evaton; Weekly Mail* 7.9.90.
11 *Sunday Star* 11.11.90.
12 *Daily News* 23.3.91; *Sunday Star* 24.3.91.
13 *Sunday Star* 5.8.90.
14 *New Nation* 10.8.90; *Daily Telegraph* 11.8.90.
15 *Cape Times* 20.4.90; *Star* 20.4.90.
16 *Independent* 21.5.90.
17 *BBC Summary of World Broadcasts* 17.5.90; *Weekly Mail* 18.5.90.
18 *Daily Dispatch* 20.12.90.
19 *Daily News* 7.12.90; *Eastern Province Herald* 31.12.90.
20 HRC 1992, p 18.
21 *Human Rights Commission Special Report SR-11*, August 1991.
22 For example police used shotguns and rubber bullets to disperse a crowd of 6,000 marching on parliament, *Weekly Mail* 3.7.92.
23 *Independent* 25.3.91; *Sowetan* 26.3.91.
24 Cited in Jeffery 1991, p 101.
25 Star 27.3.92; *Weekly Mail* 27.3.92.
26 *Weekly Mail* 17.7.92.
27 Jeffery 1991, p 128.
28 *Weekly Mail* 17.7.92.
29 *Daily Dispatch* 18.5. 90; *Eastern Province Herald* 5.6.90.
30 *SouthScan* 27.4.90.
31 *SouthScan* 18.1.91.
32 *New Nation* 15.2.91.
33 *Star* 11.2.91.
34 *BBC Summary of World Broadcasts* 2.3.92.
35 *City Press* 9.12.90; *Focus* no 92, January/February 1991, p 7 Amnesty International 1992a, pp 28–9.
36 Amnesty International 1991, p 3.
37 HRC 1991, p 4.
38 *Africa Watch* 1991b.

39 *Independent* 14.9.92; *SouthScan* 11.9.92.
40 *SouthScan* 6.11.92; 19.2.93.
41 *Independent* 12.5.91.
42 Jeffery 1991, pp 39–40.
43 HRC 1991, pp 3–4.
44 HRC 1992, p 5.
45 *Human Rights Commission Special Report SR-11*, August 1991.
46 *BBC Summary of World Broadcasts* 29.1.91.
47 *Daily Dispatch* 7.5.91.
48 *Southern Africa Church News* 12.6.91.
49 *Human Rights Update*, December 1992, pp 12, 17.
50 *Human Rights Update*, December 1992, p 12.
51 Amnesty International 1991, pp 2-3.
52 Amnesty International 1992b, p 88; *Saturday Star* 6.7.91.
53 *Focus* no 91, November/December 1990, p 4; Fernandez 1991.
54 Amnesty International 1993, p. 2.
55 *Guardian* 27.7.92; *Independent* 27.7.92.
56 *Weekly Mail* 21.8.92.
57 *Weekly Mail* 11.12.92.
58 Amnesty International 1993, p. 4.
59 Consultative Business Movement 1991, p 2.
60 Amnesty International 1992b, p 3.
61 *Human Rights Commission Special Report SR-11*, August 1991, p. 5.
62 See for example Amnesty International 1992a.
63 Case 1991.
64 For example, Africa Watch 1991, Amnesty International 1992b ICJ 1992.
65 Institute of Criminology 1991; ICJ 1992; Simpson *et al.* 1991; Independent Board 1992b; Collin 1992.
66 Case 1992, p 2; Independent Board 1992b, p 24.
67 Brooks & Brickhill 1980, pp 219–22.
68 Institute of Criminology 1991, p 8; Simpson *et al.* 1991, p 17–9.
69 Africa Watch 1991a, pp 60–2; *Focus* no 90, September/October 1990, p 3; *Financial Times* 27.7.90; *New Nation* 24.8.90.
70 *Government Gazette* 24.8.90.
71 *City Press* 16.9.90.
72 *Sunday Telegraph* 16.9.90.
73 *Guardian* 26.9.90.
74 *Guardian* 20.9.90.
75 *Star* 7.5.91.
76 *Star* 7.5.91.
77 *Independent* 17.6.92.
78 *SouthScan* 2.10.92, 30.10.92.
79 *Weekly Mail* 28.9.90.
80 *SouthScan* 10.5.91.
81 *Daily News* 21.5.91.
82 Commonwealth Observer Mission 1993, p. 63.
83 IBIIR 1991.
84 *Weekly Mail* 14.12.90.
85 *Star* 13.5.91; Amnesty International 1992b, pp 50–2.
86 Amnesty International 1992b, pp 48–50.
87 *Independent* 19.6.92; *Weekly Mail* 26.6.92.
88 *Weekly Mail* 19.6.92.
89 *Independent* 21.6.91.

90 *New Nation* 24.7.92.
91 *Guardian* 4.11.92.
92 *Guardian* 24.7.90; *Telegraph* 24.7.90; Africa Watch 1991a.
93 *Financial Times* 14.9.91; *Observer* 16.9.90.
94 *BBC Summary of World Broadcasts* 17.9.90.
95 *New Nation* 19.7.91.
96 *Argus* 19.2.92; Independent Board 1992a, p 18.
97 *Evening Post* 23.1.92.
98 Independent Board 1992a.
99 ICJ 1992, p 17.
100 Commonwealth Observer Mission 1993, p 18.
101 Cited in *Weekly Mail* 19.7.90 – translation from the Afrikaans by the author.
102 Amnesty International 1992b, pp 43–6; Sunday Times 24.6.91.
103 Amnesty International 1992b, pp 57–9.
104 *Report to the Commission of Inquiry Regarding the Prevention of Public Violence from the Committee Established to Inquire into the Events at Mooi River on 3 and 4 December 1991.*
105 *Weekly Mail* 20.4.90; Africa Watch 1991, pp 43–4.
106 *Amnesty International Urgent Action*, 76/92.
107 Amnesty International 1992a, pp 63–74.
108 ICJ 1992, p 13.
109 *Star* 7.5.92.
110 *Vrye Weekblad* 21.9.90.
111 *Sowetan* 21.9.90.
112 *New Nation* 14.9.90; *Sunday Star* 16.9.90.
113 *Weekly Mail* 11.10.91.
114 *Guardian* 9.10.91.
115 HRC Press Statement and Briefing on Political Assassination in the Nineties, 21.5.92.
116 *Sunday Star* 24.3.91.
117 *Weekly Mail* 8.5.92.
118 *Observer* 5.5.91.
119 *City Press* 5.5.91.
120 *BBC Summary of World Broadcasts* 18.3.92.
121 *War on Peace*, BBC-TV 2, 10.3.92.
122 *Weekly Mail* 16.4.92; *Sunday Star* 19.4.92.
123 *Human Rights Update*, vol 5, no 4, April 1992.
124 Amnesty International 1992a, p 22.
125 *War on Peace*, BBC-TV 2, 10.3.92.
126 Amnesty International 1992a, pp 20–1.
127 *Weekly Mail* 8.5.92, 15.5.92.
128 *Weekly Mail* 30.10.92.
129 Press Statement by the Honourable Mr Justice RJ Goldstone 16.11.92; *Times* 17.11.92; *Business Day* 25.1.93.
130 *Independent* 24.6.92.
131 Annual Report of the Commissioner of the SAP, 1990, p 33; *Weekly Mail* 17.7.92.
132 Commonwealth Observer Mission 1993, p 13.
133 *Business Day* 19.5.92.
134 Simpson *et al* 1990, p 27.
135 *Memorandum: Meeting of the SACC Church Leaders Delegation with the State President and his Delegation*, 22.5.92.
136 *Resister*, no 35, December/January 1985, p 16.
137 *Servamus* February 1991, p 15.
138 *Cape Times* 4.1.91.

139 BBC Summary of World Broadcasts 31.12.90.
140 *Guardian* 25.3.93.
141 Amnesty International 1992a, pp 75-81; Collin 1992.
142 *Weekly Mail* 21.2.92.
143 BBC Summary of World Broadcasts 18.2.92.
144 *Business Day* 17.6.92.
145 *Guardian* 25.3.93.

THE POLICE IN A
NEW SOUTH AFRICA

White minority rule in South Africa will almost certainly end in the 1990s, in form if not entirely in practice. The first few years of the decade have seen the beginning of this transition: by mid-1993, although disagreements remained, negotiations had resulted in broad agreement on the installation of a multi-party Transitional Executive Council (TEC) to prepare the ground for non-racial elections to a Constitution-Making Body, which would also become South Africa's first democratically elected legislature.

The police have a crucial role to play in this transformation – they are essential to its success although they also threaten it. And the SAP itself needs to be transformed if it is to flourish as an institution in a new South Africa: even a change of name, or the formal inauguration of a new body drawn from the SAP, the bantustan forces and the ANC, will not alter the fact that the basis of any new police service will be the institutions and personnel of the SAP.

The ANC has begun to formulate recommendations for revamping the police. In this it has drawn on the work of individuals and organisations researching ways of changing the SAP – a difficult task given the habitual secretiveness of the force. Different views about the best ways forward are held by the various parties in South Africa, and it is clear that no one step alone will provide a breakthrough. Action is needed on many fronts: within the police force, in the external environment in which they operate, and in communities themselves. Democrats broadly agree that the main aim is to restore public confidence and involvement in policing so that a genuine partnership between police and community can emerge, in which consensus rather than coercion is the norm. This is no mean task, and, given the cleavages in South African society, the very concept of community accountability is problematic.[1] The different communities in South Africa have radically divergent expectations of the SAP. It is clearly asking a lot for the same police force to be accepted in a right-wing white suburb where the residents regard blacks as a threat, and a neighbouring black squatter settlement ravaged by years of conflict which has been mobilised politically against the government. But the fundamental problem, which the SAP admits, is that the police do not enjoy the confidence of the majority of South Africans.

Ultimately, public confidence in the police is dependent on public support for the government which controls them, a condition which can be satisfied only through political transformation. Part of this process is the establishment of democratic control over the police, and the extension of community involvement and responsibility for policing.

Alongside this political process, steps which would facilitate trust in the police have been identified by researchers and opposition parties in South Africa. Step one is greater openness. The habit of secrecy so deeply ingrained in the SAP inevitably leads its critics to draw the worst conclusions – for their own good, the police need to learn to explain their actions to the media and to the public at large. This will entail public codes of conduct, the proper investigation of police delicts and misdemeanours (preferably by an external authority), an end to covert operations, full disclosure of expenditure, structures and operations, and a willingness to engage with the press.

It is important, too, that new laws, rules and regulations, and codes of conduct are drawn up and enforced. Some progress has already been made in this regard through the adoption of an enlightened code of conduct, the removal of some of the more draconian laws which gave police such extensive powers and scope for deviance, and agreement that a Bill of Rights, guaranteeing freedom from arbitrary action by the state, will be entrenched in a new South Africa. Some regulations – such as those governing detainees – have also been improved. However, the problem with all such initiatives is to make them stick when and where it matters: with police officers in their day-to-day work.

No reform of the police force is likely to be effective without improvements in the criminal justice system, in particular the prosecution process which allows police undue influence over the prosecution, and in which magistrates and prosecutors enjoy a close professional relationship and follow a similar career progression. A situation in which the police not only arrest and investigate, but actually construct the case, is clearly undesirable: the introduction of an independent prosecution service at an earlier stage would lead to greater objectivity and provide some supervision. Close attention also needs to be paid to the prisons, which all criminologists now recognise as a major factor in the reproduction of crime. These issues have been acknowledged by the ANC:

> There will be no respect for the institutions that enforce law and order unless the people respect the law. This they will do if the laws are just and if they participate both in their making and enforcement. A just criminal justice system will enhance respect for the courts and obedience to the law.
>
> ... Apartheid's overcrowded and authoritarian jails are crime factories which dehumanise their inmates, feeding a culture of violence and despair.... The ANC

proposes programmes that promote reparation and compensation to the victims and service to the community in place of incarceration. The ANC is against any inhumane and cruel punishment.[2]

The biggest challenge in transforming the police is to change the culture of the force itself through new methods of formal training, civilian input, re-education, a new style of management and the inculcation of democratic attitudes. To restore public confidence, it is essential that some of the most notorious units are disbanded, hard-line commanders are replaced and those involved in political killings are brought to book. In general the police need to adopt a more professional, even-handed and caring approach to the public. The police should reflect the composition of the society they serve: in other words, more black police and women officers, especially in positions of responsibility.[3] Perhaps even more importantly, they need to respond to the needs of society: today many blacks do not even bother to report crime because there is no expectation of an effective police response – there is a widespread belief, rooted in experience, that police take only crimes against whites seriously. So, too, with women. Many studies have shown that the police are incapable and insensitive when it comes to dealing with crimes against women, especially domestic violence and rape.[4] If the police are genuinely to provide a service to society as a whole then a reorientation of priorities and skills will be needed.

Beyond reforms to the police force as an institution, and the environment in which it works, lies the challenge of changing community attitudes and drawing communities into responsibility for social ordering and policing.

The SAP's Strategic Plan

From many of their statements, and the steps they have taken to ameliorate some of the worst aspects of policing, it is evident that many senior policemen have recognised the imperative for change. The force as a whole has done some soul-searching and is now formally committed to a different way of operating, although often, as we have seen, this has not been translated into practice. Aspects of these changes, notably the SAP's partially improved approach to crowd control and the management of political opposition, and the restructuring of the force, have been discussed in previous chapters. The overall framework within which these changes are taking place is the SAP's Strategic Plan, finalised in outline in November 1991.

The Strategic Plan is the SAP's response to the onset of negotiations and the prospect of majority rule: it was motivated by concern over the survival and credibility of the force and is meant to direct change in the SAP. As an internal briefing on 'The Role of the South African Police in a Changing South Africa' puts it:

it is clear that the South African Police finds itself almost daily within a changing South Africa. In order to adjust in time to these changes which take place in its external environment, but particularly on the political level, the South African Police was obliged and prepared to introspectively reassess its own abilities, strategies and objectives. Strategic planning is the only way in which to bring about the repositioning and re-orientation which is necessary to enable the South African Police to effectively strive towards its mission in a politically changing South Africa.[5]

While the plan includes a recognition that 'the SAP is in the process of transformation from a closed system to an open system',[6] it was drawn up without any significant external input in the evaluation and planning process, and has not been publicised: the old habits of secrecy die hard. Despite the lack of publicity, the bones of the plan are known. In general, it is long on organisational theory – often of a pseudo-philosophical nature – and short on detail. The guiding principle of the plan is that the SAP should become a service organisation. An official document described as 'the theory of the philosophy of the SAP of the future' asserts that:

A new paradigm (framework of thinking, rules and contents of life, guideline for philosophy of life) must be developed. The future cannot be understood, explained and anticipated from the present frameworks any more. The jump to a new paradigm is huge, therefore management and the employee must undergo a mind shift.[7]

The document goes on to argue that the SAP must become a 'learning organisation' and goes on to make vague assertions along the lines of 'the future is increasingly complex, unsure and unpredictable' and 'organisational culture makes empowerment possible'. Another document, dealing with the environment in which the SAP operates, is more specific and endorses the concept of community policing more emphatically than previous SAP publications. It also recognises that the SAP is not alone responsible for policing:

Policing is a wide concept and includes those actions which are undertaken by other organisations such as security companies, Self Defence Units, private armies and the like. The Police is an institution which has been called into being by law and policing is merely a function. This function can also be undertaken by persons and bodies other than the SAP and can therefore not claim sole right to the function of policing.[8]

This means that 'the ability/capacity of the SAP to combat crime, can be increased if alliances/cooperation with the other role players can be brought about': a coded call for a partnership in policing with ANC and other structures. The document goes on to argue that community policing implies decentralised decision-making and more careful selection of officers who must be allowed to use their initiative: police officers should behave in a self-regulatory way according to a system of values rather than 'being controlled by rules and regulations'. It also argues that 'the military rank structure must make way for more informal, and simpler structures, with fewer levels' and that 'community policing implies less specialisation with a greater emphasis being placed on style in general'.[9]

These broad principles have been reflected, the SAP claims, in many of the changes introduced in the 1990s, including the adaptation of training methods, the establishment of community liaison structures and the implementation of the National Peace Accord, issues which are dealt with later in this chapter. Further changes envisaged between 1992 and 1995 are listed in an internal briefing as:

- Focus on pro-active policing
- Improved partnership relations between the community and the South African Police
- Depoliticising the South African Police
- Internal structural adaptions in line with constitutional development in the RSA
- Shifting of the emphasis from a semi-military authoritative organisation to a service-rendering organisation
- A management process which focuses strongly on the cost-effective application of resources and economic principles
- Greater emphasis on the maintenance of standards
- Extension of cost recovery for certain services rendered to other departments and institutions.[10]

These objectives would be welcomed by many critics of the SAP, and if met would go a long way towards restoring the credibility of the force. Unfortunately, as events have demonstrated, the changes are filtering through to policemen and women on the ground only slowly, and the ethos of policing in the SAP remains largely unchanged.[11]

Engaging the Police

For many years the ANC and kindred organisations assumed that in the revolutionary seizure of power, the SAP would be swept away and a new force, based on the mass movements of the new order, would replace it. Now that it is clear that change in South Africa will take place not through an armed seizure of power but a negotiated end to apartheid, the ANC and the broader democratic movement have started to consider ways of bringing the SAP under democratic control and ensuring that it is a suitable instrument for maintaining law and order during the transition period. The ANC and its allies have continued to criticise and oppose many aspects of the SAP: it does so, as Nicholas Haysom has pointed out, not to score political points or to 'draw any pleasure or glee from [the] crisis', but because the SAP is viewed as a crucial institution during and after the transition.[12]

The anti-apartheid movement has also started to consider how, in the longer term, the SAP can be transformed into a force suited to a democratic system, and ANC policy now incorporates a clear vision of a new way of policing, symbolised by pointed references not to a new police force, but to a 'police service'. The principles of this 'new approach to policing' were set out in the ANC's policy guidelines adopted by the movement, after much debate and consultation, at a national conference in May 1992:

- The police service shall respect the ideals of democracy, non-racialism, non-sexism, national unity and reconciliation and act in a non-discriminatory fashion. The police shall be non-partisan and no member of the service shall hold office in any political party;

- Policing shall be based on community support and participation;

- Police shall be accountable to society and the community it serves through its democratically elected institutions;

- There shall be a professional police code governing standards and suitability of membership to the service, and a code of conduct to which police will adhere;

- Policing priorities shall be determined in consultation with communities they serve;

- Policing shall be structured as a non-militarised service function;

- The police service shall carry out its work primarily through non-violent means;

- Policing shall be subject to public scrutiny and open debate;

- Allegations of police misconduct shall be dealt with by independent complaints and investigations mechanisms;

- Members of the service shall be entitled to form and join employee organisations, of their choice, representing their interests;

- The police shall strive for high performance standards.[13]

In this chapter we will explore the implications of some of these proposals in more depth, examine the processes which gave rise to them and look at progress made.

The ANC's willingness to engage with the SAP was first publicly articulated by Penuel Maduna, the ANC representative at one of the first conferences held in South Africa to examine the prospects for democratic policing:

In some circles it is felt, rightly or wrongly, that [the security forces] cannot be entrusted with the security of the process of transition.... Relying on these forces for security, it is said, would be tantamount to placing the new South Africa at the mercy of the current ruling class, which has a well-known record as a violator of human rights.

[But] the political and economic reality confronting us all is that there is no question of the apartheid-oriented, non-representative South African Police force, which is rooted in the gross denial of human rights to the oppressed black masses, being dismantled and replaced with a new police force. At the same time we cannot take the SAP over as it is, with its wrong orientation, tendencies and value systems, and hope that it will be the best policing servant of the new, united, non-racial, non-sexist and democratic constitutional and political order. Trapped as we are between Scylla and Charybidis, as it were, we are constrained to talk about the need to transform the existing forces and instruments of the law – including the courts, civil service, the army and the prisons – and infuse them with new, humane and democratic values and personnel.... The alternative of us throwing them out lock, stock and barrel is just not feasible.[14]

The framework for this approach had been set at an earlier conference, in May 1990 in Lusaka, when representatives of the security forces had met with leading members of the ANC, including commanders of MK, to discuss the implications for the security forces of the negotiations to end apartheid. While General Malan, then head of the SADF, repudiated the conference, and the SAP was not formally represented, it was nevertheless a remarkable meeting of minds which pointed the way forward. A commission of the conference put forward proposals relating to policing and 'internal security', although these proved more controversial than those relating to external defence. The proposals included:

* Both the police and defence force have to be strictly subordinate to and controlled by a civilian authority, such as a parliamentary committee;

* Police should receive improved crowd control training with emphasis on minimum force....

* It was agreed that in the future SA some form of internal [security] agency must exist but their powers must be severely curtailed and subject to a bill of rights ....

* It was agreed that legislation should be passed to restrict the carrying of weapons. In the long run a process of disarmament must occur;

* In the long term it was felt the communities must be involved in their own policing....[15]

The conference also endorsed proposals for the monitoring of SAP actions, which it stressed should involve the participation of mass-based movements and professional associations, and should include as many political groups as possible. Monitoring structures, it said, should have 'some power of enforcement' to ensure their recommendations were implemented.

Many of the proposals put forward at the Lusaka conference proved to be premature. With the institution of transitional multi-party authority repeatedly delayed during the course of negotiations, the democratic movement gained little say over the police. Nor did the government wait for direction from the ANC and its allies in shaking up the SAP. Initiatives in restructuring and reorienting the force were presented as moves to make it more accountable and to depoliticise it, to fulfil De Klerk's public promise at the beginning of 1990 that the SAP would turn its attention to the fight against crime. But many of the most important moves were made without consultation and lacked the approval of the government's main negotiating partners. These included the changes to the Security Branch or CCI and the plans for a separate and specialised riot control division – the 1990 Lusaka conference had specifically opposed 'the creation of a paramilitary force for internal security', and the ANC protested strongly when the Internal Stability Division was announced.[16]

Controlling the Police

Although the State of Emergency was still in force when the ANC and government met for their first formal talks in early May 1990, and the ANC remained committed, for that time at least, to its armed struggle, the two delegations emerged from the talks a committed to a peaceful end to apartheid through negotiations. Problems of policing and political violence occupied a prominent place in the Groote Schuur Minute, the agreement issued after the talks, which were held at the old Dutch colonial homestead Groote Schuur near Cape Town. The minute spoke of 'a common commitment towards the resolution of the existing climate of violence and intimidation'. The government also undertook to review security legislation, to 'work towards the lifting of the State of Emergency' and to set in motion a process which would lead to the release of political prisoners and the return of exiles. The most significant indicator for policing policy was the announcement that 'efficient channels of communication between the government and the ANC will be established in order to curb violence and intimidation from whatever quarter effectively.'[17]

Police killings and the aggressive response of the force to demonstrations threatened further talks (see Chapter 4), and the 'channels of communication' called for in the minute were not implemented effectively. The SAP provided a list of 96 officers with whom the ANC and local community groups were expected to liaise.[18] But many of the officers were Security Branch members known to local communities as the very men who had tortured and terrorised activists during the emergency years; the ANC leadership that encountered grassroots resistance when it came to appointing its liaison officials.

In a few areas local conditions resulted in community-police initiatives which, although tenuous, provided a *modus vivendi* to resolve conflicts. These positive moves were isolated, but they occurred in some of the areas where political violence had been most acute. In Uitenhage, the crucible of resistance in the Eastern Cape, leaders of ANC-aligned mass organisations met with the Minister of Law and Order to establish a local liaison committee. Another was set up in Welkom, scene of right-wing vigilante operations.[19] Some breakthroughs also took place in parts of Natal, where police officers facilitated local peace pacts between the ANC and Inkatha – agreements were made in the Lower Umfolozi and Shongweni areas in 1990–1.[20]

A second round of national negotiations was held in Pretoria early in August 1990. The ANC announced the suspension of its armed struggle while the government made firmer pledges to remove politically repressive measures and agreed on a way to define political prisoners. The two sides also undertook to develop local, regional and national 'mechanisms of communication' and to 'enable public grievances to be addressed peacefully and in good time, avoiding conflict.'[21] In effect, the Pretoria agreement moved the ANC and the government closer to joint monitoring and control of the SAP and other security forces. Like Groote Schuur, it resulted in a few local successes, but progress was painfully slow.

In Natal, Patrick Lekota, a leader of the mass movement and the ANC, argued:

> Our communities on the ground have been defenceless for a long time. We consider that implementing the agreements will make it possible for our members to enjoy some measure of protection from Inkatha intimidation and even some instances of intimidation from some elements in the security forces.[22]

Joint SAP–ANC monitoring committees were set up in Durban and Northern Natal to monitor the implementation of the national agreements. Consisting of senior ANC officials and police officers, they considered any issue where either party thought the spirit of the agreements had been violated by a resort to violence or intimidation. Any deadlock would be referred upwards to more senior officials of the two organisations.[23]

Despite these local – and sometimes temporary – breakthroughs, the Pretoria Minute masked fundamental disagreements between the ANC and the government, particularly over the questions of political violence and the role of the security forces. The government tried to argue that the ANC's commitment to ending violence meant that it should curtail its campaigns of mass action – protests, demonstrations, strikes. These actions, it said, were linked to the strategy of armed struggle and inevitably led to violence. The ANC refused to forego the option of mass struggle: until Africans had the vote, they could only redress their grievances through street protests and collective actions.[24] It claimed in a series of press advertisements explaining the Pretoria Minute to its supporters that the suspension of its armed struggle was conditional on restraint by the police, and Nelson Mandela declared: 'Until the government tames the police we will continue to be dissatisfied.'[25] The atmosphere was soured further by the eruption of Inkatha-linked violence in the Transvaal, continued shootings by the police and government slowness in implementing the agreements.

Ending the slaughter in the Transvaal and Natal became an overriding concern of the ANC: without peace there could be no progress in negotiations, and while its supporters were being killed it could not get on with organisational work. The ANC was thrown off-balance by the ferocity of the violence and it took some time for the movement and its allies to agree on an overall approach. At one point different structures appeared to be issuing contradictory calls, one calling for the police to stamp out the violence and the other demanding the withdrawal of security forces from townships.[26] By early 1991, however, the ANC had settled on several core demands, mostly short-term measures which in its assessment would prevent the security forces from playing a covert role in the political violence. They were demands which the government could quite easily have met, had it the political will to do so, at relatively low cost and with little disruption to the functioning of the police and army. The ANC summarised these demands in April 1991 as:

- legislation be passed in this session of parliament to ensure no carrying of weapons of any kind at public gatherings

- the public disbandment of those bodies that have been, and continue to be, responsible for death squad activities, namely CCB and Askaris

- the removal from our country of mercenary forces, specifically the notorious 32 Battalion and Koevoet

- that security organs use civilised methods of crowd control so that lives can be protected

- that immediate efforts be made to address the whole hostel system

- and that there be an independent commission of inquiry into all the violence.[27]

The movement also called for security force members involved in massacres to be suspended from the force. Mandela provided the government with a list of names of policemen the ANC believed to be involved in orchestrating township violence.[28] But De Klerk appeared to be unmoved by the mass killings – nearly 3,000 dead in 1990 – and did his best to shrug off the ANC's calls. The movement concluded that 'the extensive loss of black people's lives has made no impact on [De Klerk] or his government',[29] and, after further stonewalling by De Klerk, it declared that it would pull out of constitutional negotiations unless its core demands relating to policing and violence were met. De Klerk rejected the ANC's 'ultimatum' but nevertheless undertook to set up a permanent commission to investigate violence and to give attention to some of the demands, such as phasing out the hostels and controlling dangerous weapons. The government was slow to implement these promises and little progress was made in the next twelve months.[30] But the ANC achieved a breakthrough of sorts by opting for multi-party initiatives which led to a comprehensive peace agreement which, had it been properly implemented, could have paved the way for community-based policing and abated the violence.

NATIONAL PEACE ACCORD

As Inkatha-linked violence continued into 1991 the ANC came to believe that peace could be achieved only by drawing both Inkatha and the government into a formal agreement to which they could be bound. This approach was shared by some religious and business leaders, who were alarmed at the slide towards anarchy and wanted to get all parties to formally pledge themselves to peace. By May 1991, pressure for a national peace conference was mounting. The ANC committed itself to 'a conference that reaches multilateral, binding agreements with obligations on all parties to act in accordance with these agreements'.[31] The government hastily tried to convene its own peace summit on 24–25 May, but the ANC and other organisations boycotted it.[32]

Lengthy and often acrimonious talks between the ANC, Inkatha and the government eventually gave rise to a document called the National Peace Accord, which was signed on 14 September by De Klerk, Buthelezi and Mandela and was subsequently endorsed by many of South Africa's political parties and organisations. The Conservative Party and other right-wing groups, notably the Afrikaner Weerstandsbeweging, did not attend the discussions and refused to sign the agreement. The PAC and the Azanian People's Organisation also refused to sign, on the grounds that the accord lent legitimacy to the government and its security forces.

The military council running the Transkei homeland, although it agreed to support the accord, regarded it as too weak and would not sign. It argued that the source of the violence was not properly identified, that the agreement needed to be underwritten by the State Security Council, and that the police and military commanders of the government, homeland administrations and liberation movements should be integrated into an executive authority. Buthelezi's support for the accord was open to question – he told the BBC that he did not believe it would work and was signing it only because 'some people clearly are very keen that it should be signed'. As if to underline his disdain, 3,000 Inkatha supporters armed with spears and other weapons demonstrated outside the hotel where the agreement was made, openly defying its provisions.[33]

The accord was greeted in the South African press as a breakthrough in the creation of a new society. The ANC was less optimistic. Noting that the government had broken previous accords, Sidney Mufamadi, one of the ANC's peace negotiators, argued that it was up to anti-apartheid forces to 'mobilise their resources to compel the government to honour the agreement.'[34]

The language of the National Peace Accord is that of the new South Africa – non-racism, non-sexism, equal rights for all – but many weaknesses become apparent on closer analysis. While the accord maps out for the first time a role for opposition parties in the management of political change and security control, it also limits that role. Many of the provisions in the accord were in fact already being put forward by the government, although couched in somewhat different terms. Nor is the accord a substitute for an agreement on the issue of political power – it leaves control over the security forces firmly in government hands.

Despite its weaknesses, the National Peace Accord will remain a touchstone throughout the transition period and beyond. It implicitly locates the problem of political violence in the context of the social, economic and political maladies of apartheid and calls for 'measures to facilitate socio-economic reconstruction and development'. It sets out a code of conduct for political parties with the aim of establishing a climate of tolerance and free political association, and providing for liaison with police and other authorities over public meetings, demonstrations and other events. Three distinct structures are envisaged to implement the agreement and to monitor and control political violence: a permanent commission of inquiry; a National Peace Committee; and a National Peace Secretariat with Regional and Local Dispute Resolution Committees underneath it.

The most challenging provisions in the accord are reserved for the SAP – it calls for a break with the policies and attitudes which have determined operations throughout its entire existence:

> The police force, which by definition shall include the police forces of all self-governing territories, has a central role to play in terminating the violence and in preventing the future perpetration of such violence. However, the perception of the past role of the police has engendered suspicion and distrust between the police and many of the affected communities. In recognition of the need to promote more effective policing, a commitment to sound policing practices and a co-operative relationship between the police and communities are necessary.[35]

GOLDSTONE COMMISSION

One of the first of the peace accord structures to take effect was the permanent Commission of Enquiry Regarding the Prevention of Public Violence and Intimidation, otherwise known as the Goldstone Commission, after its chairman, Justice Goldstone, who had earlier investigated the Sebokeng massacre. The legislation for the establishment of the Commission was already in place, through an Act introduced earlier in the year in response to ANC demands for an investigation into the violence, and the Commission soon set to work investigating some of the more notorious cases. Later, in the hothouse political climate which followed the Boipatong and Bisho massacres, the Commission took on wider roles in response to ANC demands for the government to do more about the violence.

While Goldstone's even-handed conduct and determination to get to the bottom of issues has impressed most observers, the Commission has been hampered by its limited powers. Although it can make proposals on a wide range of issues, including legislative and administrative steps, it can only put recommendations to the State President and has no power to ensure that they are acted upon. Indeed, some of the few concrete recommendations made by the Commission in its first months of work – that the SADF's mercenary unit, 32 Battalion, be removed from townships, that 'a strong and effective police presence' be established at hostels, that policing in the Mooi River area be improved, and that an apparent police conspiracy to murder an ANC leader be investigated – were *not* acted upon. In July 1992 Goldstone remarked: 'The Commission by no means expects that recommendations made by it should necessarily be accepted or implemented. It does expect, however, that they will not be ignored.' This public criticism of the government at last led De Klerk to respond: he ordered the dissolution of 32 Battalion and Koevoet, and instructed the police to seal off hostels at the centre of violence. [36]

Goldstone's ability to investigate is constrained. Although he can order anyone to appear before the Commission, and demand access to documents – anyone hampering the work of the Commission can be guilty of an offence – in his own words 'the Commission consists of five members and a small staff' and 'it is obviously unable to enquire into every one of the many tragic incidents of violence which regrettably have become a daily occurrence in South Africa'.[37] The Commonwealth Observer Mission which visited South Africa in 1992–3, noted that:

> Despite its public stature and prodigious workload it has assumed, the Goldstone Commission would still seem to be a very thinly resourced body. Its members have in many cases not been able to relinquish fully other responsibilities.... The investigatory staff would also appear to be overstretched, and there is an apparent shortage of experienced and trustworthy police officers available in the country to bolster their numbers.[38]

Goldstone's investigative deficiencies are compounded by the fear of witnesses to appear before the Commission. Even though there are provisions for evidence to be given in secret, people who have given evidence to the Commission or who have associated with witnesses have been murdered.

However, in July 1992 Goldstone reported that he had entered into discussions with the Department of Justice to draw up regulations to protect witnesses. Given the suspicion with which so many South Africans regard all the institutions of the state, this may not solve the problem.[39]

The Goldstone Commission is not equipped to investigate covert security force actions. If the police or military decide to cover up, there is little it can do about it.[40] This aside, the Commission's reports have provided no small indictment of the police, although these have been balanced by criticisms of the ANC and its allies. In its second interim report in 1992 the Commission included in its list of 'causes of violence':

> A police force and army which, for many decades, have been the instruments of oppression by successive White governments in maintaining a society predicated upon racial discrimination. This involves a police force and an army that for the majority of South Africans have not been community based or oriented. For many South Africans, the police and army are not perceived as fair, objective or friendly institutions....
>
> A history over some years of State complicity in undercover activities, which include criminal conduct ... the well-documented criminal conduct by individual members of the South African Police and the KwaZulu Police exacerbates the perception of so many South Africans that the Government or its agencies are active parties responsible for the violence ... the Government has failed to take sufficiently firm steps to prevent criminal conduct by members of the security forces and the police and to ensure that the guilty are promptly and adequately punished.[41]

POLICING THE POLICE

Traditionally the police have responded to public outrage at their more notorious actions by setting up internal inquiries. The track record of these investigations does not inspire confidence. The police investigation into the Langa massacre in 1985 is a case in point: primed with information provided by the police, the Minister of Law and Order told parliament that the crowd had been throwing petrol bombs and stones, which was later shown to have been a fabrication. The police response to the 1990 Sebokeng massacre was equally suspect. Justice Goldstone, who was appointed to look into the event after the police had held their own investigation, found that the internal inquiry had been 'haphazard and unprofessional' and would have resulted in a 'biased and one-sided picture'.[42]

The SAP's investigations into more routine allegations of transgressions against its officers have been equally lax. In 1992, when the campaigning newspaper, the *Weekly Mail*, published a list of 30 cases in which police had been accused of torture, assault, misconduct, unlawful killing, theft and other offences, General Mulder van Eyk, the Deputy Commissioner, promised to investigate them personally. The newspaper provided the general with details of the cases and the names and phone numbers of the lawyers involved. Nearly three months later, none of the lawyers had been contacted – but Van Eyk claimed that in four of the cases the lawyers had refused to respond to requests for information, in nine the matter was 'under investigation', and in 10 the case had not been reported to the police (even though the lawyers had case record numbers for some of them and others had been the subject of civil claims or supreme court interdicts). In a further three cases, the attorney-general had declined to prosecute, in one he had confirmed an inquest court finding of suicide following a death in police detention and three cases were the subject of civil claims – in other words, in not one of the 30 incidents had the police officers concerned been disciplined or prosecuted.[43]

The destruction of evidence is a major problem in police investigations – whether this is done deliberately or through sheer incompetence is a matter of interpretation. Lawyers have repeatedly claimed the police fail to investigate incidents properly and destroy evidence.[44] After the Boipatong massacre police confiscated weapons from those suspected of carrying out the killing, but because they made no attempt to record which weapon was taken from which person, they effectively destroyed any possible evidence.[45] All records of police radio communications on the night of the massacre – vital to establish whether there was police involvement in the killings – were 'accidentally' erased. A British team, headed by Dr Peter Waddington, which was brought in by Justice Goldstone to investigate the SAP's reaction to the Boipatong massacre, heavily criticised the investigative capability of the police. 'Superficial scenes of crime investigation seem to be endemic,' reported Waddington, and the systems used by detectives 'undermine evidence-gathering'.[46]

The National Peace Accord established structures for the investigation of allegations of police misconduct, through the office of a Police Reporting Officer. Special police units, under the supervision of an SAP general, are required to investigate complaints and report to officers drawn from the legal profession or the SAP itself. But no reporting officers had been appointed by June 1992, and the special investigation units have, by and large, confirmed the belief that the police cannot be expected to investigate themselves.

When the peace accord was signed, the SAP revealed that it had already set up 25 investigative units around the country, although they were looking into 'all allegations of violence' and not merely those against the SAP.[47] The Political and Violent Crime Investigation Units were headed by Major-General Ronnie van der Westhuizen until the end of 1991, when he was replaced by a former security policeman, Major-General Hannes Gloy. The investigations seldom got to the bottom of issues, however, and the ANC complained that 'too many of these units are former security policemen who lack the trust of members of communities in which violence occurs.'[48]

Only in Natal, in the Trust Feeds case, was there a breakthrough, but this came almost entirely as a result of investigative work by one man, Captain Frank Dutton. As a result of his work, another police captain, Brian Mitchell, and four of his colleagues were found guilty in the Natal Supreme Court in April 1992 of killing 11 people three years earlier. The judge found that there was evidence of a cover-up at a regional and national level, which amounted to 'obstruction of justice'. He called for an independent investigation: the Minister of Law and Order responded by ordering a departmental inquiry.[49] Captain Dutton was widely regarded as an 'honest cop' and his investigations did not go down well amongst some sections of the SAP – attempts by the CID to sabotage his inquiries were reported, and he may have been on a police hit list.[50] His investigative unit was disbanded after the Trust Feeds prosecution and he was transferred.[51]

In view of the general failure of the SAP to investigate police involvement in killings satisfactorily, calls were made for the Goldstone Commission to be given investigative powers independent of the police, like the special prosecutor systems which have been used in the USA and other countries. Lawyers for Human Rights, a group of campaigning South African lawyers, argued that a special investigative unit, involving human rights groups, private specialists like insurance investigators, carefully selected SAP members and others should be established as an adjunct to the Commission.[52]

Minister of Law and Order Hernus Kriel said early in 1992 that the government was considering establishing an independent unit to investigate the police, and was 'sending representatives overseas to look at what is happening in other countries'.[53] In August 1992 he announced the establishment of an independent investigative body to look into allegations of crimes committed by police. It would be headed by a judge and fall under the justice ministry, and it would involve attorneys-general, advocates, lawyers and overseas experts as well as the SAP and the National Intelligence Service.[54]

In addition to a body capable of investigating specific allegations, it is evident that an external watchdog is needed to scrutinise the day-to-day functioning of the SAP and respond to complaints of poor or biased service. Amongst those who have argued the case for such a body is Clifford Shearing, who played a major role in the introduction of an ombud system for the Canadian police. He has argued that an ombud body in South Africa should be recognised as impartial by the population (which might well mean international representation) and have the power to hold the police accountable by measuring their actions against a code of conduct and making remedial recommendations to every level of command. The limited watchdog provisions in the National Peace Accord do not measure up to these standards.[55]

In its policy guidelines, the ANC has committed itself to a 'full-time independent office of the Ombud', appointed by and answerable to parliament, and with 'wide powers to investigate complaints against members of the public service and other holders of public office and to investigate allegations of corruption, abuse of their powers, rudeness and maladministration'.[56] While this institution would not be specifically charged with monitoring and investigating the police, it is clear that the SAP would fall within its ambit.

MONITORING POLICING AND POLITICAL VIOLENCE

During the State of Emergency, when the government attempted to suppress information about security force actions, human rights groups played an important role in monitoring conflict, maintaining records of violence and analysing and publicising police actions. Organisations like the women's civil rights group Black Sash, the Human Rights Commission, Lawyers for Human Rights, Peace Action, the Independent Board of Inquiry, church organisations and unrest monitoring groups in the Democratic Party began to pool information and resources. By 1992 they were loosely structured as a national monitoring network and planned to set up a formal Network of Independent Monitors consisting of more than 70 organisations across the country.[57]

While the ANC and its allies have been willing to resolve the security conundrum without armed intervention from the international community, they have long believed that some form of external monitoring would help bring the armed forces into line. The Boipatong massacre led to renewed ANC calls for external monitoring, and the movement approached and the UN Security Council for help. The UN sent a special representative, former US Secretary of State Cyrus Vance, to look at ways of ending the violence and bringing about a return to negotiations.[58] After a ten-day visit, he reported to Secretary-General Boutros Boutros Ghali who recommended round-the-clock monitoring of flashpoints and a non-partisan inquiry into the SAP and other armed forces (including MK). He called for the UN to send in 30 observers and for the structures set up under the National Peace Accord to be strengthened by the establishment of permanent local and regional offices and 'operations centres' at 'the major flashpoints'. His recommendations were supported by Justice Goldstone and later accepted by De Klerk. Justice Goldstone was quite blunt: 'Unless the SADF and SAP are fully investigated by a neutral and reliable body they will have no prospect of receiving the trust, confidence and cooperation of the public.'[59]

The European Community and the Organisation of African Unity also sent in monitors, while the Vatican and the World Council of Churches set up a scheme to send groups of international observers to South Africa on visits of six to eight week. In South Africa, the observers would link up with the Network of Independent Monitors.[60]

The National Peace Committee joined the monitoring process after the

Boipatong massacre and announced that up to 150 monitors would be deployed on marches and demonstrations.[61] Its monitors played an important role during the wave of popular anger and grief that gripped the country after the assassination in April 1993 of ANC and Communist Party leader Chris Hani. Equipped with two-way radios and clearly identified, monitors not merely observed the marches but at times actively intervened to defuse potential flare-ups.[62]

Apart from providing a reasonably objective source of information about controversial incidents, the mere presence of monitors, especially from the international community, is often enough to ensure that the SAP and political organisations involved stick to the rules – though the monitors, including those from the National Peace Committee, proved powerless to stop the Bisho massacre. During the marches that followed the killing of Chris Hani it was evident that, although they carried weight with organisers and security force officers, their status was not recognised by all. In Boksburg, near Johannesburg, for instance, a group of PAC-aligned youth chanted 'Peace monitors out!' and the presence of peace-keepers failed to stop sporadic looting.[63]

It has been suggested that monitors, whether local or international, should accompany police on their operations, but the logistical problems involved would probably preclude this as a day-to-day practice.[64] There is no reason why police deployment at pre-planned demonstrations should not be monitored, however, or why monitors should not accompany police on specific tasks where their past conduct is known to be an issue. This principle appeared to be endorsed by the Goldstone Commission when it investigated the Boipatong massacre: lawyers accompanied police when they raided a Koevoet police unit believed to have been involved in the killing.

Monitoring of police actions would be made easier by improved record-keeping and recording processes. Police officers, although not auxiliary members of the force, are supposed to record incidents in their notebooks, and various records are kept at police stations, such as incident books, records of ammunition and weapons issued, vehicle logbooks and so on. Ensuring that these records are kept properly and are made available as a matter of course to external monitors will be one way of increasing accountability. The introduction of video and tape recording of interrogations, as has been done in other countries, would also help in monitoring and controlling the police (although it could be argued that these are doubled-edged swords which can be turned against suspects by the police). Schemes allowing civilians to inspect detainees would also help to prevent abuses.[65]

TOWARDS DEMOCRATIC CONTROL AND ACCOUNTABILITY

The National Peace Accord for the first time provided for structures in which community and political organisations can have a say – albeit limited – in determining policing strategy. The implementation of the accord itself is supervised by the National Peace Committee, chaired by a prominent businessman, John Hall, and with representatives from the main political organisations. A National Peace Secretariat, with regional branches, oversees Regional and Local Dispute Resolution Committees. These committees draw in representatives of political organisations, churches, trade unions, businesses, local government, the police and the SADF. They are charged with 'creating trust and reconciliation between grassroots community leadership of relevant organisations, including the SAP and SADF'; also with settling disputes, making rules and conditions for marches and other public events and liaising with local police and magistrates.

While the local and regional bodies have no management authority over the SAP, they have facilitating and monitoring powers and have played an active role in marches and demonstrations. During the Chris Hani commemorations in the Witwatersrand area, for example, the Wits–Vaal Peace Secretariat was convened with police, ANC, Inkatha and other political representatives and UN observers present. It received situation reports every few hours during the demonstrations and advised the SAP on deployments.[66]

The accord also calls for special local Justices of the Peace (JPs), to be appointed after consultation with the Local Dispute Resolution Committees, who would investigate complaints about public violence and help in the mediation of disputes.[67] In addition, for 'the swift but just dispensation of justice', the accord somewhat vaguely refers to the establishment of Special Criminal Courts using 'special procedural and evidential rules'.[68]

It has proved difficult to set up these structures. The idea of Special Criminal Courts was later abandoned. They were motivated by concerns about the slowness of the criminal justice system and the failure of the authorities to prosecute the perpetrators of political violence, but the legal fraternity expressed concern about the possibility of the courts undermining the rights of accused.[69] Instead, legislation was enacted in October 1992 to allow ordinary courts to speed up the cases identified as involving political violence. JPs had not been appointed by mid-1992 because the legislation defining their tasks had not been enacted[70] and, although 11 regional Dispute Resolution Committees had been established, they were still not operating properly.

The delay in implementing the accord was partly caused by government reluctance to provide the facilities. The scheme is supposed to be funded and serviced by the Department of Justice and other government departments. But the regional committees lack resources and have relied largely on secretarial and other back-up provided by a business organisation, the Consultative Business Movement.

The COSATU representative on the Natal regional body, Sipho Guebashe, reported in July 1992 that the Inkatha delegates failed to turn up for meetings and had not briefed their supporters about the peace accord. Funding from the Department of Justice was not forthcoming, and the committee members lacked the resources to investigate transgressions. Eighteen local flashpoints had been prioritised as areas to establish local dispute resolution structures, but only three had been set up, largely because of Inkatha's unwillingness or inability to put forward representatives, he said. The police were also being uncooperative, refusing to heed the committee's recommendations and failing to promote the accord amongst police and communities.

In the Western Cape, the regional body was reported to be meeting regularly but achieving little as it was serviced only by a part-time secretariat and its participants all had other political obligations. Ten local bodies had been set up, but none were functioning properly.[71]

Nearly a year after it was set up, the chairman of the National Peace Committee, John Hall, confessed that it was not effective, and that 'the Local and Regional Dispute Resolution Committees are by-and-large not working.'[72] The ANC called for the bodies to be strengthened through the provision of full-time personnel and financial resources and the establishment of permanent meeting places. It also argued that delegates should be mandated by their organisations to take decisions, and that they should have greater say over local policing activities.[73]

The Police Board, another structure established by the National Peace Accord, met for the first time only at the beginning of June 1992. With 12 representatives from political organisations, including senior ANC officials, and an equal number of SAP representatives,[74] the board's powers are limited to carrying out research and making public recommendations to the Minister of Law and Order 'in regard to the policy relating to the training and efficient functioning of the police'. It is specifically excluded from any role 'in regard to the day-to-day functioning of the police'.[75] Its achievements are likely to be modest, but it nevertheless marks an important break with the past, in that it recognises the right of community and political organisations to help set police strategy.

Even when they are functioning effectively, however, the structures of the National Peace Accord will go only part of the way to making police accountable to the communities they serve. Only when an authority which is perceived as legitimate and representative of the majority of the population has control over the SAP will the conditions be established for democratically accountable policing. At a national level, the ANC and its allies have concentrated during the negotiations process on pushing for a multi-party transitional authority or interim government with firm hands-on control over the security forces.

The importance opposition forces attach to control of the security forces was reflected at the Patriotic/United Front Conference in October 1991, which brought together 90 anti-apartheid organisations and resulted in a declaration of common intent to press for 'a sovereign Interim Government/ Transitional Authority that shall at the very least control security forces and related matters.'[76]

Security featured prominently when the negotiations proper began in December 1991, at the Convention for a Democratic South Africa (CODESA) involving the government, the ANC and 17 other political parties, including three of the 'independent' homelands. The bones of an agreement were settled by May 1992: phase one of the transition would entail the establishment of a multi-party Transitional Executive Council to monitor the activities of the government and ensure a 'climate favourable to free and fair elections'. Sub-councils would exercise at least some executive authority over their areas of responsibility, and security legislation would be reformed. In phase two of the transition an elected constituent assembly would take over the running of the country, and leading to the establishment of a new constitution and government.[77]

During phase one, the ANC envisaged that the various bantustan forces would be brought under single command and that a sub-council of the transitional executive, dealing with Law and Order, Stability and Security (LOSS), would exercise some control over the police (although top-down control would be limited), and would investigate intimidation and destabilisation. The sub-council would be serviced by a national inspectorate, drawn mainly from the SAP, which would monitor the implementation of decisions and investigate policing activities. The ANC also discussed the prospect of establishing an 'election police' unit, drawn from the SAP's Internal Stability Units, the bantustan police forces and various political parties, which would be responsible for public order policing, specifically controlling political meetings and demonstrations.

Behind these proposals, however, lurked key disagreements – notably with Inkatha. The government, for its part, would agree to only limited and indirect control of the police and army by the transitional authority. The sticking point proved to be the extent of the vote needed to approve the new constitution in the projected constituent assembly. The National Party wanted it approved by 75 per cent; the ANC, which stood for a two-thirds majority, accused it of seeking a white veto (the National Party and its allies will arguably take over a quarter of the vote in an election).[78]

The talks resumed again in early 1993 (the National Party having abandoned its insistence on 75 per cent), resulting in agreement on the intro- duction of a multi-party Transitional Executive Council. The ANC argued strongly that a sub-council should control the security forces – as well other armed formations, including MK. But the government continued to try to downgrade the powers of the council: Minister of Law and Order, Hernus

Kriel, declared that 'We are not interested in joint control over criminals.'[79]

The continuing disputes underlined the difficulties the various parties have had in coming to agreement on control of the security forces – an issue likely to remain disputed until the adoption of a new constitution. It may well continue to be picked over even then. In terms of ANC–National Party agreements, a government of national unity is envisaged after the adoption of a new constitution, in which a cabinet will be drawn from the major political parties, probably according to the percentage of the vote they obtain. Given the National Party's historic concern with controlling the security forces, which it sees as a guarantor of stability, it may well make a strong pitch for the Ministries of Law and Order or Defence.

Multi-party structures themselves will provide no panacea – institutional defences put up by the police will make control difficult, and this will persist even when a democratic government is elected. The SAP has traditionally paid little heed to parliament, and ministers of law and order have at times appeared to be prisoners of their generals, deferring to them when taking strategic decisions and relying on them for information which has often proved unsound. At the very least, a multi-party policing committee in an elected parliament will be needed to bring the force under democratic control and scrutiny, and the new government will have to make sweeping changes to personnel and outlook in the Ministry of Law and Order.

A persistent demand of community organisations is for local control or influence over policing. While many countries, including Britain and the USA, have decentralised systems of policing, the SAP is controlled from Pretoria with little provision for regional or local input. The picture is complicated somewhat by the bantustan police – on paper, there are 11 separate forces, although in practice many of them are mere adjuncts of the SAP. The SAP itself has argued in favour of decentralised decision making in recent years. Its 1989-90 restructuring was aimed in part at achieving this,[80] as was the 1991 Strategic Plan, although the effects have not been noticeable on the ground. It has also set up police–community liaison forums at a local level around the country, but these function as consultative bodies and do not lead to full democratic accountability. Their work has been hampered by police insistence on chairing the meetings, indicating, as the Policing Research Project has put it:

> The police is the 'dominant partner' in the police-community relationship and the community is not seen to have the right (or indeed the capability) to co-determine the nature of policing practice.
>
> ... There is little evidence that the police are generally aware of the issues of representativity, or that forums lead to substantive input and positive responses on the part of the police. This is borne out by the experiences of those involved in the Local Dispute Resolution Committees of the National Peace Accord. As with many

liaison forums the police are often unwilling (or unable because of organisational policy) to regard the views of the 'community representatives' as necessarily relevant or deserving of an organisational response.[81]

While local say over the SAP is clearly essential to community-style policing, devolution of control to local and regional levels will not necessarily lead to democratisation, and may well have the opposite effect. The National Party and other parties intent on preserving white dominance have seen devolution as a way of entrenching inequalities and preserving ethnic segregation or white privilege – and denying an ANC-dominated government effective control over the security forces and other institutions of the state.[82] As Nicholas Haysom, a Johannesburg human rights lawyer and law professor, has argued:

> Building police accountability to the community and forming a collaborative partnership with the members of the community is facilitated by decentralised policing structures by which the police are accountable to a local electorate ....
>
> However a radically decentralised police force, as in the United States, is inappropriate to South Africa. Such a decentralised police force could, as in the United States, lead to a high degree of proximity between foci of political and policing power; could replicate regional and local prejudices within local police forces leading to a persecution of outsiders; and could promote the formation of local militia in police uniform.[83]

The police have taken several steps to move the centre of power from Pretoria to the regions, in keeping with other government attempts to edge South Africa towards federalism. Regional commanders have been given increased powers at the expense of Pretoria. Even the 'purging' of 13 generals in September 1992 – seen by some as an attempt to clean out the force – was consistent with a policy of weakening the centralised command structure.[84] Despite these developments, the SAP remains a national body, and the lines of command within the SAP's five functional divisions run to Pretoria. With the exception of the Western Cape and Natal regions, budgets are set by national headquarters. Only the 'independent' TBVC forces have autonomous functional structures, although they too remain dependent on Pretoria in many ways (see Chapter 2).

The extent of the devolution of control over policing will partly depend on the future of the bantustans and the way regional and local government structures evolve. Reportedly, the SAP has drawn up plans to integrate city traffic police and bantustan forces not into a national force but into regional, federal forces. This could entrench the position of the KwaZulu, Ciskei and other forces opposed to the ANC and make it difficult for an ANC-dominated government in Pretoria to reform the police. The ANC, however, is not likely to accept such a scenario: while it is not opposed to strong regional and local governments, as long as they are not ethnically based, it is determined that South Africa should remain a unitary state and that central government should be able to control key national institutions such as the police. It calls for the reintegration of the bantustan forces, and for a single national police service. It is opposed to autonomous regional police forces while favouring local and regional influence, control and supervision of the police.[85]

New Ways of Policing

The National Peace Accord has much to say about the way police work should be carried out, and much of what it says the police, not too many years ago, would have dismissed as propaganda or meddling. It declares that the SAP should serve all the people of South Africa in an unbiased and even-handed way, be accountable to communities, exercise restraint and follow the principles of minimum force policing. While the accord has been criticised for not going far enough, its 'general provisions' relating to security force actions amount to a manifesto for fundamental change:

> The police shall endeavour to protect the people of South Africa from all criminal acts and shall do so in a rigorously non-partisan fashion, regardless of the political belief and affiliation, race, religion, gender or ethnic origin of the perpetrators or victims of such acts. . . .
>
> The police shall be guided by a belief that they are accountable to society in rendering their policing services and shall therefore conduct themselves so as to secure and retain the respect and approval of the public. Through such accountability and friendly, effective and prompt service, the police shall endeavour to obtain the co-operation of the public whose partnership in the task of crime control and prevention is essential. . . .[86]

The accord goes on to specify a code of conduct for the police. The code stresses that the police have an obligation to 'preserve the fundamental and constitutional rights of each individual' in South Africa, to secure the 'favour and approval of the public', to use 'the least possible degree of force', to be sensitive to the 'balance between individual freedom and collective security' and to act in a professional and honest way.

All police officers were required to commit themselves to abide by the code under threat of dismissal – but with knee-jerk secrecy the SAP refused to disclose if any officers had refused or been dismissed. The National Peace Accord as a whole was not taken up enthusiastically by the SAP, and its effects on the force have been limited. Rank and file police resisted it, regarding it as political interference, while a month after the agreement was signed, the most senior policeman in the Western Cape admitted to the press that he had not yet received a copy of it. The army proved even more recalcitrant – a separate code of conduct for soldiers was supposed to be drawn up, but by 1993 it had not been agreed.[87]

The problem with the code, as researchers have pointed out, is that it is a set of principles – which the SAP claims is little different to any previous sets of principles governing its members – with no concrete mechanisms of enforcement. It has been imposed from the top down and is widely resented by rank and file police. Existing SAP disciplinary procedures are used to deal with violations of the code: these consist mainly of closed internal disciplinary hearings which lack public credibility.[88] If the code is to be effectively enforced, the SAP will have to be seen to be enforcing it publicly, investigating breaches and disciplining those flouting it. It will also have to do far more to educate police officers about the code to win them over to it and also to publicise it amongst the wider community so that people are aware of their rights. The expectations of the police in many communities are very low: people will only start insisting on their rights when they know what they can expect.[89]

Fundamental to the code of conduct was the notion of establishing good relations between the police and public. Even before the code was adopted, the SAP argued that it had adopted a new philosophy of service and 'partnership with the public'. The Deputy Commissioner, Lieutenant-General Mulder van Eyk, in an address on 'The Principles and Problems of Policing in a Changing South Africa', put it this way:

> The South African Police realises that the organisation must not only be attuned to the community but also function in the context of the community. Effective policing therefore means the strengthening of relationships through which co-operation and voluntary obedience to the law will be maximised.
>
> This philosophy is a matter of great concern to the South African Police. An attempt is being made to implement this principle of partnership with the public in every possible facet of policing.[90]

Van Eyk stressed that the public needed to take the initiative in the partnership, although he did not press for measures which would give communities control or influence over policing. Similar views have been expressed by Minister of Law and Order Hernus Kriel:

> It is high time that the communities of South Africa – and especially the political leaders – start recognising their responsibility in restoring trust between themselves and the SA Police. . . . The fact remains that, if the community does not engage with the Police in breaking the pattern of confrontation policing, we will never succeed.[91]

Apart from the half-hearted efforts at implementing the National Peace Accord, and the introduction of the liaison forums, the SAP has done little to promote its declared policy of partnership. The Waddington Commission, which investigated the police response to the Boipatong massacre, was devastating in its analysis of police–community relations:

> it was suggested [by police officers] that community relations is not a function of non-commissioned ranks on the street. On the contrary, the first duty of all police

officers is community relations: that is the only way that police can function effectively in a democracy.

All parties in this situation are in danger of creating a self-fulfilling and vicious spiral: hostility and non-cooperation from the community comes to be expected; this justifies the unwillingness to persevere in the face of hostility; which further reinforces hostility and non-cooperation; this in turn encourages communities to seek their own retribution; thus creating further disorder and driving police and the people further apart.[92]

A delegation of Dutch police which visited South Africa in 1993 and witnessed police operations at first hand were equally damning about police–community relations. The delegation leader, Gert van Beek of the Amsterdam police, said that 'as far as the relationship between the police and the black population is concerned, apartheid is alive and kicking', and that there had been no improvement in relations with the community since he last visited the country during the State of Emergency in 1986.[93]

MINIMUM FORCE

The SAP's new code of conduct sets out detailed provisions for the control of crowds and stipulates that 'the police shall exercise restraint ... and shall use the minimum force that is appropriate in the circumstances'. It calls for clear guidelines to be issued for the dispersal of illegal gatherings, which should include addressing the crowd through a public address system, negotiating, and allowing a 'reasonable time' for a crowd to disperse. The code specifies:

The commanding officer shall only authorise the use of injurious or forceful methods of crowd dispersal if he believes that the crowd constitutes a danger to [people or valuable property] and if he has reason to believe that less injurious methods will not succeed in dispersing the gathering. The least possible degree of force should be used in attaining the aim of policing. Unless circumstances prevent it, persuasion, advice and warnings should be used to secure co-operation, compliance with the law and the restoration of order.[94]

As we have seen in Chapter 4, the police have been slow to change their attitudes, and, although there has been a partial improvement in their approach to the dispersal of crowds, they have too often continued to resort to the use of firearms. This was illustrated graphically in April 1993, during the events which followed the killing of Chris Hani. While the police behaved with commendable restraint in many parts of the country – in part because they were willing to leave the control of demonstrations to marshals, stepping in only when organisers lost control – in some places they were still far too quick to resort to lethal force. At Protea in Soweto, the time-honoured scene of police opening fire on a largely peaceful crowd was replayed, leaving at least four people dead and over 200 injured. It was Sharpeville 1960 again: panicky, ill-prepared and outnumbered police firing live ammunition without warning into an angry but non-violent crowd protesting outside a police station.[95]

Part of the problem is that the police are as a matter of course issued with lethal weapons. Given the level of criminal and other violence, and the widespread availability of firearms in South Africa, it would be unrealistic for the police to be disarmed. The ANC has repeatedly called on the government to demilitarise the police, however. Some critics, such as Transkei leader General Holomisa, have suggested that they should be equipped only with pistols and batons. The SAP argues that it needs heavier weapons – R5 rifles especially – because it often has to match AK47 rifle fire. But the use of the R5 in crowd control inevitably leads to casualties, and shotguns also take their toll.

The police do not appear willing to move over to the use of less-lethal and non-lethal equipment: the new Internal Stability Division is issued with the same equipment used during the State of Emergency.[96] One change in the 1990s has been the more widespread use of bullet-proof jackets. As police are likely to feel less threatened when better protected, this is to be welcomed as a measure which could lead to reduced use of force, but police often do not wear them in situations where they are likely to come under fire, and apparently they are in short supply.

Command and control in 'unrest' situations is also inadequate, which all to often means that conflict spreads rapidly and the police can do little but resort to force to try to re-establish some control. These weaknesses were identified by Peter Waddington in his report on the Boipatong incident:

> Senior officers showed a lack of basic strategic planning and tactical implementation. The division of responsibility between the internal stability unit and ordinary units of the SAP, on the one hand, and the detectives, on the other, frustrated an adequate investigation.[97]

This incompetence was exacerbated by a lack of contingency planning. According to the Waddington report:

> The SAP has guidelines on contingency planning, but it is clear from this inquiry that, to judge from Boipatong, there is a significant gap between prescription and practice. More thorough contingency planning would seem to be essential, especially when there appear to be a number of distinct organisations ... that might participate in any peacekeeping operation.[98]

Waddington was even more critical of police crowd control during the protests after the massacre, which resulted in police shootings. As on previous occasions, police officers were deployed in front of hostile crowds 'unprotected and holding a lethal weapon in both hands'.

These problems were addressed in a 79-page report drawn up by a panel of local and foreign experts appointed by Justice Goldstone to look into crowd control measures after Boipatong. Drawing on police experience in many countries, and considering the specific circumstances of South Africa, the panel argued that the police should use lethal force only in life-threatening situations, and 'every effort' should be made to ensure, through planning, training and the issuing of correct equipment, that such events did not occur.

The panel argued that responsibility for demonstrations and protests rested on three parties: the organisers, the local or state authorities, and the police. Proper management of a demonstration required 'combining and co-ordinating tangible and intangible resources of three parties'. To prevent marches and demonstrations from becoming illegal, and to ensure that organisers were able to play their role in maintaining order, the three bodies should coordinate advance plans. Any dispute between them should be referred to a supreme court judge.

Organisers should give notice of marches to local authorities, but not be required to get permission; however demonstrations inciting racial, tribal or religious hatred should be banned. Even if marches were illegal, this alone should not be grounds for their forcible dispersal, and minimal force meant that 'all particular uses of force can only be justified by the specific dangers they are intended to prevent'. Force should be proportionate to the need, reasonable and minimal. Lethal force should only be used 'when delay in its use and the use of anything less would subject police and others to a severe risk of death'.[99]

The panel also set out detailed proposals for police powers of arrest, examined various scenarios such as blockage of traffic in a central city area, stone-throwing or occupation of buildings, and considered different ways in which the police might handle the situation without risking escalation of conflict. It called for specially trained arrest units, capable of moving into crowds to arrest people violating the law. It also examined 'the hardest case': police being surrounded by hostile demonstrators intent on attacking them, an event often cited by the SAP as a distinguishing trait of demonstrations in South Africa. The panel concluded that:

> Every effort should be made to plan, equip and train police so that the dangerous situation does not occur. Explicit advance discussion with the organisers, the use of physical barriers, the movement of reinforcements, the availability of sub-lethal equipment, the development of sophisticated tactical contingency plans – all these and more must be directed to avoiding the situation we have described. For once it occurs, there is no satisfactory solution.[100]

At ordinary demonstrations police should be equipped only with handguns, but where demonstrators were likely to vastly outnumber police, armed units should be deployed but maintain a low profile. New rules for the use of rubber bullets and teargas should be drawn up, and proper systems of command and control introduced, in particular to prevent individual officers opening fire, which 'can trigger a massive escalation'. Police would have to be retrained, especially in human relations issues such as racism, communication skills and cultural sensitisation.

The panel's proposals were endorsed by the ANC and its allies, as well as Inkatha, but the SAP's public relations section issued a statement claiming that the measures would allow its members to be attacked with impunity by demonstrators. It was left to Justice Goldstone to explain that the panel had given considerable attention to the need to protect police and to train and equip them properly.[101]

While the panel's recommendations, if implemented fully, will reduce the likelihood of violence during public gatherings, improvement is likely to be slow until police attitudes change: this will require a comprehensive programme to manage, reorient and retrain police.

MANAGEMENT

Within the SAP – and even more acutely in some of the bantustan forces – there is a discernible failure of management and planning, as the Waddington investigation into the Boipatong events demonstrated. In part, this has been due to the routine promotion of individuals who have spent their entire working lives in the SAP and whose upward mobility has been determined as much by their political fidelity to the National Party and their experience in counter-insurgency war as by their technocratic and managerial skills. The Policing Research Project at the University of the Witwatersrand has pointed out that the SAP's historical emphasis on counter-insurgency and intelligence-gathering has resulted in an 'autocratic bureaucracy' in which there is little room for specialised managerial skills. The result is 'a failure to bring specialised knowledge to bear on management issues which deserve it'. Furthermore, 'the absence of a culture of collective leadership or participatory management means that suggestions and recommendations from lower-ranking officers with direct knowledge of specific problems is often ignored.'[102]

The Policing Research Project believes that at middle-management level there are many competent and experienced officers with a technocratic orientation who are often frustrated by the general staff. They argue that management could be improved by demilitarisation (including the abolition of military-style rank structures), a thorough review of organisational processes, a change in style of management and better strategic planning.[103] The introduction of civilian managers and administrators would also improve matters, as well as freeing thousands of trained police currently involved in administrative tasks for deployment on the streets: indeed, the SAP is investigating the possibility of replacing up to 13,000 police officers in administrative posts with civilians.[104] In another development, a civilian expert has been brought in to manage the SAP's Human Resources Management division.[105]

NEW APPROACHES TO TRAINING

Rightly, the training or retraining of the SAP and its auxiliary forces has been perceived as a key area requiring change. Addressing African constables passing out of initial training in June 1991, the Commissioner of Police, General Johan van der Merwe, declaimed:

> Several discrepancies in our training programme were pointed out to us by the community – and we listened. In the past, police training programmes were inclined to centre on mere knowledge of the law and the application of the laws. But we realised that this was not enough. Since a police official primarily functions within a society and therefore has to deal with perceptions, subjective belief systems and emotion, rather than logic, it is most important to prepare him or her for this.
>
> As the demands on policing in South Africa have changed, we have made the necessary changes to deal with those demands. Today the emphasis in training falls on task-oriented policing with a knowledge and understanding of police-community relations and interaction.
>
> Subsequently, police training has adapted and undergone a great change.[106]

Training is one of the few areas where the SAP has been prepared to allow outside scrutiny and input, and it has been possible, therefore, to examine General van der Merwe's claims in some detail. The Policing Research Project at the University of the Witwatersrand carried out a comprehensive survey of police basic training colleges in 1992 and put forward a programme for change on the basis of their findings.

By early 1992 the colleges were still largely segregated. The main college for Africans at Hammanskraal still catered exclusively for African students, and although the colleges previously reserved exclusively for white, Indian and coloured cadets had been opened up, they still maintained their old identities and the staff were almost exclusively drawn from the racial group concerned. There had been little change in the curriculum, although a more practically oriented four-week training block at the end of the course was to be introduced to give trainees more hands-on experience. Training continued to be highly regimented and militaristic, and largely closed to outside input.[107]

The Policing Research Project proposed that the SAP develop a training policy which

> would move away from the racial and military style of training, towards a new emphasis on skills. This must be based on a fundamentally different view of police work, defined in terms of the exercise of discretion....
>
> In the longer-term, we need to develop a vision of training as a 'thread' running continuously though all types of policework. That is to say, a culture of learning and training needs to be developed within the police force....
>
> This process can only succeed if the police organisation demonstrates its willingness to be subject to public scrutiny, criticism and input.[108]

The project argued that the Police Board should oversee desegregation of the colleges and the introduction of a new basic training curriculum, which would integrate 'legal, community relations and social skills content', draw on external advisers and civilian lecturers (including foreign expertise) and emphasise the teaching of human rights, accountable policing, professionalism and the development of skills like conflict management, investigation and decision making. Training should also take place at police stations as an ongoing process, and not merely in the colleges.[109]

The Policing Research Project did not examine the SAP's other training institutions. The majority of new African recruits are now being brought into the force as police assistants and do not pass through the basic training colleges. The training they get is even more militaristic, rudimentary and rigid than that at the basic training colleges (see Chapter 2). The new Police Academy, which trains officers, is reported to hold to syllabuses which 'appear to reflect old prejudices' – yet retraining at senior level is obviously critical to changing the culture and orientation of the SAP.[110] Counter-insurgency and riot control training, carried out mainly at Maleoskop, is also crucial. Any revamping of the training programme will have to incorporate these institutions, especially the auxiliary centres, to have any success.

While the proposals of the Policing Research Project would aid the process of producing police officers capable of acting sensitively and with discretion, the eradication of racism and rigid reactive values – the 'cop culture' – will entail far more. Police work is largely learnt on the job and the attitudes of peers and superiors are crucial to the making of a police officer: basic training can quickly be unlearnt in the day-to-day activities which follow. It is far more difficult to change the values and attitudes of police with many years' service than to inculcate new values in raw recruits. As one researcher has remarked 'the liberalising effect of police training is undercut once probationers enter the occupational culture of the station and are resocialised into its values by wisened [sic] colleagues.'[110]

Changing the outlook of long-serving police officers, steeped in racism and a way of work inimical to the new South Africa, is one of the stiffest challenges facing the SAP. The force has appointed Jacobus Neethling, a US-trained expert in creative thinking, to advise senior officers on the skills involved in generating rapport and open-mindedness, but it is unlikely that one man will be able to make much difference.[112] The SAP has also begun to test psychometrically both new recruits and existing members destined for 'sensitive units' like Internal Stability.[113] These cosmetic changes will have little effect unless they are followed up by a comprehensive programme of retraining and sensitisation, and the removal from the force of officers not willing to cooperate with the new order.

External pressure will be vital – indeed, police culture will not be reconstructed without a change in broader social and political conditions.[114] In other countries, 'cop culture' has been combated – although not always successfully – by extending the role and influence of civilians in the police force. Links with communities, through monitoring groups or community–police forums, will also gradually erode the exclusivism of police sub-culture.[115]

The SAP would also benefit from input from other police forces, including the training of senior officers abroad and the posting of international advisers, both civilians and police. This is already happening to some extent: Dr Waddington's appointment after the Boipatong massacre was followed by the introduction of two senior policemen, from Britain and Germany, to help with the Hani murder enquiry. Furthermore, the major political parties, and the government, have accepted an offer from the European Community to provide training and advice for the SAP. It was expected that the advisers would be not only policemen and women but also academics, lawyers and criminal justice experts.[116] Dutch police, acting at the behest of their unions and anti-apartheid groups, have also visited South Africa and expressed their willingness to help, particularly to support the fledgling police trade union, the Police and Prison Officers' Civil Rights Union (see below, 'Democratising the police').

RECRUITMENT AND PERSONNEL POLICY

If the bantustan and auxiliary forces are taken into account, the proportion of the police force which is black is about 65 per cent – while blacks make up about 80 per cent of the population as a whole. This gap could be closed fairly easily by intensified recruitment drives targeted in black areas. The catchment areas for recruitment need consideration: enlistment campaigns for Africans have been concentrated in rural areas, thus avoiding the more politicised townships. By and large the police are not drawn from the areas in which they serve, making the establishment of trust between police and the community much more difficult.

A far bigger problem is that blacks occupy so few senior positions and are increasingly recruited only as police assistants. The abolition of the auxiliaries and their incorporation into the regular force, and the reintegration of the bantustan forces, where there are many high-ranking black police officers, would at one sweep make a significant difference to the nature of the SAP. Although some of the bantustan officers, particularly those in KwaZulu, Ciskei, Bophuthatswana and QwaQwa, are likely to be even less acceptable to the broad African population than many of their white counterparts, others, especially in Transkei, Venda and KaNgwane, like other officials in these homelands, have developed a more receptive attitude to change. Some of these officers could find themselves in prominent positions in a new police force.

For effective policing, the ANC and its allies, and other organisations rooted in townships and other black communities, will need to be brought on board. One way of doing this will be to integrate ANC marshal structures and other informal ordering groups into the policing task (see below, 'Self-defence and self-policing'). In addition, at some point – and soon – ANC members and supporters will need to be brought into the SAP. This could happen in two ways: firstly through the incorporation or integration of trained ANC personnel, and secondly through the recruitment of ANC supporters who would then be trained from scratch in the same way as other recruits.

The ANC does not have sufficient trained personnel to make a significant difference to the composition of the SAP. MK has an estimated 8,000 people nominally under its control – although more have been trained – of whom perhaps 5,000 might be ready (but not necessarily willing) to join a new security force. It is doubtful if a tenth of them are trained for policing tasks. Most of these are in the ANC's intelligence and security organs and their training and experience, which mainly entailed counter-intelligence work, is not immediately suitable for police work in its broader sense. MK members without police-type training could of course be integrated or recruited into the SAP rather than the SADF, but because of their lack of policing training it would be some time before they could assume leadership roles or make much contribution to transmuting the SAP. At the very top, however, especially in the civilian bureaucracy, political appointments will redress some of these imbalances.

Once the composition and structure of the new force has been decided – which will largely be a process of horse-trading, reflecting the political strengths of the various parties – the process of training and promoting black officers will have to run its course. The SAP is publicly opposed to promotion on any basis other than merit but it is not averse to measures of positive discrimination or affirmative action which would seek to 'level the playing field'.

Political and ethnic criteria have patently underpinned promotion in the past, and the SAP has recognised that it at least needs to undo past injustices. When 13 police generals were retired in August 1992, Minister of Law and Order Hernus Kriel indicated that some of them would be replaced by black officers. 'Up to now', he admitted, 'it has been the policy of the SAP not to appoint people of colour to the position of general.' He also said that officers who had been passed over for promotion or demoted for discriminatory reasons would have their seniority restored and would 'be promoted once they have passed the necessary developmental courses.'[117]

Given the tiny proportion of women in the force, the SAP has a tremendous amount of work to do before it can claim that it reflects the composition of society: affirmative action for policewomen is needed.[118] The induction of more women, and their use in active policing rather than in administrative tasks, might also help to change some of the sub-cultural police values which are based on male chauvinism, although any effects would be likely to be minimal until a 'critical mass' was reached.

Better selection of recruits is an essential aspect of reforming the force. Pay, conditions and opportunities for advancement will have to be improved if better-qualified recruits are to be found, and consideration should be given to ways of recruiting people with experience in other sectors of society (business, for example) such as by a system of incentives. Improvements to the professional status of the police, and to its internal organisation, will also help to counter police culture.

For community policing, the focus of recruitment has to shift to the local area, and a balance struck between rural and urban recruitment. Proper assessment of personality and attitudes, to find a new breed of recruit committed to problem-solving rather than authoritarianism, has already been recognised by the SAP as a key factor in changing the character of the force, but there needs to be more open consultation about the criteria being employed. This alone will have little effect, however, such is the potency of institutional culture and effect of day-to-day police work on moulding attitudes.

As well as bringing in new personnel, the force will have to deal with the problem of removing those police whose track record is such that they could not be expected to serve the new South Africa. Peter Waddington has apparently recommended to the SAP that its general staff should be pruned gradually during the negotiations process and that police generals should be sacrificed 'like redundant ballistic missiles' rather than got rid of as a 'unilateral act'.[119] The compulsory pensioning off of 13 generals and the voluntary retirement of another six in August 1992 might have been the opening shots in such a strategy – but it was significant that the most powerful SAP men associated with the Total Strategy era and involved in security and covert operations were not affected by the move.

Another indicator of a failure to face up to and make a clean break with the past has been the government's refusal to identify police responsible for human rights violations, and its determination to amnesty those responsible for torture and political killings.

In October 1992 parliament was presented with the Further Indemnity Bill, which allowed the government to indemnify anyone who has 'advised, directed, commanded, ordered or performed ... acts with a political object.' The ANC and its allies objected strongly, and parliament rejected the Bill, but President de Klerk forced it through by referring it to the President's Council, where the National Party had an inbuilt majority. The move was widely condemned. Amnesty International called for 'thorough and impartial investigations into allegations of human rights violations' and said that it believed that 'national reconciliation can only be achieved on the basis of truth and justice'.[120] Similar views, drawn from an analysis of the effects of different policies adopted by Latin American governments which replaced dictatorships, were expressed by the human rights group Africa Watch. 'The Latin American experience shows that general amnesties for the armed forces are hugely unpopular, divisive, and widely regarded as illegitimate,' the study concluded: 'South Africa is at a crossroads. If it decides that the crimes of apartheid are to go unacknowledged and unpunished, then the result will be that they will continue to be committed, and will not be forgotten or forgiven.'[121]

DEMOCRATISING THE POLICE: TRADE UNIONISM?

Significant initiatives for democratisation have emerged from black police in the SAP, many of whom are concerned about their future careers in a force that in all likelihood will be controlled by an ANC-dominated government, or who have a genuine desire to be accepted and respected by their communities. Black police have grievances against the existing order in the SAP, which has denied them career opportunities, subjected them to racism and driven a wedge between the police and the community. This has given rise to an aspiring trade union, the Police and Prisons Civil Rights Union (POPCRU).

POPCRU was founded in 1989 by a feisty 30-year-old SAP lieutenant, Gregory Rockman, third-in-command at the Mitchells Plain police station in a coloured suburb of Cape Town. Rockman came to prominence in September 1989, at the time of the parliamentary elections, when he broke ranks publicly to denounce a local riot squad. The incident which precipitated his stand came when a group of 20 to 30 children held a peaceful demonstration in a shopping centre in Mitchells Plain. Rockman gave them 20 minutes to disperse, but they were attacked without warning by a riot squad contingent which arrived on the scene before the time was up. The next day Rockman approached a reporter and told him that the riot squad behaved like a 'pack of wild dogs' and they 'were just beating indiscriminately, running and attacking'.[122]

Rockman's claims attracted world attention. As he already had a reputation in Mitchells Plain as a 'good cop', thanks in part to his efforts to mediate in gang warfare, he became a local and national hero. He also attracted support from other police, including his commander, Colonel John Manuel, the highest-ranking coloured officer in the country.[123] The SAP took disciplinary action against Rockman, forbade him from speaking to the press and, when he refused to be silenced, dismissed him from the force. Colonel Manuel was transferred and Mitchells Plain police station was put under the command of Colonel Alwyn Burger – second-in-command of the local riot squad.[124]

POPCRU was formed at Rockman's home by about 30 police and prison officers in November 1989; its first action was a demonstration in which Rockman, another police officer and 11 prison warders were arrested.[125] The union grew rapidly, but it had difficulty in signing up police, who were summarily suspended or dismissed if they became members. It had more success amongst prison officers, although around 300 POPCRU members in the prisons service were suspended without pay when they went on strike in March 1990.[126] While the prisons service accepted that warders had a right to join the union, they drew the line at them going on strike. POPCRU responded to the suspensions by protest sit-ins and strikes around the country. But all the 52 police who took part in the strike were dismissed from the force – 38 of them were in East London and King William's Town in the Eastern Cape. The sight of policemen in uniform singing freedom songs and shouting anti-apartheid slogans touched off popular demonstrations of support.[127]

The dismissals and suspensions slowed POPCRU's growth, deterring others from joining, and embroiling the organisation in long legal and administrative challenges over reinstatement, in which it was eventually only partially successful. Its membership in 1991 was put at 2,300, but virtually all of this was in the prisons service.[128] POPCRU held its first full conference in June 1992, at which it elected a new executive and drew up plans to expand the union beyond its core of support amongst prison warders in the Western Cape.

While POPCRU has received broad popular support, some sections of the democratic movement have been reluctant to endorse the principle of trade unionism in the police, arguing that police officers cannot afford to play too political a role and that trade unionism in the security forces could undermine efficiency which is dependent on the obeying of commands. Others, however, believe that the police should reflect the democratic ethos of the new South Africa, that police forces elsewhere – notably in the Netherlands – have successfully introduced trade unionism without destroying discipline, and that organisations like POPCRU have a vital role to play in changing the ethos of policing.

At the ANC's national conference in June 1992, those arguing in favour of the right to organise within the security forces won the day. The ANC now believes that police should have the right to belong to political parties – but not to hold office – and should be entitled to form and join 'employee organisations'.[129] While attempts to set up a full-blown trade union may be before their time, some form of professional organisation representing rank-and-file interests is almost certain to take hold amongst the police once this becomes legal.

POPCRU argues that there is no necessary contradiction between the professional concerns of the police and the interests of the community they serve. But it has no illusions about the extent of the transformation needed. In the face of official hostility, it has a long way to go before it can claim to represent rank-and-file police and implement its aim of fostering 'recognition and respect for basic human rights of its members and those with whom they deal in the performance of their duties'.[130]

REPLACING THE TROOPS

More attention has been paid to the transformation of the SADF than the SAP. Much hope has been pinned on the concept of integrating MK and other armed formations with the SADF and the bantustan armies to create a new and more representative defence force. The contours of this process are not yet clear. It is likely to take place by degrees, even in the face of public opposition from SADF commanders. However, given the vast superiority in numbers and resources of the SADF, it will be an unequal process.[131]

A significant proportion of the army is involved in policing work and over 10,000 soldiers are deployed daily in internal security tasks:[132] in March 1993, following a security crisis in Transkei which resulted in the mobilisation of SADF troops, it temporarily rose to perhaps double that figure. In effect the SAP still relies on the SADF for much of its law-and-order functions and the fate of the army will have a profound impact on policing policy. The call by mass movements during the State of Emergency for 'troops out of the townships' has lost some of its sting since the SADF has generally proved more acceptable to communities than the SAP, especially in Natal (with the exception of the notorious 32 Battalion). By and large, however, the ANC and its allies have argued that the army should not carry out policing functions – its role should be restricted as far as possible to external defence.[133] This assessment is shared by some analysts close to the security establishment. The Institute for Defence Politics has argued:

> However well-trained and orientated military forces are for their use in the maintenance of law and order, the application of force within an internal law and order situation and on a battlefield differs fundamentally. The ethos of policing and soldiering are not the same and should not be confused. The control of our spiralling internal violence is the task of the police and para-military forces. Every effort should therefore be made to remove the military from this involvement as soon as practically possible.[134]

Recognising the extent of army involvement in policing, however, the institute goes on to argue that 'large portions of the SA Army (including personnel, equipment and facilities, the commando militia system, regional command headquarters, parts of organisations such as military intelligence, etc)' should be transferred to the SAP. They argue that this would help the army cut its operating budget, allow it to concentrate on its military functions and stop its degeneration into a 'low-technology counter-insurgency force'. It would also provide the SAP with a countrywide structure which would be administratively efficient. This may well be the case, but the inevitable effect would be to further militarise the police – even with retraining – and, given that many of the most active commandos are in right-wing areas, this would be playing with political fire.

Nevertheless, the problem remains that the police would be short-changed by the withdrawal of troops from township duties. As they can barely cope with their tasks at present, the dilemma of how to fill the gap is an acute one. In the best-case scenario the establishment of a credible and trusted police force would reduce the need for armed policing and communities would largely police themselves. The ANC and other organisations have demonstrated on many occasions that they are quite capable of maintaining order on marches and at mass rallies – through their extensive network of marshals they can control crowds 50,000 or 100,000 strong.[135] While the control of the marshals might not always be complete, the price to be paid in civic disorder (such as the scattered looting during the Hani commemorations) is probably less than that which would result from SAP or SADF attempts to maintain hands-on control. This principle of self-policing could be extended to cover a wider range of activities, and is examined in more detail later in this chapter.

RIOT CONTROL

While the SADF's principal contribution to policing the townships is in the provision of personnel and vehicles to relieve the overstretched police, it also gives the police added punch through its armoured vehicles and heavier weaponry, and it is routinely called in to restore order when violent or armed conflict erupts. In security circles the preferred option for filling this gap when the SADF withdraws from policing operations appears to be through the establishment of a separate paramilitary riot-control force along the lines of the French gendarmerie or the German Bundesgrenschutz, an idea with which the securocrats have long flirted. The development of the Internal Stability Division reflect this line of thought, although it remains, at least for the present, part of the SAP and not a separate force.

The great advantage of a separate, militarised riot-control unit is that it would, at least in theory, remove the need for the army to be deployed in civil unrest and free ordinary police from riot-control tasks, thus easing the process of demilitarisation. Proponents of the idea also argue that such a force could receive more specialised training and would be better able to prevent incidents where police acted with lethal force against crowds not so much out of malice as through incompetence. But there are many dangers: the image of the unit would inevitably be one that would imply trouble and confrontation, and its mere arrival at the scene of a demonstration could spark conflict. Its 'lean and mean' character could also lead to an over-reliance on offensive action. Problems of operational command and control would be exacerbated, especially if the unit did not fall under the SAP, and tensions between ordinary police and the paramilitary unit would inevitably arise because of the latter's élite nature. And the training of, and control over, the unit would have to be closely monitored lest it became a law until itself, or worse, a kind of Praetorian presidential guard to be used selectively by political leaders to protect their interests.

It is difficult to reconcile the ethos of a professional anti-riot unit with the idea of community policing. The track record of such units in South Africa – the riot squads and latterly the Internal Stability Units – does not inspire confidence in this solution: indeed, reasonably good relations between local police and the community have often been disrupted when the Internal Stability Units, or their predecessors, were brought in.

In a measured consideration of the pros and cons of such a solution in South Africa, the panel of international experts which examined the policing of demonstrations for the Goldstone Commission concluded that the advantages of maintaining central responsibility in the hands of local commanders, with the aim of encouraging community policing, outweighed the benefits of a specialised paramilitary unit. They recommended instead that the British or Dutch models be followed, where local commanders remain in charge but can call on a 'menu of specialised units'.[136]

A variant of the paramilitary proposal, favoured by some opponents of the National Party, is a multi-party élite unit drawing on personnel from MK, the existing security forces, 'private armies' and even vigilante formations, who would all be thoroughly retrained for use in political peace-keeping. This concept is linked to the idea of a special multi-party 'election police' which could be used to police public order during the election process. While this would have the advantage of integrating the various armed forces in South Africa, and would help to ensure that the public order force remained politically neutral, the practical problems involved would be immense. It would take considerable time to weld a corporate identity from such disparate forces.[137]

SELF-DEFENCE AND SELF-POLICING

In the wake of attacks by Inkatha and other vigilantes, the ANC has encouraged the establishment of self-defence units (SDUs), building on the long tradition of self-policing in the townships (see Chapter 2). These have sometimes been viewed as possible alternatives to the SAP: or at least, it is argued, they could take some of the burden off the SAP and possibly fill the gap after the withdrawal of the SADF.

The ANC had little option but to respond to community demands for protection, following the escalation of political violence after it suspended its armed struggle. As one MK leader reported in 1990:

> During our visits to the townships, a desperate call for arms became deafening. And at meetings, unless a speaker said something very specific on the question of self defence and arms, his message fell on deaf ears.... The desperation reached levels where even [Archbishop Desmond] Tutu and Reverend Frank Chikane [Secretary-General of the South African Council of Churches] were asked to provide arms.[138]

When it endorsed the call for self-defence units in 1990, the ANC visualised that MK fighters would form the core of these units, which would be based on community structures and made accountable to the community through the mass organisations like the trade unions and civic associations. They would carry out defensive tasks, ideally acting not as instruments of the ANC and its allies but as a force representing the community as whole.[139]

The scheme has been plagued by organisational problems and dilemmas of legality, and many of the units rapidly spun out of the ANC's control and resorted to banditry. One of the problems has been the question of arming the units. If the ANC authorises MK to use its caches of AK47s and other weapons, it is breaking the law by encouraging the carrying of illegal weapons; if it relies on registered firearms, it has the problem of persuading the bureaucracy to grant firearms licences; if it argues that the self-defence units should not be armed, it opens itself to accusations from the community that it is leaving them defenceless.

There have been even greater problems over the control of the SDUs: in some areas tensions have arisen between MK units returning from exile and other anti-apartheid groups, and many of them have been infiltrated extensively by police agents. In Sebokeng, for example, many SDU's flatly refused to cooperate with MK and fought amongst themselves.[140] Others turned to crime or set themselves up as maverick 'people's courts':[141] the Minister of Law and Order claimed in 1992 that 'nearly 23 per cent of identified SDU members have at some time or another been arrested for crimes'.[142] Chris Hani remarked in August 1992:

> We have seen an alarming revival of kangaroo courts and kangaroo justice and even the horrifying necklace. Some elements have used defence units to obstruct the police when the police have been engaged in justifiable crime prevention activities. Defence units must never seen to be sheltering criminals.'[143]

Growing alarm at the activities of the SDUs led the ANC to try to rein them in, and a code of conduct was drawn up at the end of 1992. However, the situation did not improve in the following months.

Not surprisingly, the government has refused to legitimise self-defence units – indeed it has not been willing to publicly recognise even MK as a legitimate force. National Party ministers have repeatedly argued that MK is a 'private army' which has to be disbanded.[144] The ANC argues that communities have no option but to protect themselves. Furthermore, MK is a liberation army established long before the current period of negotiations and still based largely outside the country: its demobilisation should be undertaken in terms of bilateral agreements with the government. An agreement on how to tackle the supplies, activities and membership of MK was reached with the government, ANC executive member Sidney Mufamadi revealed to the National Peace Committee in August 1992. He said that MK was keeping to the letter and the spirit of the National Peace Accord, 'notwithstanding the fact that its continued existence and operations are regulated by bilateral agreements and hence fall outside the accord.'[145]

The SDU experiment has not been successful and there are clearly problems related to the exercise of armed force by groups associated with one or another political party – even if they do it in the name of the community. Indeed, the ANC has argued forcefully for stronger restrictions on firearms, both legal and illegal, with an eventual aim of disarming the civilian population. In a submission to the Goldstone Commission in April 1993, Professor Haysom, representing the ANC, said the movement regarded the bearing of arms as a privilege, not a right. Self-defence should not be recognised as a legitimate reason for requiring a firearm licence, he argued, but he acknowledged that SDUs – and other groups – were demanding guns. This, however, was a result of their lack of faith in the security forces.[146]

Nevertheless, it is not a vast conceptual leap from the idea of neighbourhood watch – in principle accepted by most parties in South Africa – to SDUs. Indeed, the notion of self-protection units is endorsed by the National Peace Accord, although it draws a sharp distinction (and which is often one hard to make in practice) between 'private armies' attached to political parties, and non-partisan community groups:

> The Law accords all individuals the right to protect themselves and their property and to establish voluntary associations or self-protection units in any neighbourhood to prevent crime and to prevent any invasion of the lawful rights of such communities. This shall include the right to bear licensed arms and to use them in legitimate and lawful self-defence.[147]

The CODESA group considering law and order also endorsed this principle, recommending that the Local and Regional Dispute Resolution Committees 'take urgent steps to encourage the formation of nonpartisan community based self protection groups/neighbourhood watch groups ... [which] should work in close cooperation with the relevant police authorities.'[148]

Informal social ordering processes are key to the maintenance of law and order: the extent of the breakdown in South Africa has led many to argue that the problem of crime and violence will only be cracked by the more active involvement of communities in their own policing. White neighbourhoods and businesses have already taken matters into their own hands through energetic privatisation of policing – notably armed response units and security guards (see Chapter 2). This has the advantage of reducing the burden on the state, but it also means that the rich get more effective policing than the poor and that policing becomes 'exclusionary' in that certain groups are protected, often against other groups (blacks in white neighbourhoods are automatically treated with suspicion).

While security guards can be seen as freeing the police for more active tasks by the routine protection of property, the same is not true of the rapid response units which patrol the suburbs and respond to burglar alarms – clearly they have usurped the police, and their reliance on armed force has led to many problems of control. While the ANC believes that 'the role of the security forces shall not be usurped by private security companies', and has called for the regulation of the private security industry so that it 'performs its functions in a manner that is consistent with democracy',[149] the privatisation of policing is here to stay.

In black communities, there is a long history of vigilantism, self-policing and informal social ordering – from both the left and right – of which the SDUs are the latest manifestation. These groups have differed widely in their make-up and functions – street patrols, 'people's courts', street and zone committees, cultural and ethnic groups – and their track record is uneven. At worst, they have degenerated into gangsterism and preyed on the people, using violent and arbitrary methods to advance their own narrow interests. At best, they have functioned as community-based bodies using non-coercive methods to protect the greater good of the community, to smooth out social conflicts and to reintegrate offenders into society. Even when they dispensed rough justice, as in Alexandra in 1984–6, they were sometimes effective in combating crime.[150] They often started out with the best of intentions, and with considerable community participation, but degenerated as the conflicts of township life, not to mention the often hostile attentions of the police and other authorities, took their toll.

Despite this mixed record, it is evident that the scale of the problem demands the involvement of communities in their own policing: furthermore, it is only through such involvement that consensus-type policing will become possible. The recognition of the role of self-defence and neighbourhood watch groups in the National Peace Accord is the beginning of the process of legitimising and formalising community policing organisations. The challenge is to prevent them from becoming politically polarised and fractured, and to channel them into primary and pre-emptive policing tasks: day-to-day monitoring, ordering, controlling and community problem-solving, without the use of force. Public involvement in policing should be seen as part of the empowerment project in the new South Africa, where people start to take control of their own destinies, and where a flourishing civil society interacts with the institutions of the state to build a sense of purpose and belonging.

NAMIBIA: TRANSFORMING THE SAP

The challenges facing the SAP – political, organisational, managerial, personnel-related and operational – are immense. But one offshoot of the SAP, the South-West Africa Police (SWAPOL), has experienced the process of being taken over by an elected government controlled by a liberation movement it was at war with and has had to reorient itself to deal with radically different political conditions. Despite the many differences between the Namibian and South African situations – not least because many of the most problematic police personnel decamped to South Africa – the Namibian experience is a pointer to the way the SAP might be changed, if only because the South-West Africa Police was in practice a limb of the SAP.

The new Namibian Police (Nampol) is a different animal to its predecessor, although to many Namibians it remains a member of the same species. Before independence the strongest elements in the police were the poorly disciplined auxiliary special constables and Koevoet, the most ruthless counter-insurgency unit in the South African security forces. Namibia's new minister of home affairs described it 'an instrument of suppression in the hands of the state' with 'militaristic and anti-people features'. The government set itself three priorities: to demilitarise the force, to create a more representative service, and to restore public confidence and cooperation.

Changes in policing in independent Namibia have been facilitated by a constitution which stresses human rights. It entrenches the rights of individuals, severely restricts the powers of the security forces to arrest and detain, and contains a detailed bill of rights. It also outlaws the death penalty.[151] To symbolise the break with the past, new non-military police uniforms and rank structures were introduced and (except for a special task force) counter-insurgency training was stopped. Police were instructed that weapons could only be used if lives were threatened, and in most cases they no longer carry firearms as a matter of course. The worst elements were weeded out and, although the officer corps is still largely made up of white officers from the old force, at least a third of rank-and-file members were recruited from Swapo's army, Plan. Training and re-training was prioritised, under the supervision of British experts. To restore public faith in the force, Public-Police Relations Committees were set up, with representation from churches, businesses, trade unions and community organisations.[152]

The Namibian experiment has not been entirely successful. Violent crime has increased since independence[153] – in part due to rampant unemployment and the demobilisation of thousands of soldiers from both sides who have little hope of finding jobs – and recruits with a background in the liberation army and those who fought on the other side have at times been at odds. Many black Namibians, including policemen and women, feel that the government's policy of national reconciliation has allowed racist whites to entrench themselves in the new force, as whites still occupy a large proportion of top posts. Nor has the force gained the full confidence of the Swapo government. The relationship was described by Commissioner Siggie Einbeck as 'strained' – a comment precipitated by an incident on 3 March 1992 when four senior officers were suspended after they had sjambokked demonstrators during an industrial dispute.[154] This was not the only time Namibian police used violence to disperse demonstrators.[155]

Nevertheless, the Namibian government has demonstrated that it is possible to transform a militarised and biased force into one with a more genuinely national representation. In other countries, too, police forces have been fairly successfully transformed from partisan instruments of repression to modern, 'liberal' forces, though this has not always been an easy task.[156]

A NEW BASIS FOR POLICING

The transformation of the SAP's Namibian branch into a new service points the way forward, but for the broader challenge of involving communities in their own policing and of establishing new forms of policing which are not reliant on a professional force provided by the state, there are fewer examples to follow. Whatever happens – and there are not likely to be any easy victories or unproblematic solutions – South Africa, with its unique social and political composition, will make a contribution to the theory and practice of policing which will be of interest to many countries.

The flowering of a new ethos in the SAP cannot be a one-way process, as the SAP points out. Indeed the police often try to put the blame for poor police-community relations on what they perceive to be a campaign by the ANC and its allies to denigrate and undermine the force.[157] The ANC has moved on from its insurrectionary politics of the 1980s, however, when it openly called for the killing of policemen and those collaborating with the SAP. Since it suspended its armed struggle and began the process of negotiating, it has instead concentrated on ways of winning over sections of the police and of making the force accountable. It has taken to task organisations and people continuing to call for armed attacks on the police.[158] It has also begun the long, slow process of weaning popular opinion away from the notion of armed force as a solution to political ills and attempting to counter the culture of violence with an alternative community-based vision of political tolerance and openness.

But in the end the successful transformation of policing in South Africa will entail not merely changes to the police force and to the way it interacts with society, but to the political, social and economic conditions which are the poisonous legacy of apartheid. This was recognised by Mathew Phosa, the ANC's spokesperson on the police, when he addressed a conference on policing in South Africa in the 1990s:

> We cannot escape the fact that centuries of domination, oppression and exploitation of the black majority has left us with a legacy of mistrust, conflict and a deeply divided society.
> The most important consideration should be to look at policing in a socio-

economic context. A future democratic government has to address the relationship between effective law enforcement and crime prevention and the accessibility of the majority of people to adequate housing, education, food, healthcare, decent standards of living and employment.[159]

These sentiments find expression in the ANC's policy guidelines for the new South Africa, which, alongside specific proposals for reforming the police, talk of tackling the 'crime-producing conditions that prevail in our society' through social and economic transformation and the sweeping away of 'ideologies and practices that diminish the value of life or place one life above another'.[160] While these policies are unlikely to be implemented in their full form – the realities of political power usually entail the revision or dilution of policy, the ANC will be locked into a 'government of national unity' and South Africa's vast social and economic afflictions will not be dealt with easily – at least policing in a democratic South Africa will retain some of the flavour of this new approach.

NOTES

1   See for example Scharf 1989, p 231.
2   ANC 1992, p 12.
3   These suggestions have been gleaned from Marais 1991; Haysom 1991; Scharf 1991a; Brogden 1991; Brewer 1991; Cawthra 1992; Rauch 1992.
4   Shearing & Mzamane, 1992.
5   SAP 1992, p 4.
6   SAP 1993.
7   SAP 1993.
8   SAP 1993, Schedule A.
9   SAP 1993, Schedule A.
10 SAP 1992, p 8.
11 Marais & Rauch 1992.
12 Haysom 1992, p 1.
13 ANC 1992a, pp 73–4.
14 Maduna 1991, pp 5–6.
15 *Joint Press Statement on the Idasa–ANC Conference on the Future of Security and Defence in South Africa,* 27.5.90.
16 *Joint Press Statement on the Idasa–ANC Conference on the Future of Security and Defence in South Africa,* 27.5.90.
17 *Groote Schuur Minute* 4.5.90.
18 *Financial Mail* 10.8.90.
19 *Daily Dispatch* 30.4.90.
20 Cawthra 1992, p 30.
21 *Pretoria Minute* 6.8.90.
22 *Daily News* 22.8.90.
23 *Daily News* 22.8.90.
24 *BBC Summary of World Broadcasts* 14.8.90.
25 *New Nation* 10.8.90.

26   Haysom 1991, p 1.
27   *ANC Comment on President De Klerk's Statement* 6.4.91.
28   *Guardian* 28.1.91.
29   *ANC Comment on President De Klerk's Statement* 6.4.91.
30   *Financial Times* 3.5.91.
31   *Press Statement of the Extended National Executive Committee Meeting of the ANC* 18.5.91.
32   *Times* 19.4.91.
33   *Weekly Mail* 20.9.91; *Observer* 15.9.91; Holomisa 1992, pp 2–28.
34   *New Nation* 30.8.91.
35   *National Peace Accord*, preamble.
36   *Independent* 7.7.92; *Statement Read by Justice Goldstone* 6.7.92.
37   *Statement Read by Justice Goldstone* 6.7.92.
38   Commonwealth Observer Mission 1993, pp 32–33.
39   Evidence given at the *International Hearing on Violence in South Africa and the Implementation of the National Peace Accord*, London, 14–15.7.92.
40   Address by Frank Chikane, Secretary-General of the South African Council of Churches, *International Hearing on Violence in South Africa and the Implementation of the National Peace Accord*, London, 14–15.7.92.
41   *Second Interim Report of the Commission of Inquiry Regarding the Prevention of Violence and Intimidation*.
42   *Sunday Star* 9.9.90.
43   *Weekly Mail* 30.5.91.
44   *International Hearing on Political Violence in South Africa and the Implementation of the National Peace Accord*, London 14–15.7.92.
45   *Business Day* 23.7.92.
46   *Report of the Inquiry into the Police Response to, and Investigation of, Events in Boipatong on 17 June 1992*.
47   *Financial Mail* 27.9.91.
48   ANC 1992b, p 2.
49   *Amnesty International* 1991, p 95; *Guardian* 4.5.92.
50   *Weekly Mail* 24.4.92.
51   *Anti-Apartheid News* July/August 1992.
52   *International Hearing on Violence in South Africa and the Implementation of the National Peace Accord*, London, 14–15.7.92.
53   *Weekly Mail* 29.5.92.
54   *Sunday Times* 9.8.92; *Business Day* 28.8.92; Media Statement by the Minister of Law and Order, Mr Hernus Kriel, 27.8.92.
55   Shearing 1991c.
56   ANC 1992, p 11.
57   *SouthScan* 25.9.92.
58   *Citizen* 20.7.92.
59   *Report of the Secretary-General on the Question of South Africa*, S/24389, 7.8.92; *Independent* 10.8.92.
60   *SouthScan* 25.9.92.
61   *SouthScan* 25.9.92.
62   *Star* 15.4.93.
63   *Star* 15.4.93.
64   Jeffery 1991, pp 209–12.
65   Brogden 1991, pp 21–22 deals with some issues involved in this procedure.
66   *Star* 15.4.93.
67   *National Peace Accord*, Chapter 7; Marais & Rauch 1991.
68   *National Peace Accord*, Chapter 10.

69 *International Hearing on Violence in South Africa and the Implementation of the National Peace Accord,* London, 14–15.7.92.
70 *Weekly Mail* 24.4.92.
71 *International Hearing on Violence in South Africa and the Implementation of the National Peace Accord,* London 14–15.7.92.
72 *Citizen* 26.8.92.
73 ANC, 1992b, pp 6–7.
74 *Weekly Mail* 29.6.92, *Argus* 30.4.92.
75 *National Peace Accord,* Section 3.3.
76 Declaration of the Patriotic/United Front Conference.
77 *Guardian* 13.5.92.
78 *SouthScan* 22.5.92.
79 *Times* 31.3.93.
80 SAP 1990.
81 Marais & Rauch 1992, p 3.
82 Cawthra 1992, p 30.
83 Haysom 1991, p 6.
84 *SouthScan* 4.9.92.
85 Haysom 1992, p 8.
86 *National Peace Accord,* sections 3.1.1 – 3.1.4.
87 *Weekly Mail* 13.3.92.
88 Rauch 1992b.
89 Shearing & Mzamane 1992.
90 Van Eyk 1991, p 3.
91 Kriel 1992, p 16.
92 *Report of the Inquiry into the Police Response to, and Investigation of, Events in Boipatong on 17 June 1992,* p 34.
93 *SouthScan* 2.4.93. Dutch Violence Observation Mission 1993.
94 National Peace Accord, section 3.2.5.1(vi).
95 *Star* 15.4.93.
96 Haysom 1987a; Jeffery 1991, pp 221.
97 *Report of the Inquiry into the Police Response to, and Investigation of, Events in Boipatong on 17 June 1992,* p 3.
98 *Report of the Inquiry into the Police Response to, and Investigation of, Events in Boipatong on 17 June 1992,* p 27.
99 Heymann 1992.
100 Heymann 1992, p 62.
101 Heymann 1992, *Weekly Mail* 10.7.92, *Business Day* 17.7.92.
102 Marais & Rauch 1992, pp 5–6.
103 Marais & Rauch 1992, pp 11–3.
104 Kriel 1992, p 12.
105 *Media Statement by the Minister of Law and Order, Mr Hernus Kriel,* 27.8.92.
106 Van der Merwe, 1991.
107 Rauch 1992a.
108 Rauch 1992a, p 28.
109 Rauch 1992a, pp 29–34.
110 Brogden 1991c, pp 4–5.
111 Brewer 1991, pp 7–8.
112 *Weekly Mail* 22.3.92; Jeffery 1991, pp 173–4.
113 *Sunday Star* 19.5.91.
114 Rauch 1992, p 3.
115 ICJ 1992, p 24; Brogden 1991, pp 15–9.
116 *Weekly Mail* 25.9.92.

117 *Business Day* 28.8.92.
118 Gouws 1991.
119 *Weekly Mail* 28.8.92.
120 *Amnesty International Weekly Update* 18.11.92 .
121 *AfricaWatch* 1992, pp 23–24.
122 *Weekly Mail* 6.10.89.
123 *Sunday Star* 17.9.89.
124 *Cape Times* 22.11.89.
125 *Guardian* 8.11.89; *Daily Telegraph* 14.11.89.
126 *Guardian* 21.5.90.
127 *Daily Dispatch* 22.3.90; *New Nation* 23.3.90.
128 Cawthra 1992, p 34.
129 ANC 1992, pp 73–4.
130 *Constitution of the Police and Prisons Civil Rights Union.*
131 Military Research Group 1992.
132 *Argus* 27.1.92.
133 See for example *Joint Press Statement on the Idasa–ANC Conference on the Future of Security and Defence in South Africa*, 27.5.90.
134 Cilliers & Mertz 1992, p 13.
135 As the ANC did in the mass demonstrations of August 1992.
136 Heymann 1992, pp 68–70.
137 Jeffery 1991, pp 212–14.
138 Mapetho 1990, p 8.
139 *Daily Dispatch* 29.4.91.
140 *Weekly Mail* 29.5.92, 27.11.93.
141 Stavrou 1992.
142 Kriel 1992, p 8.
143 *Weekly Mail* 7.8.92.
144 Kriel 1992, pp 7–8.
145 *Business Day* 7.8.92.
146 *Citizen* 8.4.93.
147 *National Peace Accord*, section 3.7.1.
148 CODESA 1992, p 6.
149 ANC 1992, p 72.
150 Stavrou 1992.
151 *Constitution of the Republic of Namibia*, 9.2.90.
152 Nathan 1990.
153 Kazombaue, 1992, p 1.
154 *Focus on Africa*, July–September 1992.
155 Kazombaue, 1992, p 2.
156 In the context of the challenges facing the SAP, Brewer 1991 cites the experience of the Spanish police after the death of Franco and the civilianisation of the Royal Ulster Constabulary in Northern Ireland in the 1970s.
157 Jeffery 1991, pp 75–82.
158 *BBC Summary of World Broadcasts* 13.1.92.
159 Phosa 1992, pp 2, 4.
160 ANC 1992, pp 11–2.

BIBLIOGRAPHY

Africa Watch, 1991a, *The Killings in South Africa: The Role of the Security Forces and the Response of the State*, Africa Watch, New York.

Africa Watch, 1991b, *Out of Sight: The Misery in Bophuthatswana*, Africa Watch, New York.

Africa Watch, 1992, *South Africa: Accounting for the Past*, Africa Watch, London.

Aichison, John, 1990, *Interpreting Violence: The Struggle to Understand the Natal Conflict*, Centre for Adult Education, University of Natal, Pietermaritzburg.

Aichison, John, 1991, 'Can the Inkatha gate be closed?', *Work in Progress*, No 77', Johannesburg.

Amnesty International, 1978, *Political Imprisonment in South Africa*, Amnesty International, London.

Amnesty International, 1991, *South Africa: Statement by Amnesty International to the United Nations Ad Hoc Working Group of Experts on Southern Africa*, Amnesty International, London.

Amnesty International, 1992a, *South Africa: Oral Statement by Amnesty International to the 48th Session of the United Nations Commission on Human Rights*, Amnesty International, London.

Amnesty International, 1992b, *South Africa: State of Fear*, Amnesty International, London.

Amnesty International, 1993, *South Africa: Oral Statement by Amnesty International to the 49th Session of the United Nations Commission on Human Rights*, Amnesty International, London.

ANC, 1979, *Forward to Freedom: Strategy, Tactics and Programme of the African National Congress South Africa*, African National Congress, Budapest.

ANC, 1991, *Advance to National Democracy: Guidelines on Strategy and Tactics of the African National Congress*, African National Congress, Johannesburg.

ANC, 1992a, *Ready to Govern: ANC Policy Guidelines for a Democratic South Africa*, African National Congress, Johannesburg.

ANC, 1992b, *Submission of the African National Congress to Working Group 1 Sub-Group 2 on the National Peace Accord*, African National Congress, Johannesburg.

Anti-Apartheid Movement, 1979, *Fire Force Exposed: The Rhodesian Security Forces and Their Role in Defending White Supremacy*, Anti-Apartheid Movement, London.

Barber, James and Barratt, John, 1990, *South Africa's Foreign Policy: The Search for Status and Security 1945–1988*, Cambridge University Press, Cambridge.

Baynham, Simon, 1987, 'Political violence and the security response', in Blumenfeld, Jesmond (ed), *South Africa in Crisis*, Croom Helm, London.

Benson, Mary, 1985, *South Africa: The Struggle for a Birthright*, International Defence and Aid Fund, London.

Bernstein, Hilda, 1978, *No 46 – Steve Biko*, International Defence and Aid Fund, London.

Black Lawyers Association, 1986, *Dark City: Report on Unrest in Alexandra*, Black Lawyers Association, Johannesburg.

Brewer, John, 'South Africa', in Brewer, John; Guelke, Adrian; Hume, Ian; Moxton-Brown, Edward; Wilford, Rick, 1988, *The Police, Public Order and the State: Policing in Great Britain, Northern Ireland, the Irish Republic, the USA, Israel, South Africa and China*, Macmillan Press, London.

Brewer, John, 1991, 'Re-educating the South African police: comparative lessons', *Conference on Policing in the New South Africa*, University of Natal, Pietermaritzburg.

Brogden, Michael, 1989, 'The origins of the South African Police: institutional versus structural approaches', in Faculty of Law, University of Cape Town, *Policing and the Law*, Juta and Co, Cape Town.

Brogden, Michael, 1991, 'Social accountability of policing – an alternative agenda', conference paper, Conference on Policing in the New South Africa, University of Natal, Pietermaritzburg.

Brooks, Alan, and Brickhill, Jeremy, 1980, *Whirlwind Before the Storm*, International Defence and Aid Fund, London.

Buchner, Major-General Jac, 1992, 'Building the partnership: practical steps towards and enhancement of police–community relations', *Policing in South Africa in the 1990s Conference*, Johannesburg.

Bunting, Brian, 1986, *The Rise of the South African Reich*, International Defence and Aid Fund, London.

Campbell, Kurt M., 1987, *Southern Africa in Soviet Foreign Policy*, Adelphi Paper 227, International Institute for Strategic Studies, London.

CASE, 1991, *Inkatha/ANC Responsibility for Reef Violence: Case Research Statistics*, Community Agency for Social Enquiry, Johannesburg.

CASE, 1992, *Political Violence in the PWV, Late 1992–Early 1992*, Community Agency for Social Enquiry, Johannesburg.

Cawthra, Gavin, 1986, *Brutal Force: The Apartheid War Machine*, International Defence and Aid Fund, London.

Cawthra, Gavin, 1992, *South Africa's Police: From Police State to Democratic Policing?*, Catholic Institute for International Relations, London.

Cawthra, Gavin and Navias, Martin, 1992, 'Apartheid's armies: South Africa's homeland forces', *RUSI Journal*, Royal United Services Institute for Defence Studies, London, December.

CIIR, 1988, 'Vigilantes and the new policing system in South Africa', conference paper, *Conference on Death Squads and Vigilantes: Block to Third World Development*, Catholic Institute for International Relations, London.

Cilliers, Jakkie, 1985, *Counter-Insurgency in Rhodesia*, Croom Helm, London.

Cock, Jacklyn and Nathan, Laurie, 1989 (eds), *War and Society: The Militarisation of South Africa*, David Philip, Cape Town.

Codesa, 1992, 'Draft report of Sub-Group 2 Working Group 1', Convention for a Democratic South Africa.

Coetzee, Gen P.J., 1983, 'Urban terror and counter measures', conference paper, *Revolutionary Warfare and Counter-Insurgency*.

Coker, Christopher, 1987, *South Africa's Security Dilemmas*, Center for Strategic and International Studies/Praeger, New York.

Collin, Susan, 1992, *Police Deviance in the Western Cape Taxi War*, Centre for

Intergroup Studies, Cape Town.

Commonwealth Observer Mission, 1993, *Violence in South Africa: The Report of the Commonwealth Observer Mission to South Africa*, advance copy, Commonwealth Secretariat, London.

Consultative Business Movement, 1991, *CBM Memorandum on Violence*, Consultative Business Movement, Johannesburg.

Cook, Allen, 1982, *Akin to Slavery: Prison Labour in South Africa*, International Defence and Aid Fund, London.

Corder, Hugh, 1989, 'The record of the judiciary', in Corder, Hugh (ed), *Democracy and the Judiciary*, Institute for a Democratic Alternative for South Africa, Cape Town.

Cosatu, 1989, *The Role of the Police in Relation to the Violence in Pietermaritzburg*, Congress of South African Trade Unions, Johannesburg.

Crail, Brian, 1992, 'Security: a town council's perspective', *Policing in South Africa in the 1990s Conference*, Johannesburg.

Dippenaar, Marius de Witt, 1988, *The History of the South African Police 1913–1988*, Commemorative Albumn, South African Police, Pretoria.

Douglas, R.S., 1990, *Interim Report on the Violence in Natal*, Commission of Enquiry into the Township Violence in Natal, Durban.

Dutch Violence Observation Mission, 1993. *Violence in the Vaal*, Dutch Violence Observation Mission to the Vaal Triangle in South Africa, Amsterdam.

Ellis, Stephen and Sechaba, Tsepo, 1992, *Comrades Against Apartheid: The ANC and the South African Communist Party in Exile*, James Currey, London.

Fernandez, Lovell, [1991], 'Police abuse of power: an historical review'.

Fine, Derrick, 1989, 'Kitskonstabels: a case study in black on black policing', in Faculty of Law, University of Cape Town, *Policing and the Law*, Juta and Co, Cape Town.

Foster, Don and Luyt, Clifford, 1986, 'The blue man's burden: policing the police in South Africa', *South African Journal of Human Rights*, Centre for Applied Legal Studies, University of the Witwatersrand, vol 2, part 3, November.

Foster, Don and Sandler, Diane, 1985, *A Study of Detention and Torture in South Africa: Preliminary Report*, Institute of Criminology, University of Cape Town.

Frankel, Philip, 1980, 'South Africa: the politics of police control', *Comparative Politics*, July.

Frankel, Philip, 1984, *Pretoria's Praetorians: Civil–Military Relations in South Africa*, Cambridge University Press, Cambridge.

Gouws, Amanda, 1991, 'Of gender, vice and policemen', *Work in Progress*, No 79, December 1991, Johannesburg.

Grant, Evadne, 1989, 'Private policing', in Faculty of Law, University of Cape Town, *Policing and the Law*, Juta and Co, Cape Town.

Grundy, Kenneth W., 1983, *Soldiers Without Politics: Blacks in the South African Armed Forces*, University of California Press, Berkeley.

Grundy, Kenneth W., 1988, *The Militarisation of South African Politics*, Oxford University Press, Oxford.

Grundy, Kenneth W., 1991, *South Africa: Domestic Crisis and Global Challenge*, Westview Press, Boulder, Colorado.

Hanlon, Joe, 1986, *Beggar Your Neighbours: Apartheid Power in Southern Africa*, Catholic Institute for International Relations, London.

Hansson, D.S., 1989, 'Trigger-happy? An evaluation of fatal police shootings in the greater Cape Town area from 1984 to 1986', in Faculty of Law, University of Cape

Town, *Policing and the Law*, Juta and Co, Cape Town.

Hansson, Desireé, 1990, 'Changes in counter-revolutionary state strategy in the decade 1979 to 1989', in Hansson, Desireé and Van Zyl Smit, Dirk (eds), *Towards Justice? Crime and State Control in South Africa*, Oxford University Press, Cape Town.

Haysom, Nicholas, 1983, *Ruling with the Whip: Report on the Violation of Human Rights in the Ciskei*, Centre for Applied Legal Studies, University of the Witwatersrand, Johannesburg.

Haysom, Nicholas, 1987a, 'Licence to kill part I: the South African police and the use of deadly force', *South African Journal of Human Rights*, Centre for Applied Legal Studies, University of the Witwatersrand, Vol 3, Part 2, July.

Haysom, Nicholas, 1987b, 'Licence to kill part II: a comparative survey of the law in the United Kingdom, United States of America and South Africa', *South African Journal of Human Rights*, Centre for Applied Legal Studies, University of the Witwatersrand, vol 3, part 3.

Haysom, Nicholas, 1989a, 'Policing the police: a comparative survey of police control mechanisms in the United States, South Africa and the United Kingdom', in Faculty of Law, University of Cape Town, *Policing and the Law*, Juta and Co, Cape Town.

Haysom, Nicholas, 1989b, 'Legal intervention and the State of Emergency', in Haysom, Nicholas and Plasket, Clive (eds), *Developments in Emergency Law*, Centre for Applied Legal Studies, University of the Witwatersrand, Johannesburg.

Haysom, Nicholas 1989c, 'International human rights norms and states of emergency', in Haysom, Nicholas and Plasket, Clive (eds), *Developments in Emergency Law*, Centre for Applied Legal Studies, University of the Witwatersrand, Johannesburg.

Haysom, Nicholas, 1989d, 'Vigilantes and militarisation of South Africa', in Cock, Jacklyn, and Nathan, Laurie (eds), *War and Society: The Militarisation of South Africa*, David Philip, Cape Town.

Haysom, Nicholas, 1990, 'Vigilantes and the policing of African townships: manufacturing violent stability', in Hansson, Desireé and Van Zyl Smith, Dirk (eds), *Towards Justice? Crime and State Control in South Africa*, Oxford University Press, Cape Town.

Haysom, Nicholas, 1991, 'The police in a new South Africa: accountability and control', *Conference on Policing in the New South Africa*, University of Natal, Pietermaritzburg.

Haysom, Nicholas, 1992, 'Police and constitution in a new South Africa', unpublished paper.

Herbstein, Denis and Evenson, John, 1989, *The Devils Are Among Us: The War for Namibia*, Zed Books, London.

Heymann, Philip B, and others, 1992, *Testimony of Multinational Panel Regarding Lawful Control of Demonstrations in the Republic of South Africa Before the Commission Regarding the Prevention of Public Violence and Intimidation*, Cape Town.

Holloway, Patrick M., [1989], 'Privatisation of policing: the private security industry', unpublished thesis, University of Cape Town.

Hope, P.J., 1989, 'Who are the terrorists? An account of security police operations in the Forbes and Yengeni trials', unpublished thesis, University of Cape Town.

HRC, 1991, *Review of 1990*, Human Rights Commission, Johannesburg.

HRC, 1992, *Review of 1991*, Human Rights Commission, Johannesburg.

IBIIR, 1990, *Memorandum on Extreme Rightwing Organisations in South Africa*, Independent Board of Inquiry into Informal Repression, Johannesburg.

IBIIR, 1991a, *Incidents where the IBIIR has Alleged Collusion between Inkatha and the South African Police*, Independent Board of Inquiry into Informal Repression, Johannesburg.

IBIIR, 1991b, *Who Lied? Discussion of the Findings of the Harms Commission of Inquiry Prepared by the Independent Board*, Independent Board of Inquiry into Informal Repression, Johannesburg.

ICJ, 1990, *Natal Violence: Joint Statement by ICJ Mission to Natal*, Mission to Natal, International Commission of Jurists, Johannesburg.

ICJ, 1992, *Agenda for Peace: An Indpendent Survey of the Violence in South Africa*, International Commission of Jurists.

IDAF, 1971, *South Africa: The BOSS Law*, International Defence and Aid Fund, London.

IDAF, 1980, *The Apartheid War Machine: The Strength and Deployment of the South African Armed Forces*, International Defence and Aid Fund, London.

IDAF, 1982, *Apartheid's Army in Namibia: South Africa's Illegal Military Occupation*, International Defence and Aid Fund, London.

IDAF, 1989, *Namibia the Facts*, International Defence and Aid Fund, London.

IDAF, 1990, *Review of 1989: Repression and Resistance in South Africa and Namibia*, International Defence and Aid Fund, London.

IDAF, 1991, *Apartheid the Facts*, International Defence and Aid Fund, London.

Independent Board, 1992a, *Blood on the Tracks: A Special Report on the Train Attacks*, Independent Board of Inquiry, Johannesburg.

Independent Board, 1992b, *Fortresses of Fear*, Independent Board of Inquiry, Johannesburg.

Institute of Criminology, 1991, *Violence in South Africa during the First Four Months of 1991: A Comment from the Institute of Criminology*, Institute of Criminology, University of Cape Town.

Jagwanth, S., [nd], 'Report on the perception study on policing'.

Jeffery, Anthea J., 1991, *Riot Policing in Perspective*, South African Institute of Race Relations, Johannesburg.

Katjavivi, Peter, 1988, *A History of Resistance in Namibia*, James Currey, London.

Kazombaue, Lindi, 1992, 'Policing of Violence', *Policing in South Africa in the 1990s* conference, Johannesburg.

Kentridge, Matthew, 1990, *The Unofficial War in Natal: Pietermaritzburg under the Knife*, Project for the Study of Violence Seminar Programme, Department of Applied Psychology, University of the Witwatersrand.

Koch, Eddie, 1978, 'The development of a police force on the Witwatersrand 1886–1906', *Africa Perspective* No 8, Johannesburg.

Kriel, H.J., 1992, *The Influence of Criminal and Political Violence on the Internal Stability of the RSA*, Issup Bulletin 6/92, Institute for Strategic Studies, University of Pretoria.

Landgren, Signe, 1989, *Embargo Disimplemented: South Africa's Military Industry*, Oxford University Press, Oxford.

Laurence, Patrick, 1990, *Death Squads: Apartheid's Secret Weapon*, Penguin Forum Series, Penguin Books, London.

Lawyers Committee, 1983, *Deaths in Detention and South Africa's Security Laws*, Southern Africa Project, Lawyers Committee for Civil Rights Under Law, Washington.

Lawyers Committee, 1990, *South Africa's Death Squads*, Southern Africa Project, Lawyers Committee for Civil Rights Under Law, Washington.

Leap, 1990, *Kitskonstabels in Crisis: A Closer Look at Black on Black Policing*, Legal Education Action Project and Criminal Justice Resource Centre, Institute of Criminology, University of Cape Town.

Legal Resources Centre, 1991, *The Role of the KwaZulu Police: Impartial Law Enforcement or Obstacle to Peace?*, Legal Resources Centre/Human Rights Commission, Durban.

Louw, H.H., 1978 (ed), *National Security: A Modern Approach*, Institute for Strategic Studies, University of Pretoria.

Lubowski, Anton, 1989, 'Democracy and the judiciary', in Corder, Hugh (ed), *Democracy and the Judiciary*, Institute for a Democratic Alternative for South Africa, Cape Town.

Maduna, Penuel, 1991, 'Popular perception of policing among blacks in South Africa today', *Conference on Policing in the New South Africa*, Pietermaritzburg.

Mandela, Nelson, 1990, *The Struggle is my Life*, International Defence and Aid Fund, London.

Marais, Etienne, 1991, 'Police–community relations and the Natal conflict', conference paper, *1991 Conference of the Association of Sociology in Southern Africa*, Project for the Study of Violence, Department of Applied Psychology, University of the Witwatersrand.

Marais, Etienne, and Rauch, Janine, 1992, 'Policing South Africa: reform and prospects', *Policing in South Africa in the 1990s* conference, Johannesburg.

Marcus, Gilbert, 1986, 'Challenging injustice: the role of the judiciary', *Indicator SA*, Vol 4, No 1.

Martin, David and Johnson, Phyllis, 1981, *The Struggle for Zimbabwe: The Chimurenga War*, Monthly Review Press, New York.

Mathews, Anthony S., 1986, *Freedom, State Security and the Rule of Law: Dilemmas of the Apartheid Society*, Juta and Co, Cape Town.

McCuen, John J., 1966, *The Art of Counter-Revolutionary War: The Strategy of Counter-Insurgency*, Faber and Faber, London.

Military Research Group, 1992, *The Integration of the Armed Forces: Report of the Military Research Group*, Johannesburg.

Murray, Martin, 1987, *South Africa: Time of Agony, Time of Destiny*, Verso, London.

Mzala, 1988, *Gatsha Buthelezi: Chief with a Double Agenda*, Zed Books, London.

Nathan, Laurie, 1990, 'Marching to a different drum: a description and assessment of the formation of the Namibian police and defence force', *Southern African Perspectives*, No 4, Centre for Southern African Studies, University of the Western Cape, Cape Town.

Nathan, Laurie, and Phillips, Mark, 1991, 'Security reforms: the pen and the sword', *Indicator SA*, Vol 8, No 4.

Neille, Gaye, 1992, 'Paper presented by Gaye Neille, President South African Neighbourhood Watch', *Policing in South Africa in the 1990s* conference, Johannesburg.

Olivier, Johan, 1991, *The South African Police: Managers of Conflict or Party to the Conflict?*, Project for the Study of Violence Seminar Programme, Department of Applied Psychology, University of the Witwatersrand, Johannesburg.

Omar, Dullah, 1990, 'An overview of state lawlessness in South Africa', in Hansson, Desireé and Van Zyl Smit, Dirk (eds), *Towards Justice? Crime and State Control in South Africa*, Oxford University Press, Cape Town.

Parsons, Neil, 1982, *A New History of Southern Africa*, Macmillan, London.

Pauw, Jacques, 1991, *In the Heart of the Whore: The Story of Apartheid's Death Squads*, Southern Book Publishers, Halfway House, Transvaal.

Phosa, Mathew, 1992, 'Building police-community relations in a divided society', *Policing in South Africa in the 1990s* conference, Johannesburg.

Pinnock, Don, 1982, 'Towards an understanding of the structure, fuction and cause of gang formation in Cape Town', unpublished thesis, University of Cape Town.

Plasket, Clive, 1989, 'Sub-contracting the dirty work', in Faculty of Law, University of Cape Town, *Policing and the Law*, Juta and Co, Cape Town.

Policing Research Project, 1991, 'Training in the SAP in 1991: observations', unpublished paper, Department of Psychology, University of the Witwatersrand, Johannesburg.

Price, Robert M., 1991, *The Apartheid State in Crisis: Political Transformation in South Africa 1975–1990*, Oxford University Press, Oxford.

Prior, Andrew, 1989a, 'The South African Police and the counter-revolution of 1985–1987', *Acta Juridica*.

Prior, Andrew, 1989b, 'The SAP and the state: first line of defence', *Indicator SA*, Vol 6, No 4.

Rauch, Janine, 1988, 'Neighbourhood watch in the white suburbs of Cape Town, 1987', unpublished honours thesis, Institute of Criminology, University of Cape Town.

Rauch, Janine, 1991, 'Deconstructing the South African police force', conference paper, *1991 Conference of the Association of Sociology in Southern Africa*, Project for the Study of Violence, Department of Applied Psychology, University of the Witwatersrand, Johannesburg.

Rauch, Janine, 1992a, *South African Police Basic Training: A Preliminary Assessment*, Project for the Study of Violence, Department of Applied Psychology, University of the Witwatersrand, Johannesburg.

Rauch, Janine, 1992b, 'A preliminary assessment of the impact of the Peace Accord Code of Conduct on police behaviour', unpublished paper, Johannesburg.

Ruppel, Hartmut, 1987, 'Namibia: Security legislation and its consequences', in Tötemeyer, Gerhard; Kandetu, Vezera and Werner, Wolfgang (eds), *Namibia in Perspective*, Council of Churches in Namibia, Windhoek.

SACBC, 1982, 'Report on Namibia', Southern African Catholic Bishops' Conference, Johannesburg.

SACBC, 1984, *Report on Police Conduct During Township Protests August–November 1984*, Southern African Catholic Bishops Conference/ Catholic Institute for International Relations, London.

Sachs, Albie, 1973, *Justice in South Africa*, Sussex University Press/Heinemann Educationanal Books, London.

Sachs, Albie, 1975, 'The instruments of domination', in Butler, Jeffrey and Thompson, Leonard (eds), *Change in Contemporary South Africa*, University of California Press, Berkeley.

SADF, 1977, *White Paper on Defence*, South African Defence Force, Pretoria.

SAP, 1990, *White Paper on the Organisation and Functions of the South African Police*, South African Police, Pretoria.

SAP, 1983, *Profile of the South African Police*, South African Police, Pretoria.

SAP, 1988, *White Paper on the Organisation and Functions of the South African Police*, South African Police, Pretoria.

SAP, 1992, *The Role of the South African Police in a Changing South Africa*, South

African Police, Pretoria.

SAP, 1993, *Strategic Plan: Efficiency Services/Corporative Planning*, South African Police, Pretoria.

Scharf, Wilfried, 1988, 'Police abuse of power and victim assistance during apartheid's emergency', *Sixth International Symposium on Victimology*, Jerusalem.

Scharf, Wilfried, 1989, 'Community policing in South Africa', *Acta Juridica*.

Scharf, Wilfried, 1991a, 'Skeletons and patriotic positivism: towards a new vision of South African policing studies', *Conference on Policing in the New South Africa*, University of Natal, Pietermaritzburg.

Scharf, Wilfried, 1991b, 'Report of Mr Wilfried Scharf', *State vs Booi and 3 Others*, Case no G/SH 40491, Regional Court, George.

Security Association, [nd], *Legal Powers of the Security Officer*, Security Association of South Africa.

Seegers, Annette, 1988a, 'Local government: state strategy – the National Security Management System and Joint Management Centres', unpublished paper, University of Cape Town.

Seegers, Annette, 1988b, 'The government's perception and handling of South Africa's security needs', in van Vuuren, D.J., Wiehahn, N.E., Rhoodie, N.J., Wiechers, M. (eds) *South Africa: The Challenge of Reform*, Owen Burgess, Pinetown, Natal.

Seegers, Annette, 1989, 'The rise of an authoritarian mode of policing in South Africa', unpublished paper, Department of Political Studies, University of Cape Town.

Seekings, Jeremy, 1989, 'Black policemen in the townships: case-studies from the Witwatersrand, 1985–86', Universities of Oxford and Stellenbosch.

Segal, Lauren, 1991, 'The human face of violence: hostel-dwellers speak', *Journal of Southern African Studies*, Vol 18, No 1.

Selfe, James, 1989, 'South Africa's National Management System', in Cock, Jacklyn and Nathan, Laurie (eds), *War and Society: The Militarisation of South Africa*, David Philip, Cape Town.

Shearing, Clifford, 1991a, 'Police deviance and accountability', *Conference on Policing in the New South Africa*, University of Natal, Pietermaritzburg.

Shearing, Clifford, 1991b, 'The relation between police and government: the quest for impartial policing', Community Law Centre, University of the Western Cape, Cape Town.

Shearing, Clifford, 1991c, 'Policing the police: the ombudsman solution', *Indicator SA*, Vol 8, No 4.

Shityuwete, Helao, 1990, *Never Follow the Wolf: The Autobiography of a Namibian Freedom Fighter*, Kliptown Books, London.

Simons, H.J. and Simons, R.E. 1983, *Class and Colour in South Africa 1850–1950*, Defence and Aid, London.

Simpson, Graeme, [nd], 'The origins of violent resistance in the Vaal Triangle 1984–86', unpublished draft paper.

Simpson, Graeme; Huber, Jill; Mokwena, Steven; Segal, Lauren; Vogelman, Lloyd, 1990, 'Political violence in 1990: the year in perspective', Project for the Study of Violence, University of the Witwatersrand, Johannesburg.

Slabbert, Mana, 1985, 'Problems facing criminological researchers in South Africa', in Davis, Dennis and Slabbert, Mana, *Crime and Power in South Africa: Critical Studies in Criminology*, David Philip, Cape Town.

Sloth-Nielson, Julia, 1990, 'Corporal punishment: acceptable state violence?', in Hansson, Desireé and Van Zyl Smit, Dirk (eds), *Towards Justice? Crime and State Control in South Africa*, Oxford University Press, Cape Town.

Smit, B.F., 1989, 'Verwagtinge teen opsigte van the SA Polisie 2000', Pretoria.

Sparks, Allister, 1991, *The Mind of South Africa: The Story of the Rise and Fall of Apartheid*, Mandarin, London.

Stavrou, Paraskevi, 1992, *The Alexandra Community Crime Survey: A Study of the Perceptions and Fear of Crime of the Residents in an Area of Alexandra*, Project for the Study of Violence, University of the Witwatersrand, Johannesburg.

Steytler, Nico, 1989, 'Policing unrest: the restoring of authority', *Acta Juridica*.

Steytler, Nico, 1990, 'Policing political opponents: death squads and cop culture', in Hannson, Desireé and Van Zyl Smit, Dirk (eds), *Towards Justice? Crime and State Control in South Africa*, Oxford University Press, Cape Town.

Suter, K.D., 1980, *The Laws of Armed Conflicts and Apartheid*, Notes and Documents 24/80, Centre Against Apartheid, United Nations, New York.

SWAPO, 1981, *To Be Born a Nation: The Liberation Struggle for Namibia*, Zed Press, London.

Swilling, Mark and Phillips, Mark, 1989a, 'State power in the 1980s: from "total strategy" to "counter-revolutionary warfare"', in Cock, Jacklyn and Nathan, Laurie (eds), *War and Society: The Militarisation of South Africa*, David Philip, Cape Town.

Swilling, Mark and Phillips, Mark, 1989b, 'The emergency state: its structure, power and limits', in Moss, Glen and Obery, Ingrid (eds) *South African Review 5*, Ravan Press, Johannesburg.

Taylor, Chief Constable AN, 1992, 'Police accountability', *Policing in South Africa in the 1990s Conference*, Johannesburg.

Umac, 1990, *Police Action and the Negotiation Process*, Unrest Monitoring and Action Committee, Cape Town.

Van der Spuy, Elrena, 1988, 'Policing in the eighties: servamus et servimus?', conference paper, *1988 Annual Conference of the Association of Sociology in Southern Africa*, Department of Sociology, University of Stellenbosch.

Van der Spuy, Elrena, 1989, 'Literature on the police in South Africa: an historical perspective', *Acta Juridica*.

Van der Spuy, Elrena, 1990, 'Political discourse and the history of the South African police', in Hannson, Desireé and Van Zyl Smit, Dirk, *Towards Justice? Crime and State Control in South Africa*, Oxford University Press, Cape Town.

Van der Merwe, Gen J.V., 1990a, 'Toespraak deur General JV van der Merwe, by the regslui onthaal te Port Elizabeth op Vryday 2 Nov 1990'.

Van der Merwe, Gen J.V., 1990b, 'Referaat deur the Kommissaris van die SA Polisie', *Quo Vadis: Suid-Afrikaanse Staatsdiens* conference, University of South Africa, Pretoria.

Van der Merwe, Gen J.V., 1991, 'Toespraak deur Generaal J.V. van der Merwe Komissaris van die Suid-Afrikaanse Polisie by die upassering van studente te Hammanskraal op Donderday 20 Junie 1991'.

Van Eck, Jan, 1989, *Eyewitness to 'Unrest'*, Taurus, Emmarentia, Transvaal.

Van Eyk, Lt Gen M., 1991, 'The principles and problems of policing in a changing South Africa', *Conference on Policing in the New South Africa*, University of Natal, Pietermaritzburg.

Van Zyl Smit, Dirk, 1990, 'Contextualising criminology in contemporary South Africa', in Hannson, Desireé and Van Zyl Smit, Dirk (eds), *Towards Justice? Crime and State Control in South Africa*, Oxford University Press, Cape Town.

Wandrag, Major-General A.J., 1985, 'Political unrest: a police view', *ISSUP Strategic Review*, October 1985, Institute for Strategic Studies, University of Pretoria.

Weaver, Tony, 1987, 'The war in Namibia: social consequences', in Tötemeyer, Gerhard, Kandetu, Vezera and Werner, Wolfgang (eds), *Namibia in Perspective*, Council of Churches, Windhoek.

Webster, David and Friedman, Maggie, [nd], *Suppressing Apartheid's Opponents: Repression and the State of Emergency June 1987–March 1989*, Southern African Research Service/Ravan Press, Johannesburg.

Williams, Rocklyn, 1990, *Back to the Barracks: The SADF and the Changing Nature of Civil–Military Relations Under the Botha and De Klerk Administrations*, Institute of Commonwealth Studies, London.

Woods, Gavin, 1991, 'Perspectives on policing', *Conference on Policing in the New South Africa*, University of Natal, Pietermaritzburg.